VASSULA OF THE SACRED HEART'S PASSION

(revised)

Michael O'Carroll, C.S.Sp.

Published and Distributed by:-

J.M.J. Publications
P.O. Box 385
Belfast BT9 6RQ
United Kingdom
Fax: (1232) 381596

His Holiness Pope Paul VI has confirmed on October 14, 1966, the decree of the Sacred Congregation for the propagation of the Faith, under number 58/16 (A.A.S.), permitting the publication of writings about supernatural apparitions, even if they do not have a "nihil obstat" from ecclesiastical authorities.

Vassula of The Sacred Heart's Passion

© All rights reserved worldwide
US Library of Congress copyright no: TX 3-800-423
ISBN: 0-9519973-3-5
Printed in Canada

First Printing, Canada, April 1993 - 10,000 copies
Second Printing (revised), Canada, February 1995 - 10,000 copies

See back for the addresses of distributors

Dedication

To Pope John Paul II to mark the similarity
between the message of Vassula and his teaching,
and her defence of his universal primacy.

FOREWORD

The pages that follow will make it clear why this book has been written. It is intended for anyone interested in the message and mission of Vassula Rydén. This is a lady who has changed her life-style, interests and activities totally as a result of mystical graces, by which I mean direct experience of the divine. Before the turning-point in her career she had led the life of a typical European expatriate, wife of an important official in an international agency working in the Third World. She had access to the social round at a high level, had achieved distinction as a painter and a tennis champion, was interested in fashion design. With her exotic background and linguistic attainments she could aspire to continued worldly success.

Why did she turn her back on all this? Why has she spent hours in prayer daily, in communion with God, instead of taking part in tennis competitions, arranging cocktail parties, painting attractive people or places? Why has she given her time to addressing meetings in different countries on spiritual themes? Why is she so much in demand for this work? Why have her writings been so widely distributed? Why so many demands for translation rights? Why so much acclaim from those qualified to judge?

The complete answers to such questions are open to those who read Vassula's writings. I do not offer this book as a substitute for this essential source. But my pages may facilitate reading and avoid waste of time. All references in this book unless otherwise stated refer to *True Life in God* Volumes I, II, and III.

I owe a special word of thanks to Mrs. Christine Lynch, publisher of Vassula's writings. She has undertaken to bring out this book with exemplary speed and competence; my thanks include her daughter Christine and Moira Smith, her associate.

Michael O'Carroll, C.S.Sp.
Blackrock College
25 March, 1993
Feast of the Annunciation

TABLE OF CONTENTS

INTRODUCTION

The writings of Vassula Rydén are widely known and demand constantly increases for further distribution and translation. I have aimed, in the following pages, at providing two things: information on Vassula's personality and background, which will explain the origin of her writings; and an overall survey of the message which they convey, an analysis of the principal themes, the spiritual insights, which she has been given, which I consider, as do so many others, very relevant to Christian life today.

I knew very little about Vassula when Lord John Eldon, a friend of hers, telephoned me in February, 1991 and spoke about her. I had seen but not read an article about her by the French Marian theologian, Fr. Rene Laurentin in the periodical *Chrétiens Magazine*. Lord Eldon asked me to meet Vassula who would be in Ireland in March of that year. I knew the organiser of a Marian congress in Pittsburgh, which she wished to attend. He also raised the question of a possible meeting in Dublin to hear Vassula. It was then too late to look for a hall in the city, so the College authorities very kindly offered the theatre where meetings and assemblies take place. She spoke there to the largest attendance it has ever contained, over eleven hundred. Entry had to be restricted to ticket holders, so great was the demand.

Lord Eldon had sent me a photocopy of Vassula's writings and from these and from conversations with her then and later I began to appreciate her personality and her message. My experience and intellectual pursuits explain the sympathetic response I felt towards one and the other. In an Appendix I have listed such items in my *Curriculum Vitae* as would illustrate this statement; I have, to the same end, provided an outline bibliography of my written work.

In the years which I spent in Fribourg (Switzerland) studying theology I, like so many others at the time, came under the influence of Bishop Marius Besson, the most important ecumenist in the Catholic Church at the episcopal level since Cardinal Mercier. His outlook was expressed in two books, *La route aplanie* and *Après quatre cents ans*, which were read avidly by those conscious of the problem of Christian unity, but with little effect in wider circles.

i

In the Dublin of the forties I took an active part in the work of the Legion of Mary, something which enriched my life with the friendship of the founder, Frank Duff. I worked especially in the area of contacts with Protestants and Jews. When an inter-faith group, the *Mercier Society*, was founded I was invited to become a member and was so from the outset. Its motto was "Towards a Better Understanding", its purpose honest dialogue. In the quality and quantity of its members it was a prodigious success, the first venture of its kind in Ireland since the Reformation. Among the members were three future Catholic bishops (one of them Archbishop of Teheran)[1] and two future Church of Ireland bishops, Dr. Otto G. Simms, archbishop of Armagh and of Dublin, and the outstanding patristic scholar, bishop of Clogher, assistant bishop of Manchester, R.P.C. Hanson. A future president of the United Nations came, as did future ambassadors, distinguished theologians from all the Christian communions.

To me this was the dream fostered by Marius Besson come true. We were doing something about Christian Unity. In passing, I mention that I also was a member of the Pillar of Fire Society, aimed at dialogue with the Jewish community - we were just then in the time of the Jewish genocide in Europe. But in the climate of opinion then prevailing in the Catholic Church, especially in countries like Ireland, we were suspect. Canon Purdy, in his book on Pius XII and John XXIII, says that before Vatican II those working for Christian Unity in the Catholic Church were a "persecuted minority", a slight exaggeration but I know what he meant. We were suppressed, with all the legal proprieties. We may have been under a cloud thereafter, but these clouds do not do much harm.

I mention this event in my personal experience to explain why I welcomed wholeheartedly one like Vassula who is totally dedicated, in the name, and with the explicit encouragement, of Jesus to the task of Christian unity. Members of the Mercier Society and of the Pillar of Fire Society have been vindicated by the Second Vatican Council. Without any triumphalism I rejoice in this official change of policy. I cannot conceal my satisfaction that from the Orthodox communion, which all my recent studies have led me to respect profoundly, has come an outstanding witness to Christian unity, one ready to make every sacrifice for this cause. For that reason I decided to support Vassula's apostolate.

There were other reasons which led me to become completely identified with her mission. I was profoundly disturbed - I do not think that I was alone in this - by what appeared abandonment within the Catholic community of one of the priceless treasures in our spiritual and devotional life, the sense of the Saviour of mankind as the Sacred Heart of Jesus, his own revelation of this wondrous mystery, which Pius XI could say was a summary of the Christian religion.

A saintly and learned theologian about the time that the decadence was fully apparent, told me that in a sector of the Church where it would be expected it was now dead. "But" he added "we believe that there are still faithful ones who will help one day to revive it." I was given a similar assurance from another important source. I scarcely thought that the revival would come from outside the Catholic body, and with a force which has proved already in many places irresistible. To know of such a spiritual stirring and not encourage it would be for me a kind of treachery. I assume that elementary steps would be taken towards discernment.

I would have felt similar remorse had I in any way opposed or thwarted one who so convincingly spreads a message of Marian devotion and spirituality. I have served the Marian apostolate in various ways and laboured over the years to acquire a sound theology of the Mother of God. I learned that such an aim would lose nothing from choice of the most perfect methodology. But I learned also that here as in the theology of Jesus Christ, Mary's divine Son, there must be a place for genuine mystics.

This is now a problem acute, at times even poignant, in the Catholic Church. It is impossible to give an accurate account of the number of people who presently are receiving apparitions, revelations, locutions directly from Our Lady.[2] This is not a challenge to the institutional Church; it is so decidedly to some of those who hold office for they seem ill equipped to deal with it. They are in some cases truly concerned that private revelations should not threaten the influence of lawful authority. But when faced with a difficult case some of them resort too readily to condemnation. There is an a priori assumption that this, if not an act of aggression, is a menace, and measures to nullify its effect must be taken at once.

Faith is necessary to all involved. Even in presence of a miracle faith which, at its root, is a gift and for which those responsible may have to pray, is indispensable. A French novelist once said that if all the miracles worked at Lourdes were genuine he still would not believe. Some of those in authority faced with a manifestation of special graces do give the impression that they see no place for the exercise of faith. This ultimately compromises their own authority; for their subjects have to make an act of faith in them. I would not say that this thought occurs to them too often.

As I point out in the course of my text certain guidelines have been issued from Rome in regard to special graces, especially apparitions. They represented practically a turnabout from a statement published by Mgr. (later Cardinal) Ottaviani, then at the head of the Holy Office (now the Congregation for the Doctrine of the Faith), a document almost totally negative, rendered out of date anyway by the explicit teaching of Vatican II.

I do not claim that to follow the positive view which I advocate will be always easy, that human error will not creep in. But the formally negative approach is in itself erroneous, in some cases a direct insult to Almighty God. His special action is thereby ruthlessly excluded from His Church, which would not exist without His divine power. The attitude is counter-productive in many ways, as was the tendency, denounced by speakers during Vatican II, of multiplying mortal sins. At its best the practice maximised the innate legalism of the Latin Church, still heavily overshadowed by Roman law; at its worst it exposed immortal souls, made in the image of God, redeemed by the precious blood of the incarnate God, to the ignorance, prejudice, emotional whim of an inadequate prelate.

Sad but with space easily documented. The relevance to Vassula Rydén is not immediately apparent. For she is not a Roman Catholic. She does not come under the jurisdiction of our ecclesiastical authorities. But she has now an international Catholic constituency. This prompts Catholic writers to pass judgement on her. Catholics even Catholic prelates, should be wary of intruding here on the jurisdiction of the Greek Orthodox Church, to which Vassula belongs. We, for our part, should resent any such intrusion by the Orthodox in the life and apostolate of Catholics.

But the reader may reasonably ask what experience I have had in the area of what may be broadly called extraordinary graces, mystical phenomena. As a member of a religious institute dedicated to the Holy Spirit and the Immaculate Heart of Mary I have felt the duty of investigating contemporary Catholic attitudes towards one and the other. The results of my research are in print.[3] More specifically I may recall that during my theological studies in Fribourg I followed the course on Mystical and Ascetical Theology given by a well-known theologian, Fr. Benoit Lavaud, O.P. My doctorate dissertation was prepared under his direction, the subject being "Spiritual Direction in the Writings of Ven. Francis Libermann." Libermann, a convert Jew, was acknowledged as a truly great spiritual director.

In the course of a varied pastoral ministry, mostly in the field of education and various sectors of the lay apostolate, I have been fortunate to encounter individuals who were patently instruments of the Spirit in the life of the Church. Foremost among these I would place Frank Duff, founder of the Legion of Mary, with whom I was bound by the ties of intimate friendship, with whom I discussed more than once some of the problems of mystical intervention in the Christian life. This was important because he did not wish his association to appear anything but a logical sequel to the ordinary belief of the Church. Since life is larger than logic, Frank had on the Vexillum or standard of the Legion a reproduction of the Miraculous Medal!

I have also been privileged to enjoy the friendship of Mr. Justice Coyne and his wife, Judy, widowed for many years, who inaugurated and sustained the recognition of Knock Shrine, leading to its status as a national centre of Marian piety. One who spent himself in bringing this movement to its present day glory, Mgr. James Horan, gave me his confidence unremittingly.

Of a different kind was the priestly apostolate of an English lady resident in the last decades of her life in Ireland, a convert from Dialectical Materialism, Mrs. Anne

F.E. Partridge. I supported her Priests' Crusade, enjoyed her total confidence up to the moment of her death.

Among religious who deeply influenced my life I would name a Carmelite sister, Thérèse of Blackrock Carmel, Prioress for a time, a very distinctive personality, favoured with special graces, communications from Our Lady; and Mother Agnes, Abbess General of the Poor Clares, Newry, the superior who received Briege McKenna into the congregation, guided her first steps in the religious life. For a number of years I gave eight day retreats annually to sisters in Irish, occasionally Scottish and English convents, was called on to act as counsellor.

I should enlarge the range of my experience of souls recipients of special graces, which is just to relate facts, not to claim any special degree of favour before the Lord. I have reflected a good deal on the apparition at Knock in 1879[4]. I had the good fortune to meet the last surviving witness living in Ireland, Patrick Beirne. I also met Mariette Beco, the visionary of Banneux,[5] though I did not talk to her about the apparitions of Our Lady, which have been declared authentic. I found Maria Concepción (Conchita) Gonzales quite communicative, though I did not question her on the detail of her extraordinary experience at Garabandal; I had read the literature. I refrained from questioning at any length the one Medjugorje visionary whom I met, Marija Pavlovic. I saw them in ecstasy a number of times, and had abundant material from utterly reliable sources to satisfy my research.[6] At the times I was there I felt they had too much exposure to the curious. Over the years and latterly especially I have become acquainted or friendly, sometimes in the role of adviser, with individuals claiming to have received special divine favours, charisms if one must use the proper term. I respect confidentiality in these cases and mention them solely to assure the reader that I did not come to the case of Vassula without some experience, as well as theoretical knowledge, of the special world in which she has found her vocation. I have had to point out in the following pages that her critics feel no obligation to declare any such credential. I fear that in some cases there are none to declare. Nor does this in any way inhibit harsh, negative opinions.

Vassula presents an interesting case, existential evidence of the action of the Holy Spirit. Still more striking, as I shall show, is the series of luminous messages on the Holy Spirit which she has received, which amount to a practical treatise, a precious guide on this presence and action in the Church. She could not have invented this, discovered it on her own. It was possibly the one feature of her teaching which convinced me that she is an accredited messenger of the Lord. This was so because I had been working on, was about to complete, a theological encyclopédia on the Holy Spirit. In the course of preparing this work I saw still more clearly the neglect of the Spirit from which we are now emerging. It has been a kind of affliction in the Latin Church. To recognise all this and to discuss it theoretically is one thing. To translate such theory into the stuff of life is something quite different. Anyone with the spiritual sensitivity to discern the need, and a talent in proposing the remedy deserves our entire support.

Another dominant theme in Vassula's writings is one which she had no means of discovering on her own. This is the union or to use John Paul II's word "alliance" of the Two Hearts. It would have needed much study and research on Vassula's part to see the validity of this intuition and its relevance to the life of the Church in our time. Acquaintance with the trends within religious institutes, or lay associations like the Legion of Mary, would have shown that invocation of the Sacred Heart of Jesus and the Immaculate Heart of Mary or the choice of one or other, or of both, as patronal titles was not unknown; one the universally distributed emblem of Marian piety, the Miraculous Medal, displays the two Hearts.

But the divine intention to bring both into one mediatorial action on behalf of the Church would have escaped the attention of many, certainly that of one outside the Catholic Church. The facts supporting this assertion are given in my book. I cannot overlook an interesting aspect of the subject. As in her teaching on the Holy Spirit, Vassula here meets most accurately and effectively the thinking of John Paul II. She does so more fully and enthusiastically than some of his Catholic subjects, even some commissioned to teach or preach Catholic doctrine. It is not surprising then that alone among writers from the Orthodox churches she constantly receives messages from Jesus and his Mother explicitly sympathetic towards the Pope, who is even named; messages too of admiration and of criticism of his opponents, even those within the clergy.

In this loyalty, which is patently disinterested, two aspects of the contemporary religious situation come into focus. One is the widespread decline in faith within the Catholic Church, the apostasy that has eaten into its membership, that leaves it open to invasion by the sects of our time, an ever increasing phenomenon, that also causes in places painful confusion in the ranks of the faithful, exposed to conflicting views from their religious guides.

The second reality calling for attention, one which also brings Vassula into intellectual and prayerful harmony with John Paul II is the epoch-making change inside Russia and in the one-time east-European satellites. The conversion of Russia, a hope prompting prayer, but unconsciously oriented towards some distant future, has suddenly begun to take place before our eyes. As a priest journalist I visited Moscow twice in the sixties. I have gone back as a member of the International Peace Pilgrimage in October of this year. What was impossible five years ago and unthinkable twenty years ago is happening. An international Catholic Youth Congress, with members from thirty eight different countries, took place in one of Moscow's biggest hotels, the Kosmos. Fifty priests with four bishops from the Philippines concelebrated Mass in the auditorium; placards announcing the theme of the Congress, the Alliance of the Two Hearts, were on display everywhere within the hotel. On 16 October the statue of Our Lady of Fatima was crowned in Red Square at 10 o'clock and, for those unable to attend, at midnight. This statue had been borne with an honour guard of priests and bishops from the plane into the Airport, with nothing but respectful curiosity from those present. This fact which I was able to observe, fits into a wider pattern of events with which I deal in the book.

That John Paul II would rejoice at news of these happenings none can doubt; he wept when he heard of the initiative taken by Bishop Hlnilica 1984. Inside the church of the Assumption in the Kremlin the Czechoslovak bishop, who enjoys his trust in all that concerns Russia and eastern Europe, consecrated Russia to the Immaculate Heart of Mary, on 25 March when the Pope was making his act of consecration in Rome.

Two questions arise. Since Vassula's thinking is so accurately focused on papal policy does she have a message for the Pope? A prior question is, do her writings agree in all things with the teaching of the Church, of which doctrine the Pope is the ultimate guardian?

Visionaries have been given special messages for Popes. The best known is St. Catherine of Siena, who told the Pope of the day that he should return from Avignon to Rome as the seat of the papacy. Leo XIII was influenced in two of his public acts by messages from mystics: from Sister (now Blessed) Elena Guerra to declare special devotions to the Holy Spirit, for which he also issued an Encyclical; from Sister Droesch-Vichering, a Good Shepherd nun, to consecrate the world to the Sacred Heart of Jesus, which he did on 11 June, 1899. It is believed that Pius XI was acting on a message from a mystic when he instituted the feast of Christ the King. Pius XII and his successors who have made consecrations to the Immaculate Heart of Mary were certainly influenced by Sister Lucia, a visionary at Fatima, now a Carmelite in Coimbra convent.

The popes have never publicly acknowledged their debt to these individuals. Thus far the problem has not arisen in the life of Vassula. The problem of an official investigation of her case and a verdict cannot arise. For she is not subject to the jurisdiction of Catholic ecclesiastical authorities. Prelates of the Greek Orthodox Church have shown no desire to institute any such procedure.

The question still remains: Is she an authentic messenger of Jesus? I shall not anticipate matters to be dealt with later. I would suggest that the reader apply the customary criteria, which are a blend of mystical theology, psychology and common-sense. Does her doctrine conform to the teaching of the Church, that is, is there variance or opposition to what Catholics hold as orthodox interpretation of the sources of God's revelation to man? In substance the answer is unhesitatingly favourable. From the brief notes offered in the preceding pages it is clear that the essentials of her spirituality, as this can be put in synthesis from the highly singular mode of expression which is hers, and this by divine intervention, are either an emphasis on most important truths which were allowed to lapse, or a most welcome revival of ideals which were being excluded from Christian instruction. There had been a loss of inspiration in the everyday business of living the teaching of Jesus Christ.

Further to this approach there is the question of Vassula's reliability, her credibility as a witness. Is she competent in perception? Is she truthful? The answer to the first question occasionally requires medical, even psychiatric examination as to normalcy. We can dispense with such things here, as we can in regard to her honesty. Anyone who knows her over any length of time can have no doubt about her integrity. (This clearly shown in the professional evaluation of her writing contained in Appendix III.) Akin to this matter is the ability to report accurately. A witness may be competent in observation, utterly truthful but faulty in narrating what he or she has seen and heard. Different factors enter here, immediate memory, retentive power, discipline of the imagination or lack of it, a subconscious craving to play a role, to meet what is known to be expectation on the part of the reader or listener. One has the feeling at times in dealing with some visionaries that they did receive at the outset genuine messages or locutions, but as these faded with the passage of time they felt justified in fabricating something which would satisfy the longing or curiosity of followers already roused. I was present once at a session, a prayer group, the identity of which cannot be guessed, where a visionary behaved in such a way as to leave me highly sceptical about the reality of what was given as of supernatural origin.

In granting to Vassula the special gift of distinctive writing the Lord has preserved her from this temptation and saved us from any justifiable suspicion. There are many pitfalls and the most highly favoured have at times passed through moments of self-scrutiny and doubt. This is the human condition. Despite the limitations which it imposes we can trust the working of the Holy Spirit and benefit by the results of His inspiration and impulse.

There is one other very important point. People often talk about prudence as needed in judging cases of the kind we are considering. It is not specifically prudence which is required, and one must add that by prudence is sometimes meant caution. Prudence is needed for the whole of human life. It is one of the basic virtues analysed by the Greek philosopher, Aristotle. Supernatural prudence is needed in the Christian life, and for difficult cases there is the special gift of the Holy Spirit, Counsel. Prudence may dictate a course of action that is, in wholly human terms, quite incautious. The most prudent thing that St. Thomas More did was to risk his life for his belief; the bishops who capitulated to Henry VIII, all but one, probably thought him imprudent.

What is specifically required in the evaluation of special graces like locutions, visions, apparitions, heavenly messages is discernment. It is not given to all, if a serious under-statement be permitted. It demands a certain apprenticeship, it cannot grow save in a whole spiritual atmosphere of humility, docility to the Spirit of God, patience, profound respect for human personality and a certain awe, a sense of the sacred, in the presence of divine munificence. The truly discerning will have very considerable distrust of their own judgement; they will know that theoretical knowledge no matter how massive, is not the key. Nor can those with massive theological learning, and insight in proportion, be ruled out. The greatest theologian of the age, author of works vast and deep, taking 55,000 pages to publish, Hans Urs von Balthasar, proved himself a most perfect practitioner of spiritual discernment in dealing with the great mystic, Adrienne von Speyr.

It would be easy to gather evidence through recent church history of people called on, officially named, to act on commissions of inquiry into mystical claims, without any evidence that they had discernment or even knew what it meant. Sad, very sad, but alas true. The victims of such clumsy performers carry for years the marks, the wounds, of their incompetence which sometimes verged on brutality. They have sometimes treated visionaries in a way that in the secular forum would have them hauled into court for mental torture: rightly.

Notes:

1. Archibishop William Barden, O.P.; Bishop Donal O'Herlihy of Ferns, Bishop Joseph Carroll, Auxiliary in Dublin;

2. Cf. R. Laurentin, *Apparitions of the Blessed Virgin Mary Today*, Dublin, 1991; he also supplies further information in the review, *Chretiens Magazine*, from time to time;

3. In two theological encyclopedias, *Theotokos*, Wilmington, 1981, *Veni Creator Spiritus*, Wilmington, 1985; further works in the appendix, Outline Bibliography;

4. Cf. my articles published over the years in *Knock Shrine Annual*, pamphlet *The Secret of Knock*, Dublin, 1942; my book *L'apparition de Knock* is awaiting publication in Paris;

5. I have discussed the apparition with members of the *Société de Banneux*, on occasion of pilgrimages with Irish and Belgian handicapped to the shrine, principally with the last president of the Société, Marie Thérèse de Theux;

6. Cf. my books *Medjugorje: Facts, Documents, Theology*, Dublin, 1986 and later editions; *Is Medjugorje Approved?* Dublin, 1991;

1

PERSONALITY

Vassula Rydén was born on 18 January, 1942 in Egypt of Greek parents, who were of the second generation in that country. She was baptized and later confirmed in the Greek Orthodox Church, the religion of her parents. She was given the education of the children of well-off families, was not notably pious. She did, as a child, on two occasions, have dreams of a spiritual, probably mystical, kind. At the age of ten it was Christ who called her to Him with irresistible force. The following year it was something more elaborate. The eleven year old dreamt that she was spiritually espoused to Jesus, Our Lady awaited her and had prepared her bridal attire. On each occasion Vassula told her mother of her experience.

This double experience was to return to her with meaning in later life. But this would be after long years of religious indifference. She travelled with her husband, an official in international agencies, to several African countries (Sierra Leone, Ethiopia, Sudan, Mozambique, Lesotho) and to Bangladesh, where she lived from 1984 to 1987.

For thirty years, 1955 to 1985, Vassula was not a church-goer; for social reasons she appeared occasionally at marriages and funerals. She had not lost her faith in God; she just felt no inclination towards any observance. She led the life of the typical expatriate in Africa and Asia: the social round, amusement, cocktail parties for her husband's business friends, such games as the climate permitted. Her choice was tennis, in which she became quite proficient; she was champion of Bangladesh. The word at the time was, "If you want Vassula, go to the tennis court." She also modelled clothes, as a hobby to while away the time. Painting she took up seriously, and with considerable success. I have seen some of her paintings. One of them, *Horses*, reminded me of a treatment of the same theme by the Irish painter, Jack Yeats, the poet's brother; it seized the imagination of Dubliners in an Irish Academy Exhibition during the war years.

A woman of culture then and through the demands of existence in different countries, a competent linguist; she speaks Greek, Arabic, French, Swedish (her husband's language), not all with the same fluency, some Spanish as well as her customary language, English. Though Greek she is Nordic in appearance, is highly articulate, sensitive, with latent strength; she is never aggressive, and has a ready sense of humour, which makes her a very easy, pleasant companion. She is devoted to her two children, runs her house efficiently, is unassumingly hospitable.

This is Vassula seen in her present phase. This is how she appears as she has come through a continuing mystical experience, and undertaken a mission which flows directly from it.

This phase began in 1985 in Bangladesh, in the last week of November. Vassula was one day writing a shopping list. But she felt her hand tremble, and she found herself writing something entirely different. She wrote under another influence. First the power controlling and using her hand wrote the words, "I am your angel guardian." He named himself Daniel. A relationship grew gradually between them, the writing being the medium. It lasted for two months, was a time of trial and purification. But she loved Daniel. She has even been assured by the Lord that no one ever so loved an angel guardian. Her husband though intrigued at first when she informed him of her experience, remained interested and supportive. Internally she went through the process of purification necessary to prepare her for the direct advent of Jesus into her life.

"The angel prepared me; it was a kind of purification. He showed me my sins as one sees them in purgatory. Little sins that had previously seemed to me to be nothing at all, I now saw with other eyes. They seemed enormous, and that made me feel so bad that I hated myself. How could I have done such things? It was a great purification."

The angel told Vassula that she should from now on read the Bible, which had meant nothing to her. She did not know where to find a copy of the sacred book, and this information too he supplied.

A principal problem was spiritual direction. This she needed, but where to obtain it? She turned to a community of missionaries in the Bangladesh city where she lived; their residence was across the road from hers. But those she approached were disconcerted, sceptical as are Catholic priests generally when presented with this kind of problem: cautious, prudent they would say. One even suspected some nefarious preternatural influence. But eventually an American priest, Fr. James Fannan, assumed the task and role of spiritual director to Vassula.

Divine Providence is over all. Sometimes this reality is manifest evident. When Vassula's husband was assigned to Switzerland she bade good-bye to her spiritual director. To whom would she now turn for advice, positive directives? The problem was, before long, resolved to her satisfaction. Fr. Fannan began to suffer from a serious malady of the eyes, cataract, which called for surgery. His superiors decided that he should come to Europe for this special treatment. In the event he found himself in Switzerland, not far from Lausanne, in the suburbs of which city Vassula had taken up residence with her husband and children. Another happy coincidence is that her mother and other members of her family have been living for some time in the very street where she came to live.

Vassula later described her moment of destiny thus:

"At the outset I was suddenly approached by my guardian angel so that he should open the Lord's way to me, I, an inveterate sinner, had no love for God. Even when my guardian angel explained things of heaven to me I was happy to be with my angel. I sought nothing more. When God approached me, taking the place of my angel, I was in a way disappointed. I felt Him to be a stranger, whilst having already made acquaintance with my angel my feelings of surprise had become feelings of love. I did not understand then why God wished to take the place of my angel. I had even come to believe that God was jealous of the love which I felt for my angel."

"Later after a painful purification given by my guardian angel God came to me a second time, again taking the place of my angel. He remained with me for a few days, opening my heart little by little and wisely so as not to frighten me. Then just as I began to open myself to Him, He moved away and hid. I turned on every side seeking my angel, but did not find him either. I had the feeling of souls coming to me, begging prayers and blessings. I prayed for them and I blessed them. Then they asked me to bless them with holy water. I ran quickly to the church to look for holy water for them, and I blessed them, sprinkling them with holy water. I took advantage of this to ask them if they had seen where my angel and the one whom I had begun to love in my heart were to be found. But I got no reply. Every day that went by seemed to be a year. I sought peace without being able to find it. I had around me many people and many friends, but I never felt more alone and abandoned than during those days. It was like going through hell; several times I cried out to my angel to come back to me, but no, he had turned his back and was gone away!"

"My soul failed me for his flight. (RSV "when he spoke"). I sought him, but found him not; I called him, but he gave no answer." (Song 5:6) I wandered thus abandoned to myself in the desert for three long weeks, to the point where I could no longer bear it. Then, in my distress, seeking Him in heaven I cried out to Yahweh: 'Father! Oh my God, take me and make of me what you will! Purify me so that you may use me.'"

"No sooner had this cry come from the depth of my heart, than suddenly heaven was opened, and as lightning, the Father's voice cried out full of emotion: 'I, God, love you!' Instantaneously, I felt as if from a tornado I had passed into a magnificently peaceful world. My angel reappeared and, with great tenderness, began to dress my wounds, the wounds I had received in the desert."

Vassula is here describing what took place in 1986. On 22 December, 1990, when she had some years' experience of messages given her by Jesus, she took down this locution from him.

"I Am; I treat you very gently so that you, as my flower, grow; I want you strong and believe Me I shall make it possible; you shall be strong, daughter, since you carry My Word; in front of you, I am, to break all barriers that come up while you are witnessing; I am the Most High, and I tell you, daughter, that I shall see to it that no power from beneath stops you from proclaiming my message. I have taken you out of the land of Egypt to respond to me in a foreign land and witness to a people not your own; so although your behaviour was appalling and your sense blemished enabling you to see the light, Mercy and Compassion was seized by your astounding misery, guilt and wretchedness and came to your rescue; No, Oh Vassula, you have not deserved any of my gifts. Why, I had servants in my hand who honoured me, never uttering but My name in holiness, who blessed Me without ceasing, who praised the Holy Trinity wholeheartedly, but yet My Heart, an abyss of love, cried out for you; you had accumulated sorrow upon sorrow in My Heart, treason upon treason; you were wrestling with Me, puny little creature... but I knew that your heart is not a divided heart, and that once I conquer your heart, it would become entirely mine. An object of your era you were wrestling with me, but I have thrown you down in the wrestle, and dragged you in the dust and into the desert, where I left you there all alone. I had provided you with a guardian angel since the beginning of your existence, to guard you, console you and guide you, but my Wisdom ordered your guardian angel to leave you and to let you face the desert on your own. I said 'you are to live in spite of your nakedness!', because no man is able to survive alone. Satan would have taken over completely and would have killed you; My order was given to him too; I forbade him to touch you. Then, in your terror, you remembered me, and looked up to heaven searching desperately for me; your laments and your supplications suddenly broke the deathly stillness surrounding you and your terrified cries pierced through the heavens, reaching the Holy Trinity's ears. 'My child, the Father's voice, full of joy resounded through all heaven.' 'Ah, I shall now make her penetrate my wounds, and let her eat my Body and drink my Blood. I shall espouse her to Me, and she will be Mine for eternity. I shall show her the love I have for her, and her lips from thereon shall thirst for Me and her heart shall be My head-rest. She shall eagerly submit daily to My righteousness, and I shall make her an altar of My love and of My Passion, and I shall send her with My message to the ends of the world to conquer an irreligious people, and to a people who are not even her own, and voluntarily she will carry My Cross of peace and love, taking the road to Calvary.' '..And I the Holy Spirit shall descend upon her to reveal to her the truth and the depths of Us. I shall remind the world through her, that the greatest of all gifts is LOVE.' Let us then celebrate! Let all heaven celebrate! I have taken you by the hand and formed you to become a living sign of My great love, a witness of my Sacred Heart, and of the renewal of my Church. I am the Resurrection."[1]

Some time earlier Jesus had spoken similar words to Vassula. He wished her to bear constantly in mind her utter dependence on him, and He clarified the danger of Satan's intentions. He had shown her a view of Hell and when Satan saw her he spat and exclaimed that "worms" were being now brought to his abode. This explains one reference in the following message:

"Child look at my lips and listen to me carefully; faith, have faith in Me and trust Me. I know your ineffable weakness and that without me you cannot raise your little finger; this is why I have chosen you. I have chosen weakness to show the world my power, I have a reason why I have chosen you in your state. Trust Me and draw your strength from Me; I shall remind you how the devil hates you, and today you felt his claws on you. Yes, if I had left him he would have torn you to pieces, but you are under my divine protection. Every single minute of his is aimed on you and all My other chosen souls. I tell you because of your nothingness and because of your poverty, puny creature of mine, you are undoing Satan's patterns, you are undoing, stitch after stitch, his embroideries; he called you a worm when he knew you are My chosen one. Yes, be like a worm and eat up and ravage his designs, see. I can use for My works even worms.. Yes, eat up like a worm his patterns. I have allowed you to feel his hatred, because the Father Himself loves you for loving me. This infuriates him beyond one's imagination. Happy is the man who does not lose faith in Me. Delight My soul and fill me with joy by remaining nothing."[2]

The foundation of the lifework thus guaranteed is linked with the dictation Vassula receives from Jesus. Other favoured souls have received communications from the Lord which he wished to see written, St. Catherine of Siena, Maria Concepcion Cabrera de Armida, the Mexican co-foundress of the *Missioneros del Espiritu Santo*, Adrienne von Speyr from whom Has Urs von Balthasar took sixteen thousand pages of dictation. But Vassula's gift is entirely singular in character. Those who have seen the published notebooks, entitled *True Life in God*, know that most of the writing, that which contains messages attributed directly to Jesus, differs in appearance from much shorter passages which express Vassula's own thought.

This mode of writing has been seriously misinterpreted. Let Vassula herself explain it. This is how she did so under the careful, respectful examination of Fr. René Laurentin:

"During the dictation were you in ecstasy? Were you withdrawn from the outside world like the seers at Medjugorje? It does not seem like it?"

"No, I see what's around me, but I am absorbed in Jesus and his message. It's a little like when you are writing at your desk, and don't think about what's around you, which is still nevertheless present to your sight."

"But you are very dependent. For the seers at Medjugorje the apparitions especially aroused their freedom."

"He asked me not to take a step without asking Him."

"But doesn't that change you into a robot? It is not even your handwriting any more; it is somebody else's. And even though it is your hand, a graphologist wouldn't dare to say that it is the same person."

"Yes, but Jesus had told me and clearly shown me that this handwriting is not automatic writing, as some people imagine. One day, he told me, 'Today you will write my message with your own handwriting, so that those who have not truly understood this grace that I am granting to you can understand, realizing that I have also given you the grace to hear my voice. Allow me today to dictate only. You listen and write.'"

At this point Vassula showed me her notebook where the handwriting changes for the message that follows. Her own small, sensitive writing begins:

"Vassula, the days are counted."

The message continues then in the normal handwriting of Vassula for two pages and then concludes with the words:

"This is for all those who think that your hand is moved by Me without your hearing or understanding that it is I, the Lord, who inspires you. Now let us continue in the way I like, My Vassula."

Then the large handwriting reappears:

"Receive my peace, be alert."

René Laurentin by judicious questioning helped Vassula to clarify still further the operation of this astonishing script.

"But in the case of these messages, is it your hand that moves, or rather is it dictated to your hearing?"

"It is dictated."

"But you said that your hand was moved in some way."

"Yes, it is simultaneous. At first, He guided my hand without dictating. One day He said to me: 'I would like you to listen to my voice, the interior voice.' And in just six weeks I learned to hear His voice. It is dictated word by word; and at times there are words that I don't even know. I have to look them up in the dictionary."

"Even in English there are some words that puzzle you."

"Yes, there are some words that I don't know. At other times he gives me a paragraph all at once, and I have to hurry to write it before I forget. But if I do forget He reminds me of the word that I skipped. One day He invited me to go to confession. I was against that. I wanted to erase the sentence I had begun, but He blocked my hand. It was as if the pencil had got stuck in a hole. Then I pushed with the other hand that felt more free. Then the pencil just twisted in my hand, flew to one side and my hand was flung back."[3]

Vassula sometimes feels obliged to rewrite what she has hastily taken down. Jesus then corrects her; He does not object to elimination of what has been personal, words of advice or warning to friends. He also guided her to draw the hearts that are to be seen here and there in the text, as the fish, symbol from ancient times of the Saviour. He prefers to take His dictation kneeling. She has taken dictation for four or five hours daily, sometimes six-four in the morning, two in the afternoon.

For some time after her entry into a way of life so utterly new Vassula kept knowledge of her gifts to herself. Only four or five people knew. Then after three years, in November 1988, Jesus instructed her - "insisted" is her word - that she should take part in prayer meetings once a month. She had no knowledge of how to do this. She protested to Jesus: "I don't know how; I don't know how to speak:

I don't know how to do anything." Jesus answered: "But it is not you who will do it; I will do it, and I will dictate the programme for you."

After the meeting the following dialogue ensued:

"I was surprised to see so many come. There must have been one hundred and thirty people."

"Vassula, I have said before - full, you shall be many."

"Lord, you must have noticed that there were some disputes because of the programme?"

"How could I not notice all this! Vassula, opposing forces there will be, but I will not allow anyone to tread on you. Detach yourself and depend on me; from now on, it is I who will organise and give you the programme of my meetings; it is I who will tell you what to say - the programme will be given to you from above. I am Wisdom and from Wisdom you will receive it. Write: first you will sanctify the place (where) you are to hold my meeting, like you have done, by praying the prayer to St. Michael; open My meeting by saying these words: 'Peace be with you.' Remember to tell my little flowers that it is I, the Lord, who gives them My peace and that these words come from My mouth. Then you will invoke, all of you, the Holy Spirit. You will pray the prayer to St. Michael - your era needs this prayer desperately. I will indicate always to you the passage to be read from the Holy Bible, just like I indicated to you in this past meeting to read Joel 3:28-32; in this way I will show you the passage to be read. My wish is that you read to them, then tell them why I chose this passage. This is to be followed by you reading to them parts of My peace and love message."

"How would I know which part I am to read to them?"

"Do not worry, am I not your Counsellor and Guide?"

"Yes, my Lord."

"After reading to them you can ask them if they have any questions - it is a time for open conversation. I will inspire you little one. Then I would like you to read to them My message concerning them. Please Me by offering them love; please Me by terminating with the holy Rosary."

"If anyone wants to talk to me should I accept?"

"Beloved, yes, talk to them."[4]

The prayer meetings opened a new stage in Vassula's life, her mission, as it would very soon appear. Such a future was outlined to her by Jesus in these words: "You are to write, to love me, and to spread my message. It is I who will do the rest." During 1988 meetings took place mostly in Switzerland. In the early stages these meetings were mostly in churches; with time other venues were chosen.

With increasing serenity and skill in spiritual, apostolic work, Vassula has had to face a growing demand for her presence and communication. She has had to become a special communicator of divine truth, not only orally but in the written word. Each promotes the other, for those who hear her wish to have her message in permanent form, and those who read her feel drawn also to listen to her.

The demand for Vassula's presence among Catholics has been worldwide. This is explainable through many factors. One is the readiness of well-known Catholic priests, many of them experienced in the relevant matters, to testify on her behalf. One of the first to do so was Dom Ian Petit, O.S.B., well-known and esteemed as a preacher of retreats. His conversation with Vassula was taped and issued as a cassette. It was very widely distributed, was to many people a delightful surprise. Several other cassettes have since been made with her cooperation; video=cassettes of meetings where she has spoken are also in circulation.

Many other priests have met Vassula, studied her message and judged her personality. Those who have been favourably impressed include - besides the outstanding expert in all the questions relevant to her mission, Fr. René Laurentin, Fr. Gobbi, founder and leader of the Marian Movement for Priests; the Italian writer, Don Luigi Bianchi; Fr. A. Gentili, specialist in mystical theology; the Canadian spiritual writer; Fr. Louis Parent, O.M.I.; Dr. Franic, former archbishop of Split, president of the Theological Commission of the Yugoslav hierarchy, a post he was pressed to retain after his resignation from his episcopal see; Fr. Richard Foley, S.J.; Fr. Henry Bordeaux, O.D.C., spiritual counsellor; Fr. Gerard McGinnity, spiritual counsellor; Cardinal Sin and Cardinal Vidal, both of the Philippines; Fr. Edward O'Connor, professor at Notre Dame Catholic University, Indiana; Bishop Hlnilica, adviser to the Pope on Russia and eastern Europe; Fr. Robert Faricy professor at the Gregorian University, the vice-president of Quito Marian Society; Père Courtil, O.F.M.Cap., exorcist in many French dioceses.

Vassula easily identifies with the Catholic ethos in her acceptance of prayers like the Rosary, which are particularly ours and not found among the Orthodox; she prays the Memorare, likes to make the Stations of the Cross, uses the prayer to St. Michael traditional among us.

In the same way this child of the Greek Orthodox Church has gone as a pilgrim to Catholic shrines of Our Lady, Lourdes, Garabandal, Fatima, and Medjugorje, as will be seen in a later chapter. She also defends the Shroud of Turin, a singular relic of the Passion which should appeal to all Christians but which has been in Catholic custody, is now, by the will of the original owner, the Italian king, the property of the Holy See. On 2 October 1987, Vassula received this message from Jesus:

> "It is I, Jesus. Let it be known that any image of Mine or of My Mother is to be honoured, for it represents us, as My Cross is representing me. Let it be known that My Holy Shroud is authentic. It is the same that covered Me."

Support for the messenger of the Sacred Heart has not been only from the clergy. Some of the dynamic lay men and women in the Catholic Church at the present time are identified with her apostolate. With no claim to advance an exhaustive list I mention Anthony Hickey, director of the Manchester Medjugorje Centre; Howard Dee, former Philippine ambassador to the Holy See; June Keightley, author, radio and television personality of the Centre for Peace, Manila; Judge Daniel Lynch, companion of the Pilgrim image of Our Lady of Guadalupe, Protectress of the unborn, witness of striking effects of the presentation of this wonderful sign of Mary's power; Paul and Evelyn Bouchard of the *Information Catholique*, influential in French-speaking Canada; Patrick de Laubier of the University of Geneva; Leon Legrand, tireless worker for Medjugorje throughout Australia.

Some of the clerical and lay names I have cited are either active in the Medjugorje apostolate or sympathetic to it. It is important to see and evaluate the link between Medjugorje prayer groups and Vassula's work. Most of those touched by the amazing outpouring of grace in the Yugoslav village take spontaneously to her message. Vassula on her side finds this spiritual atmosphere highly congenial. To document this generalization factually would take a separate monograph, which will be undertaken in due course.

The reader will scarcely need to be told that all of this continuous spiritual activity imposes an immense burden on the one at the centre of it. Her days are passed in many different places, as she is incessantly in demand to address audiences, always Catholic audiences. Any one of these journeys, especially those overseas may entail a great deal of time, in telephone calls fixing times and programmes, sending messages by fax to adjust schedules. The journeys are at times lengthy, taxing energy: not only by train to European cities, sometimes by plane. Vassula has many times crossed the Atlantic. She has flown or is in the near future due to fly to the U.S.A, Canada, Philippines, Australia, Japan, Latin America, the Middle East, Mexico, Russia, the West Indies, Central and South Africa and Poland.

This is a lady of very generous disposition, not only in terms of hospitality in her home to visitors from near and far, but in the work she undertakes to facilitate collaboration in spreading the message. Since her writings are appearing either in facsimile or in print in the original language, English, and in several translations, publishers or translators call on her advice or approval: all of which takes time and persevering industry. She is ready to send photocopies of parts of the message to persons reliably interested in one aspect or another of it. Thus she was eager to send a dossier on the "Two Hearts", as complete as possible, to Howard Dee, for he has played an active part in propagating this ideal - they met in Manila.

An apostolate free of suffering? Who, with any knowledge of mystical theology would think so? For a number of years Vassula had to endure the Passion of Christ on Fridays. It was a moving experience to witness this ordeal of love, of identification with the Saviour in His redemptive sacrifice. Generosity and cooperation were on the part of the victim total. Delicacy imposes restraint in writing of such things.

Readers of this short work, which I see as an introduction to the writings of Vassula, would be disappointed if I did not deal with critical comments which have been made and circulated about her. I have some experience of controversy, in regard for example to misrepresentation of St. Thérèse of Lisieux and at much greater length in defence of the saintly Pope Pius XII and the wartime genocidal campaign against the Jewish people. But I do not think that a controversial or polemical approach would, in the present instance, serve the only cause that interests me, namely that the message of love and peace given to Vassula would reach the widest possible audience. In the same spirit Fr. René Laurentin[5] and Fr. Ovila Melancon, C.S.C.[6] have already published informative and reassuring works on Vassula.

I remind readers that in any such investigation there are certain preliminary tests which they may apply. One is a basic imperative of our time, respect for the human person. Those who set out to assess and perhaps ultimately to criticize visionaries or favoured souls seem at times to think themselves relieved of this elementary duty. They think or assume that their zeal for the truth, which may be genuine, allows them to say things seriously damaging to the persons in question. In certain parts of the world this carelessness is accompanied by a harshness, even hardness, in expression which is anything but Christian.

Secondly it is fair and advisable to inquire what are the credentials of the critic: What evidence is there of proficiency in the relevant theological disciplines, primarily mystical and ascetical theology? What practical experience has the critic of dealing with similar cases? Does he or she speak or write from wisdom which has stood the test in the examination of alleged claims to special divine graces? Is there independent testimony on these matters? Is there any published work, written or recorded on cassette or video to substantiate important claims? The layman, that is the non-professional, is viewed with suspicion in every walk of life - which does not mean that he may not occasionally be right. Professional norms are still universally imposed.

I have a file of criticism in regard to Vassula. Thus far none of the contributors is a writer or teacher of international stature, as are those I have already mentioned who support her, think her message authentic. One item in the dossier I do not think worthy of serious consideration. It is anonymous on the plea that the signature is withheld for reasons of humility! One hopes that this does not impugn the thousands of Christian writers from the gospels to our time who have honourably signed their published work. A nasty suspicion attaches to a written product which attacks a living person by name, but hides the name of the assailant. The evil is compounded by the claim that what is in this document has come with approval from Our Lady. Has the writer been subjected to appropriate discernment? By whom? With what verdict? There is also a very unusual assertion that a message has been received from a soul in Purgatory in regard to Vassula. I shall deal with this submission when I am informed of the author's identity.

The points that are raised may be grouped under these headings: personal life, manner of divine communication, theological content of what is communicated. I must dismiss at once outright a serious error. An image is in circulation taken from Vassula's home, which is supposed to depict her dubious, if not satanic background. It shows, in a sombre atmosphere, elderly figures. They have lights in their hands. What is the origin of this image? It was copied by Vassula from the National Geographic Magazine; it had as title "Mediterranean peasants at prayer." It has nothing whatsoever to do with satanism. It is sombre because it is in the style of Rembrandt.

It is entirely objectionable to parade any item taken from the privacy of another person's home. In the present case this is doubly objectionable for in fact those who have been in her home, as I have been, know that she has a truly edifying collection of wonderful images of the Lord and his Blessed Mother! Especially prominent among them is the image of the Saviour wrought from the Shroud of Turin; so is the reproduction of the Christ of Limpias, and the Rosa Mystical statue of Our Lady - again with several other impressive images.

In the context of Vassula's personal life people are puzzled that such important messages come from a member of the Greek Orthodox Church. She is also divorced. That she remains Orthodox is her own conscientious decision, and her messages can be taken as seriously as they merit, just as certain experts at Vatican II took very serious account of the criticism of teaching published during the first three sessions: it did not provide adequate teaching on the Holy Spirit. This matter will be dealt with later. John Paul II admits in his Encyclical on the Holy Spirit, *Dominum et vivificantem* that the easterns are superior to us here. Vassula's role in regard to Christian unity will be also considered later.

She has a Catholic confessor - not me, I add - and receives Holy Communion in virtue of this Canon in the new Code of Canon Law promulgated by Pope John Paul II: "Catholic ministers may licitly administer the sacraments of Penance, Eucharist and anointing of the sick to members of the Oriental churches which do not have full communion with the Catholic Church, if they ask on their own for the Sacraments and are properly disposed." (844, 3) Her marital situation has been completely regularised by the authorities in her Church and she is in excellent standing with Archbishop Damaskinos, responsible for the Greek Orthodox in her area.

What about the manner of communication? People have attempted to show that the handwriting is "automatic writing", a form of "channelling". The source of such activity is dark, possibly diabolical, cosmic in a vague sense. But it is not related in its product to an established creed on the writer's part, is not an exercise of personal freedom, does not issue in a set of ideas entirely supernatural, related directly to the Saviour of humankind, Our Lord Jesus Christ, knows nothing about sensitive relationship with the Mother of God, with angelic society, never leads to a deepening of Christian faith, hope and love, cannot favour an approach, salutary and continuous, to St. Michael, prince of angelic society. Automatic writing could no more give a rich Trinitarian doctrine, traditional and existential, such as will be outlined in the pages of this book than stirring dirty water in a cracked bowl could turn it in vintage wine. Automatic writing does not continue over years to achieve such sublime things as people admire in "True Life in God".

The New Age has been mentioned in the same context. Vassula utterly repudiates it:

> "I fight the New Age. How could I belong to it. New Age means that there is no Eucharist, no Rosary, no Pope. And what do the messages say? The Pope is the Vicar of Jesus Christ; the Rosary it is which chains Satan; the Eucharist is what makes the life of the Church. This has reappeared a thousand times in the messages."

With the writing one is led to apply the biblical test, "Judge the tree by its fruits." Many people have been deeply influenced by reading the messages. When Vassula came to Dublin in November 1991, she was accompanied by eight friends of different nationalities, each of whom had been touched by grace as a result of reading Vassula's books or hearing her. She very frequently receives letters telling of conversion for similar reasons. Note, that her public mission began in November 1988, exactly three years after she had received her first message.

There are points of doctrine to be considered in the critical dossier, principally in regard to ecumenism and Trinitarian theology. These will be taken in their proper place.

Notes:

1. 22 December, 1990, Volume II, page 260f;
2. 30 October, 1990, Volume II, page 246;
3. Testimony of Vassula to Fr. René Laurentin, I, pp viff;
4. Programme of meetings communicated 17 December, 1988, Volume I, page 407;
5. *Quand Dieu fait signe*, Ottawa and Paris, 1992;
6. *Vassula Ryden, Messagère du Sacré Coeur, Justification Théologique*, Montréal, 1992. Apart from a refutation of errors which appeared in *The Wanderer*, after Vassula's meeting in Sacramento cathedral, I generally avoid public controversy. I have conducted such a controversy in defence of Pius XII, in the columns of the *Irish Times* during several months in 1964. I amplified my defence of Pius XII, on the basis of the Nuremberg papers, those published and those held in the National Archives in Washington, and the Vatican War Documents, in *Pius XII, Greatness Dishonoured*, Dublin, 1980. My defence of St. Thérèse of Lisieux against ideas put out by Fr. Etienne Robo was lauded by the saint's surviving sister, Geneviève de la Sainte Face. I have written to a number of persons privately to correct their erroneous opinions of Vassula. The irony of life had it that some were people whom I had defended against their critics. Life is like that - sometimes.

2

THE APOSTASY

The Catholic Church enjoyed a brief moment of euphoria after the Second Vatican Council. The worldwide media interest in what was happening in Rome, the unanimity manifested in the final voting of the vast majority of the conciliar documents, the status of hero figures, media personalities almost, conferred on prelates and theologians well-known through the Council, Cardinals Suenens and Bea for example or theologians like Fr. Karl Rahner and Hans Kung, Edward Schillebeeckx perhaps also and Yves Congar, seemed to indicate a readiness on the part of the world to change its attitude towards the Catholic Church. Would we not then see an increase in vocations to the priestly and religious life, a revival of religious practice among the masses, a warm welcome to the Catholic missionary in pagan lands and rapid steps towards Christian unity. Over all this change, those in the great Catholic intellectual centres would preside, dispensing Catholic truth coherent in itself and cogent in its appeal, ancient doctrine given a new vitality and brightness by a thorough carefully worked harmony with ultra-modern method.

The very title of one important text to issue from the assembly in Rome, *The Catholic Church in the Modern World*, seemed to express hope for such a happy future. The Pope of the Council, who was to die after its first session, John XXIII, was a universal favourite, inside and outside the Catholic body. True, as time passed, not a long time, his features were blurred from reality into something like a fairy god-father; his name would be invoked to justify theories or programmes which he would have been the first to repudiate.

True also, there were already signs of dissension within the schools of theological thought, dissension which would harden into conflict. The words "conservative" and "progressive" increasingly entered into the vocabulary of Catholics, which does not mean that they all clearly understood these words. "Traditionalist" was also soon in use to designate a particular category of conservative. But much more than exchange of names, even as these were taken as militant slogans, was to affect the Catholic Church. Events took suddenly and unaccountably a downward turn. A widely praised achievement of the Council had been the liturgical reform, though reform is scarcely the right word. Pius XII (d. 1958) had welcomed the widespread movement within the Church focused on the Liturgy, which aimed at removing the barrier between the celebrating clergy and the lay congregation. The key word was participation. Along with it went a wish to promote an intelligent understanding of liturgical rites, to highlight especially the celebration of Easter, to give universal acceptance to the concept of the Paschal Mystery. Great theologians of the liturgy, principal among them Dom Odo Casel, author of the *Mysterienlehre* insight, were recognised and valued. All that now remained to do was to translate this shining theory into practice, which meant explaining it to the faithful, or, if need be, reassuring them that change was on the road to improvement, not to destruction.

But what did happen in places was something akin to destruction. Catholic priests now liberated from a set of rigid rules, from being encased in a framework heavily overlaid with mortal sins, broke loose of all constraints. Bizarre ceremonies took place in different countries "in the spirit of the Council." Reports of such things are often exaggerated. Essays of different kinds have appeared with fairly reliable documentation. Papers on a weekly or monthly basis published eye-witness reports. For France a writer, Michel de St. Pierre, whose novel *Les nouveaux prêtres* had expressed remarkable prescience on the situation, now published two books which were irrefutable dossiers, *Les fumées de Satan* and *Le ver est dans le fruit*, factual records of thoroughly inexcusable alterations in the liturgy.[1] Nothing of the kind was intended or permitted by the conciliar Constitution on the Liturgy or the subsequent official rulings. On the contrary it was laid down in the capital document, the Constitution, that: "No person, even if he be a priest, may add, remove or change anything in the Liturgy on his own authority."[2]

Is Michel de St. Pierre the only one to have noted the deviations? They are put much more strongly in an *Instruction on Certain Norms Concerning the Worship of the Eucharistic Mystery*, issued, with the approval of John Paul II, by the Sacred Congregation for the Sacraments and Divine Worship, on 3 April, 1980. After referring to positive results of the liturgical reform, the text went on:

> "But these encouraging and positive aspects cannot suppress concern at the *varied and frequent abuses* (italics added) being reported from different parts of the Catholic world: the confusion of roles, especially regarding the priestly ministry and the role of the laity (indiscriminate shared recitation of the Eucharistic Prayer, homilies given by lay people, lay people distributing Communion while priests refrain from doing so) an increasing loss of the sense of the sacred (abandonment of liturgical vestments, the Eucharist celebrated outside church without real need, lack of reverence and respect for the Blessed Sacrament etc.); misunderstanding of the ecclesial character of the liturgy (the use of private texts, the proliferation of unapproved Eucharistic Prayers, the manipulation of the liturgical texts for social and political ends). In these cases we are face to face with a real falsification of the Catholic liturgy."[3]

Concomitant with these abuses went another upset not on the agenda of optimism: the numbers of priests who abandoned the ministry were not counted in hundreds or thousands but in scores of thousands. Nuns, in equally large numbers, left their convents not to return. Recruitment to the priestly ranks and to the sisterhoods declined sharply. The Catholic Church still maintained its institutional structures, but they were weakening visibly.

That was bad, but there was worse. It was not at first patently recognisable as apostasy, that is loss, which really means rejection, of the faith. Here we touch a sprawling mass of confusion. But apostasy was soon really upon us. Those who should have been the custodians, the reliable teachers, of the faith were heard embracing theories, giving vent to doubts, utterly at variance with the truth transmitted in the infallible Church, the Mystical Body of Christ. To cover the whole spectrum of error would demand lengthy surveys and analyses. One of the most gifted theologians of our time, Joseph Cardinal Ratzinger, Prefect of the Congregation for the Doctrine of the Faith, showed in his justly famous *Report on the Faith*, the lines along which investigation should proceed.[4] Everywhere you have to disentangle with care and discrimination subtle error presented with a show of sophistication, glibly, if not cynically, from a validly modern expression of the truth which respects the claims of both the Church and sound scholarship.

Biblical studies come to mind at once. Since the liberating Encyclical *Divino Afflante Spiritu* (1943) of Pius XII, Catholic scholars have done admirable work, witness purely by way of example and to avoid personal names, the *Sainte Bible de Jérusalem* and the *St. Jerome Biblical Commentary*. This is genuine scholarship at the service of the Church.

But along with such scholars there are the "intellectuals". These are the middlemen, not qualified as scientists or scholars, but able to pick up such results of others' research as suit their particular prejudice, and put them across suitably altered and damaging. They are articulate, often good media performers, excellent communicators, with access to the publicity openings, the best known tracks; they appear at seminars, specially organised courses, where they can intellectually manipulate innocent victims devoid of any criteria to assess their outpourings, people eager to be "with it" at any cost, looking for liberation from ideas they have come to think boring and old-fashioned because they have never really tried to understand them.

The result in practice is that a work of impeccable scholarship may be completely overlooked, while some outrageous denial of a basic Christian truth uttered in a modern sanctum of dissent, if not revolt, gets headlines across the world. Illustration would be only too easy. From biblical studies the disease spread into other areas, affecting sacred Christian dogmas such as the divinity of Jesus Christ, original sin, the very meaning of sin, the privileges of the Mother of God, the mystery of the Resurrection.

Historical revisionism offered a plum. The great Pius XII died surrounded by universal admiration. But within a few years of his death an iconoclast got to work, Rolf Hochhuth in his play, *The Representative*. This Pope was practically responsible for the Jewish genocide because of his alleged silence! Some Catholics just lost their nerve, momentarily vanquished by a skilfully orchestrated campaign of denigration masquerading as disclosure of hidden truth. But for some "intellectuals" it was all too good to be true. Here right at the very centre of the Catholic citadel was a target that appeared totally vulnerable. So they went to work with the result that the peddlers of encyclopedic information will generally castigate the Pontiff.

Modesty apart, I have examined the evidence in the case and shown the different ways in which it had been manipulated against the Pope. This is patent not only from primary documents, but from Jewish expert historians. I mention it here to show how Catholics who were turning against their religion behaved. It was in places just symptomatic of disaffection. The disaffection spread over widening areas, taking different forms, showing different symptoms. It would be characterized by open revolt when Paul VI published his Encyclical, *Humanae Vitae*, to expound traditional Catholic doctrine on matrimony with reference, among other things, to contraception. In the vanguard of the rebels were priests and professors of theology. From about this time a new kind of Catholic emerged here and there, those who called themselves Catholics but thought themselves free to pick and choose what they should believe, who thought that they should select from the known body of truths what suited them. If they were socially or culturally prominent they would welcome press, television or radio interviews in the course of which they would attempt to justify this utterly illogical stance: what looks plausible is not always valid.

Meanwhile Catholics were lining up with the advocates of purely secularist values. This would be especially evident in any question involving the relations between Church and State, especially sensitive areas like education and marriage where Church and State have each an interest. Secularism was interpreted in a conveniently narrow sense, as was ecumenism. If you uttered uncritical praise of a Protestant or atheist you were a good ecumenist or "open." If you spoke any words of praise of a Catholic you were a triumphalist. So if you advocated valid secular values, such as sound aesthetic, scientific or medical norms, if you called for integrity in professional, commercial or political life, you might pass unnoticed among the avant-garde, à la carte Catholics. But if you could slant such things in a way that would embarrass churchmen or church members about their past or present, then you were a secularist prophet.

There is no space here to deal with certain movements which are incipient, but look like growing in the immediate future, and which will throw a revealing light on the one time Catholic masses and their leaders. I refer to resurgent Islam, to the swarming sects and to the Orthodox Russian church awakening with new energy from a painful past. Nor can I deal with the sectors of the Catholic body in Third World countries which are brimful of hope: Africa which has eighty million Catholics after little over a century of evangelization, the Philippines which lead the world in one of the fruitful intuitions of Catholic theology and spirituality of our time, the Alliance of the Two Hearts, South Korea, which is the fastest growing Catholic community in the world - numbers doubled in five years. An overall balance would allow for such things. The harsh reality is that apostasy has invaded vast, hitherto or once faithful domains in western Europe and its overseas projections.

The Pope who witnessed the acceleration of decadence, the phase wherein what had been growing in secret came openly to the surface, Paul VI, did not mask his awareness or deep sorrow. Speaking to French bishops about what displeased him in their country he remarked that some thought him ignorant of these things. But his strongest language was related to the worldwide Catholic situation. He denounced what he styled apparent auto-destruction within the Church; and especially he pointed to the source of this evil, the "smoke of Satan" which had entered the Church.

The Pope knew that though global statistics appeared annually showing growth in Catholic numbers, not proportionately with the rising world population, but not in striking contrast with it, there was another question addressed with increasing accuracy by a discipline recently called into existence, the Sociology of Religion: what percentage of Catholics practise their religion, if by practice one means attendance at Sunday Mass and performance of Easter duty, that is reception of Holy Communion at least once a year? How many Catholics were merely nominal?

There had been since the nineteenth century a vague idea of the "non-practising masses." A book which appeared in France during the second world war stripped away the vagueness and made it clear that accuracy was a prime need, *France, pays de mission*, its general thesis made available to English readers by Maisie Ward's *France Pagan?* The authors contended that millions in their country were not even baptized. Here was the broad base from which came indifference and, as opinions hardened, apostasy. Data have been processed in many countries and the findings are mostly gloomy. Percentages of the practising are low.

Statistical estimates cannot measure the inner reality, the mystery embodied in the Church; they cannot evaluate how much one soul consummated in holiness compensates for many others spiritually dead. Nor do they easily test what has been another growing disease, not separable from secularization in the bad sense of the word: What is the commitment even of practising Catholics to make religion operative through the whole of life? How many think that this is even possible? How many suffer from the divided Christian mind, willingly accepting, setting up, a partition between private practice of religion and the rest of life, civic, professional, political, cultural? Do they assume that Christianity does not work? That it has no relevance to the great concerns which claim their attention, planning, energy? Do they unwittingly play into the hands of those who say that religious practice should be confined to church attendance, that the clergy have no role outside the sacristy and the sanctuary, that elsewhere "God is dead"?

But it is time to relate the life and lifework, the message of the subject of this book to this general picture of a world in apparent religious decline. What is the relevance of Vassula Rydén to such considerations?

For those who acknowledge her credibility she gives us the mystical testimony on what rational analysis enlightened by faith can discover - we have seen a summary, which I hope is broadly accurate, of the findings. What the theologian of history reaches by the method proper to his discipline, mystics are given directly by experience of the divine. In a healthy religious situation they confirm, possibly complement each other; or we may have to rely on one alone.

In dealing with the present state of the Catholic Church, whether the word apostasy be used or not, we have many descriptive studies, several mystical testimonies. I can merely allude to some of these. Since the publication of Fr. Luigi Bianchi's book, *Fatima aveva ragione: Profezia et realtá del XXO secolo*[5], we know the substance of the third secret of Fatima - there would be a general apostasy in the Church. Messages received by others have been explicit. Sister Agnes, the visionary of Akita, heard these words:

> "The work of the devil will infiltrate even into the Church in such a way that we see cardinals opposing cardinals, bishops against other bishops. The priests who venerate me will be scorned and opposed by their confreres.... churches and altars sacked; the Church will be full of those who accept compromises and the demon will press many priests and consecrated souls to leave the service of the Lord."

That was on 13 October, 1973. Over a decade before that Our Lady told the visionaries at Garabandal that there would be a decline among priests in Eucharistic faith, even affecting belief in the Real Presence.

From Vassula Rydén we have a lengthy, detailed, series of messages from Jesus on the apostasy. As she herself has remarked, references to the subject appear to be "everywhere." Like the insistence by Jesus on the manifold, immense treasury which His Heart constitutes, like the constant reminders of His Spirit of grace, our contemporary apostasy is never far from His thought and His intimate messages to her.

One of the surprising things about the message of Vassula seen in the context of the Church today is the frankness with which Jesus speaks of evil, failings, failure. Again there is a certain pedagogy traceable in His treatment of His messenger. He builds up her confidence before imposing the heavy weight of truth on her. In the early days He would just briefly refer to paganism which He "loathed" or He would express pity for her, forced to live in a wicked world:

> "My Heart rends and lacerates to see you among all this evil. Understand, My child, that I am sacrificing you to be among godless people. I suffer to have you out in exile. Daughter, many will try and hurt you. I could bear now your sufferings, but I would not bear, no, I would not bear to have them hurt you."[6]

Jesus becomes more specific as the heart of His disciple grows stronger under the influence of his Spirit:

> "Vassula, when I see how so many of My sacerdotal souls deny My signs and My works; how they treat those to whom I have given My graces to remind the world I am among you, I grieve - they are unwillingly damaging My body: *pono* (I ache). They deny My works; thus making deserts instead of making the land fertile!

Vassula questioned Jesus:

> "Lord, if they deny your works, there must be reasons!"

> "Spiritually they are dead; they are deserts themselves, and when they spot a flower in that great wilderness they made they rush to it and trample on it destroying it."

"Why?" She persisted.

> "Why? It is a misfit in their wilderness; they make sure that their desert stays arid. I find no holiness in them, none. What have they to offer Me?"

> "Protection, Lord! Protection not to distort Your word!"

> "No," Jesus insisted "they are not protecting Me; they are denying Me as God. They deny My infinite wealth, they deny My omnipotence, they are comparing themselves to Me. Do you know what they are doing? They are

promoting paganism, they are multiplying My scourgers, they are increasing spiritual deafness, they are not defending Me, they are deriding Me. I have willed, in spite of their denials, to help them so that in their turn they would help and feed My lambs. Love me, Vassula; honour Me by never denying Me."[7]

On 1 September 1987 Jesus returned to the subject:

"the world has incessantly been offending Me, and I, for My part, have incessantly been reminding them of My existence and of how I love them. My chalice of justice is full, creation. My justice lies heavily upon you. Unite and return to Me; honour Me, creation. When you will, then I will lift My justice."

"My cries resound and shake the entire heavens, leaving all My angels trembling for what has to come. I am a God of justice, and My eyes have grown weary watching hypocrisy, atheism, immorality. My creation has become, in its decadence, a replica of what Sodom was. I will thunder you with My justice as I have thundered the Sodomites. Repent, creation, before I come. I have indeed forewarned you many a time, but you have not followed My instructions. I have raised up saints to warn you, but, daughter, they have closed their hearts. My creation would rather live in lust and ignore Me. I have given them signs to awaken them."[8]

In a dialogue Vassula tried to defend the "teachers and servants" trying to cope with "negative multitudes": helpless.

"Helpless?" Jesus replies. "They should repent; they should come to Me and repent. I have through times given them signs, but they have rejected them as not from Me. I have given them warnings through weak and wretched souls, but they doubted My word. They have rejected all My blessings, grieving Me. O men with hearts of rock! Men of little faith. Had they more heart, and had they now even more heart, I would have helped them. I stirred them up from their sleep but how many times have they closed their eyes, falling back into sleep."[9]

Of his priests Jesus spoke thus: Some of them make known to the world the signs He gives

"but the majority of my sacerdotal souls have closed their hearts, doubting, fearing; many of them fear. Vassula, do you remember the Pharisees? Let Me tell you that many of them are replicas of the Pharisees, doubting, fearing, blinded by vanity and with hypocrisy. Do you remember how many times I have given them signs? I have given them signs hundreds of times, and what have they done? Times have not changed; many of My sacerdotal souls are just the same replicas of the Pharisees! I have given them signs, but they want signs which could be explained by proofs; they want proofs."[10]

Again Jesus pointed to lack of belief in His "omnipotence and His wealth".

On 28 September 1987 Jesus again pointed to the failure of priests:

"But many of My sacerdotal souls have disowned Me in the presence of men... By disowning My signs they have disowned Me, their God. Have I not said that the man who disowns Me in the presence of men, will be disowned in the presence of My angels? Have I not said that I will continue to make My name known to you? Why then do they doubt that I am among you and that it is by My Mercy I give you signs and miracles which are barely honoured; for let Me tell you, daughter, they have taken the key of knowledge. Neither have they gone in themselves, nor have they let others in who wanted to."[11]

On 12 December 1987 Jesus, who had until then spoken only of the defects of priests, gave his view of the Church at large:

"Never has My Church been in such confusion. Remember the words of your Holy Mother, 'the confusion of Garabandal was given as a similitude', to show how My Church of today is confused - it is reigning in confusion."[12]

Later in the same month He used a biblical type with which Vassula has become familiar:

"Yes Vassula, seek My interests only, be real, not just a facade of holiness like some are. I the Lord know them. No matter how hard they try to appear like Abel, they do not deceive Me - wearing a mask will not help conceal their identity. I tell you truly. I will point out to you this time those deceivers; I will come to them in an unexpected hour. Why have in My house Cains - seeking only their interests and not Mine? I will, with heavenly strength, unmask them - I will unveil that which is hidden. Do not fear, beloved, My Church I will clean; I will sweep away all those that obstruct the way to divine love."[13]

On 17 March 1988 Jesus reverted to the image of the desert:

"Your era Vassula is dead, they have made a desert by condemning My works of today, expanding this wilderness. My blood was shed to irrigate your hearts and allow you to live in My light. O creation was My blood shed in vain? This era would tell you, 'Do not listen. Shut your ears, for the voice you hear is certainly the devil's'. And as to those I blessed, giving them visions today, these blessed souls would be mocked and discouraged by My own from within My house. They would be determined and ever so ready to condemn Me. Yes, in spite of themselves they are condemning Me in the presence of men when they are denying My gifts... I wish I could say today upon you creation, 'Era of little faith' as before, but I can only say this of you today, 'O era of no faith at all!'"[14]

On March 29 of that year He is again explicit:

"I have said that out of the babe's mouth you shall hear the truth. So to those who condemn My divine works of today I tell you this: your apostasy is condemning you. All you who disbelieve and have made desolate My garden, come to Me and repent."[15]

Next month Jesus spoke again of His garden and of the apostasy:

"I will expand My Kingdom and all Heaven will rejoice. You have neglected My garden but I, the Lord, who am its Keeper love you to distraction and cannot bear to see thorns and briars choking My few remaining flowers. The time has come to clean up, extirpating those thorns and briars, allowing My buds to bloom, embellishing My garden. Justice will prevail... Peter, assemble Peter, all the nations - draw them into My Heart. I call from My Cross: 'Feed all My sheep, Peter. I ask you again Peter: Do you love Me more than these others do? If you do, do not let the Cains convince you - remain steadfast. They will ask you for laws that seem just, to treat every soul as they please; these very laws that are coming from men - do not let them persuade you. Remember how I, the Lord, am; I am meek and humble. Be My reflection. If they long for Me to come near them, then why do they not hear My voice? I am at their very doors knocking. Why do they refuse to hear? If they long for Me and do not hear Me it is because of their apostasy that has grown as thick as slime. I am here now, waiting for them to open their hearts, but they push Me aside, oppressing Me."[16]

Later in the year Jesus spoke stern words about those with the power:

"The ecclesiastical authorities will invariably deny you. I had been denied by the Pharisees because they believed they had all the power and authority; they had forgotten that they could not do anything without being given power and authority from above, and now these sons of Cains keep forgetting that they cannot do anything unless I give them power and authority. I am the authority, was, and will always be, for all eternity. Now, as it is, those that deny My providential works are blinded by their vanity which obscures them; they are those same blind guides who repeat their error, clean and polished from the outside, but all corruption and dead-men's bones from the inside."

Jesus will effect restoration:

"I will reverse these false kingdoms, and raise up in My light like a torch My real kingdom, and to Peter I will give entirely back his seat, enthroning him; and I will place into his hand an iron sceptre in which I will give him the power to reign as shepherd. I will amass My scattered lambs, and when I have done this, I will encircle this Fold with My arms and no one! no one!, not even the evil one, will be able to steal one single lamb out of this Fold. My cape I will spread over them and shelter them in My warmth, protecting them. To Peter I will give back what I had given him when I was on earth and in flesh."[17]

On the feast of the Assumption of that year Jesus was again explicit on the apostasy:

"Pray for those who need to be saved. Pray to Me, for My name is 'He who saves.' The hours are fleeing, the days of reckoning have begun, the days of reprisals are here. The iniquity of this generation is so great and the apostasy so grave that both our Hearts have been pierced through and through by their injustice and their flagrant offenses."[18]

He still held out a promise of forgiveness to those who return to Him.

This same promise was held out on the same day by Our Lady:

"I am calling you, I am encouraging you, but how many know of our calls? How many believe in these calls? My heart pains to say that only a handful of you trust these calls. This generation's heart has turned into granite - blinded by rationalism they have forgotten God's ways; they have forgotten God's wonders; they have forgotten that He is omnipotent and full of mercy. Never has God's creation fallen so low - not even in the days of Sodom and Gomorrah. Your apathy has pierced eternity, your lack of understanding is condemning you; your relentless persecutions on my apparitions (and on those whom God blessed, giving them His messages) are going to be one cause of your fall. I, your holy Mother, Mother of your Saviour, appeal and beg you to repent and change."[19]

On another occasion, Jesus evoked the *pietá* image to convey the state of his Church:

"The image of Myself, lying dead in My Mother's arms is a symbolic way of showing you all how your apostasy betrayed My Church. You see, daughter, I led you to see the correct image of the present Church; you have seen on My Mother her sorrow, and you saw in her arms My dead body, betrayed, bruised, scourged, pierced and crucified; and this is exactly how My Church of today is to be found. My Mother weeps over her with tears of blood, as she wept over My body on Golgotha."

There follows a note of hope:

"But in a short time she (the Church) will be transfigured and resurrected, as I the Lord was resurrected."[20]

The theme recurs in allusions now and then, is given concrete form in this passage:

"I have, since the beginning of this revelation, been telling you that My Church is in ruin and in this ruin vipers have nestled inside it and made their homes within its depths. Ah Vassula! How I suffer... I will have to come and untangle those snakes which are creeping all over My holiest Sacraments and throw them out of My Church all over again... My child, to live and be surrounded by this devastating wilderness is difficult and terrifying but I am near all those who love Me and worship My holy Name with love.

"I have to remind all those who tread upon my heavenly works that I am infinite wealth. Whenever I saw My creation fall into rebellion I always sent messengers carrying My word - for rebellion turns the land you are living in into deserts. Although your ancestors rebelled, their doubts were never severe as your generation's doubting that I speak to My chosen angels, giving them My messages. Today My child, I have ministers in My Church who claim to believe in Me but refuse all My divine works I am offering you in your days and that come from the Holy Spirit. Their aridity is condemning them and in the day of judgment I will judge them severely! These people should go back to Scriptures and read how My Spirit works and how I bless the gifts I am giving to the chosen ones - they all come from Me. My child, you and I, I and you are crossing this wilderness, this deadly wilderness caused by rationalism, lack of faith, lack of love, promiscuity, self-indulgence, vanity and a resentment to all that descends from the Holy Spirit. Their obduracy to listen is condemning them - anyone who rejects the works of My Holy Spirit is rejecting Me for the Holy Spirit and I are one and the same... These people are promoting this desert and are making sure that nothing will grow in it; if they see a flower, either they will trample on it and crush it, or will ignore it on purpose, and never water it so that it withers and in this way get rid of it. My cup of justice is brimming over and already they are sensing the first drops of My justice upon them. All I ask from these people especially those who serve Me yet refuse the Holy Spirit's works, is to pray, pray, pray for enlightenment and a stronger faith. Come, My child, please Me always by remembering My holy presence."[21]

Again early in the year 1989 Jesus spoke of the evils consequent on the rebellious spirit:

"I have redeemed you and lifted you up to Me and cradled you in My Sacred Heart. I descend from heaven, from My holy throne. I bend to reach this ungrateful generation; your hands still fresh with My children's blood - blood because you refused to believe My messages given at Fatima. You refused to believe then its urgency and now you are repeating your errors. New blood will be shed because of your obduracy. O My child, so many of My own are blinded by Satan's smoke! My own rebel fearlessly, and without the slightest hesitation. Sincerity is missing from them - I find no holiness in them. I search for love and I find none in them. There is no justice to be seen and Wisdom has been replaced by folly, abandoning them, because their tongues are forked, murmuring only treachery. These rebels have allowed vanity to be their crown and disobedience was accepted by them - becoming their sceptre. I find no peace in them, none. Their way of thinking is not Mine - they are heading for the havoc and the ruin of My city. O Cain, Cain! Where is the Spirit with which I endowed you? Are you heading for your own destruction again? I had known you violent since the day of your birth, and because you knew that this was not new to Me, here you come masquerading and dressed up like a High Priest. You have garbed yourself in My clothes, in gold and silver, to hide your dark robes, given to you by the Black Beast. You have no light in you, and to hide your hideous face you have placed a mask on your abominable face so that your appearance can deceive even My elect. Your mask cannot deceive Me for My eyes know that behind the lamb's mask you are hiding an immense destruction - you have armoured yourself to the teeth with evil. And now you are scheming to conquer the world - to wipe out the little light that is left in them. Your intentions are to increase lawlessness and extirpate all that is holy, removing powerful men and monopolising My sanctuary. These My child are the vipers I had shown you in a vision - creeping all over My holy Sacraments and on My Tabernacle. He will deceive many and people will be blinded, blinded because of his imposter's garments. These poor souls will be convinced that what they see before their very eyes, and in their own era, is the High Priest Himself! With his glorious disguise, he will bring a great apostasy upon all My Church - he will bring desolation. But everything will be disguised by miracles - by great portents and signs in the skies. My perpetual Sacrifice he will fling down, trampling on it and abolishing it - but all in disguise, in malice. My Holy City will be under Cain's power, because they have rejected My warnings. I have come to them unexpectedly, bare-footed, but they have scoffed on Me. Cain's power will last just for a short time, thanks to My beloved souls who repair - who pray and sacrifice themselves. All this I have taken into consideration and your sacrifices were not in vain.   Iniquity and transgression can be suppressed with your prayers."[22]

From these extracts the reader must not think that it is a panorama of hopelessness which Jesus displays to his disciple. In July of that year He expressed an idea always latent, often expressed: He will rebuild His Church:

"My Church today lies in ruin and in terrible havoc, but the days are soon coming when every man shall follow My law because of the seeds of love I am sowing in their heart. They shall carry My law deep inside their heart and they shall be called 'Witnesses of the Most High.' They shall be My people and I shall be their God, and knowledge they shall learn directly from My own lips; I will be their Master and they will be My pupils. I shall then establish order that will never pass away and they shall all know me by My holy name, even those without any merits, since I am infinite mercy, forgiveness and pity... Yes the walls of My Sanctuary will be rebuilt, layer after layer, brick after brick, all will be rebuilt by My own hand."[23]

Yes, the wilderness will become a watered garden; love will be living among Jesus' own. He will be surrounded by them, praising, glorifying Him, united under His new name.

"Rebellion shall cease and will come to its end, pierced by My Word; it shall be dead, never to rise again. I mean to deliver you from the hands of the evil one fortifying you in My light. Only for the sake of those who love Me and immolate for Me, I shall reduce My fire. For your sake, beloved ones, My hand shall not fall as hard as you were told."[24]

But He still must advert to His enemies:

"I have seen them extirpate flower after flower (in His garden). Treacherous and vicious as vipers, they come by night into My Sanctuary, unfolding without fear their despicable inclinations, such abetting of evil men that no one renounces his evil-doing."

"But Lord" said Vassula "they must know that you are watching them."

"They are rebels, rebelling against My law. It is those that Scriptures say of them, 'they dress My people's wounds without concern. Peace, peace they say, but there is no peace. They are without shame and without love, they are heartless;' but I shall overthrow these rebels with one blow of My breath. I shall overthrow all of those Cains that have enthroned themselves into high seats of falsehood. Of what use are their thrones to Me? I have been warning them and the more I warned them the more they refused to hear lest they should return to Me and be converted. These Cains have persisted in apostasy for several decades, never loosening their grip from their evil-doings; they cling to illusions and to falsehood; they trample on My devout ones and on those who keep faithful to My Peter, yes they ridicule all those who still believe in him. These Cains harm My Church to the extent that they made My eyes turn into a spring of tears, weeping all day and all night long."[25]

Jesus does not mince His words when it comes to responsibility for the disastrous decline. He calls to Him the shepherds "who have strayed from the truth", with the question "how could you say that you have left no path of lawlessness or ruin unexplored"? - continuing thus:

"Can you say now that you have governed justly? Have you ever asked yourselves in sincerity if you behaved as I, the Shepherd, would have you behave? Listen then to Me and understand and take these words as a warning, you who have exchanged your shepherd's staff for a sceptre of falsehood, and who have thousands under your rule. Was it not I who relieved your shoulders of the burden? Was it not I who atoned for you?"[26]

Jesus reminds them of "wonders and signs" He is giving them, asks them to acknowledge His graces. "Come and repent" He says, "Fill My Sacred Heart with joy today and set your eyes on Me your Shepherd so that you may no longer err aimlessly in this desert. I am present to guide your feet into the way of peace, love and unity."

Always there is a generous opening towards hope, but on the condition of repentance. Realism keeps recurring. In September of that year, Jesus took up again the subject of the shepherds:

"I want you to understand that the heart of your wise ones in the house of mourning, they tend to forget in their great stature My power and My divinity; their corruptibility blinds them, leaving in them an open space for Satan to speak to them, for they have shut their heart to love; their mind and their heart are closer to the rational world than My spiritual world. This plague has infiltrated into My Church; many of My shepherds are like those crows in the parable that I have given you - they are the cause of so much discordance. Their speeches and sermons lack spirituality, faithfulness to My word and My precepts; they repudiate My mysteries in My presence; they flout piety. Remember the deeds performed by their ancestor Cain. They have adopted his language, serving vice instead of virtue, immorality instead of purity. They have submitted without reservation to the slavery of sin - these Cains are alive to sin, but lifeless to My Spirit of truth. When My day comes they will have to answer Me and give Me accounts for not having guarded the traditions of their Shepherd. Today their mouth is condemning them and their own lips will bear witness against them. It is the fruit of their apostasy."[27]

Later in the same month Jesus spoke of "rationalism, the plague of this generation", it is deadly. "Rationalism descends from the Prince of darkness, and all those who live in darkness have this disease among other diseases."[28]

The theme was taken up in a very impressive Trinitarian setting:

"Do not suffocate My Spirit in you with immorality, rationalism, egoism and other sins; do not suffocate Me, leave My Spirit to breathe in you and lift your eyes to heaven and pray in silence as I have been praying to My Father."

In the same message He speaks of the enemy:

"So many times he is using poor souls to reduce My voice into silence, rebuking the graces of My Holy Spirit and thus injuring My Body beyond recognition. Hiding behind a cloud of darkness these souls become masters of evil and vanity, refusing to grasp My ways, these people weigh heavily on My Heart. Fearlessly they come to Me void and empty-handed; they make fun of the promise."

They renew mysteriously phases of His Passion.

Now that Vassula is formed and strengthened she can assimilate hard truths. Here is how He can now speak to her:

"If My house lies in ruin today and atheism is reigning in so many hearts, it is because your generation refuses Me a place in their heart. I come to find no love, no faith and no hope. My house lies in ruin, reduced into rubbles by rationalism, disobedience and vanity. My glorious pastures of the past are now barren because of the great apostasy which penetrated into My Sanctuary. Obedience is missing. I have given My shepherd's staff entirely to Peter to guide My lambs until My return, but in their wickedness and for their own self-interest and not Mine they have broken My shepherd's staff in two, then in splinters."[29]

On 12 May 1990 Jesus spoke of the response He will give to so much evil, a topic immense in itself, not now considered:

"I mean to extinguish all evil and wickedness, this is why in these days My veil will be thrown over the sun, the moon and the stars. I will cover the sun with dark clouds, and the moon will not be giving you its light. I will dim every luminary in heaven for you and I will cover your countries in darkness so that Babylon will cease intermarrying with sin. She shall then adopt My law of love, because her renegades I shall put up in flames. If your era has failed to appreciate My great love and has defiled My holy name, it is because of the great apostasy that penetrated in the core of My Sanctuary."[30]

Then Jesus reveals His treasures, the inexhaustible source of His munificence:

"Today, generation, My Spirit of grace comes to help you more lavishly than ever before, see? I am raising in each corner of the earth new altars to sanctify your lands and sanctify you all. It is by grace that I intend to raise you and make out of you living altars carrying My flame. For within you will be living My Spirit of holiness, a Spirit unique, subtle, unsullied and pure. Then I shall send you out throughout the earth and your message will be to proclaim My infinite love, and I promise you, you who love Me, that in those days of darkness which will come upon the whole world, I will keep you safe and I will lock you in the depths of My Sacred Heart, I shall be with you. But alas for those who spend their time breaking down and trampling on My altars! Alas for those who kill My prophets! Alas for these souls. Alas for those who follow the black beast. Alas for all those who reject My warnings, spurn and ignore them. They shall in these days of darkness call to Me, but I will not answer."[31]

Some months later Jesus asks that we listen to "the voice of My Holy Spirit, the constant reminder of My word, and all that I have given you." He asks that we pray the prayer given by our "Holy Mother" to avert the Father's justice. But soon He will deal with those marked by so-called wisdom, and by hostility towards His divinity. "I shall" He says "pull them out by the roots so that they will not thrive any more. They have apostatized from Me, yes, they have accustomed their steps to walk with apostasy, and have as their guide and travelling companion Rationalism, the weapon to combat My divinity."[32]

In this context Jesus does not fail to point to the source of evil:

"I tell you solemnly that in these coming days Satan and all the foul spirits shall not work subtly as they did before. No, the time has come now when he and those foul spirits shall show themselves openly to every inhabitant of the earth. Satan shall send false prophets and he shall multiply them like sand, creating confusion among you to deceive even the elect."

Jesus reassures his faithful ones who love Him. Yet He says:

"But alas for those who defiled My Sanctuary, bringing great apostasy in My Church, brimstone and fire shall rain upon them!"[33]

We ought not to pass over a glaring symptom of the infidelity of shepherds which Jesus evokes as He is commenting on the Ten Commandments:

"For those who sought Satan's blasphemous powers and erected them as banners to efface My divinity and My holiness, and My holy Sacrifice, I tell you: it is your fault that My name is being blasphemed among the godless. You have sullied My Sanctuary by ordaining perverted men with degrading passions; tainted all alike they do not fear Me. So if the godless today commit adultery and find it natural it is because of the great permissiveness in My Church given under instructions of the beast whose aim is to falsify the truth."[34]

In the last months of 1990 and early in 1991 Vassula heard still utterly explicit judgements on ecclesiastical corruption:

"Have you not read before to stay awake and watch so that when you see the disastrous abomination of which the prophet Daniel spoke, erected in My Sanctuary, you would know that this is the sign spoken by the prophet for the end of times? How is it that you cannot read the times? The bricks of My Sanctuary have fallen down and you are living in the middle of this great apostasy of your era. My oppressors think now they have the upper hand, and the traders think they will continue trading in My Sanctuary, but I tell them, 'you who have corrupted your wisdom by trading My image for a lifeless statue, a false god, an idol, you who struggle to erect this disastrous abomination and abolish My perpetual Sacrifice, you will drink the full winecup of My justice.' The figure daubed with assorted colours, this figure these traders are trying to make you revere and follow is not Me; it is an invention of perverted human skill to degrade the concept of My holiness and My divinity; it is false ecumenism, it is a defiance of all that is holy. I suffer because of the sins of these traders. Pray for these priests who become traders, their sin is grave. Pray that I may put My Spirit of truth in them and make them keep My laws and sincerely respect My divinity."[35]

In February, 1991 Jesus spoke to Vassula words that will be unforgettable for most readers - He had on a previous occasion spoken of dubious nominees to high places in the Church. Now He says:

"But today I look with dismay from above on this generation's crimes which now have outdone the sins of Sodom and Gomorrah. Because your hopes are built on a false Christ, this generation is vile, rebellious, and polluted with blood, and living under Satan's shadow."

Later this was the chilling verdict:

"Scriptures are being fulfilled and I tell you solemnly that the one for whom My Abels and My Jacobs were longing, will suddenly come, entering his Temple to extirpate the Cains and the Esaus who made havoc and ruin out of My Church. You have industrialized My house, the house which should have been a house of prayer. You have indeed turned this house into a den of thieves. If I am, as you say, 'the Holy One' then where is the honour you owe Me? If I am indeed your Master, where is your respect? If I am your God, where is My adoration and My incense? Where is My devotion? How is it that you cannot read the signs of the times? How is it that you cannot understand heavenly things? How is it that you do not believe anymore in My marvels? Why are you persecuting My Abels and Jacobs? if not openly, in secret? I appear as well as your Holy Mother and We manifest ourselves through souls in many nations, but our manifestations weary you, and even anger you. 'How tiresome it all is' you say, for to this day you have not understood the Heavenly things like My Abels and Jacobs. No, you have neither understood My love nor the devotion you owe My Mother. You call to faith and rely on your strength, your authority and your reasoning. My voice calling out today for repentance to the sinners disturbs your ears. When righteousness suddenly shines out with healing in its rays, you refuse My gift which is offered today in your dark era."

He tells them that they are persecuting Him, causing suffering to His Abels and Jacobs; they have closed their ears to His voice to listen to their own.

"You have deprived many of the fruits of My new vineyards because Satan has entered you and ambushed your spirit and lo, others are atoning for your crimes. Others are atoning for your vanity and your folly, to save you... You do not repent but you go astray as you pursue your course dragging millions after you."[36]

Readers will have different opinions on this aspect of Vassula's thought, thought which, as is clear, she attributes to Jesus Christ as a direct source. Principally three questions may arise: Would Jesus really speak so frankly about the state of His Church, not omitting these defects of its ruling personnel, to anyone? Would He do so to a woman, to one who for thirty years had no meaningful contact with any of the Christian churches? Secondly is the total picture so fully drawn not another instance of doom and gloom, leading to unrelieved pessimism? Thirdly, are we to expect punishment, chastisement to use the word found on the lips or in the writings of others favoured with divine messages, such as the children at Fatima, Sister Agnes Sasagawa at Akita, or Julia at Naju in South Korea?

The first question is like one occasionally prompted latterly by the multiplicity of Marian apparitions: Would Our Lady really appear so often? The answer is similar in both cases: it is not for us to tell the Lord or His Blessed Mother what they should do, to set limits to their action, to measure their free choice by our notions of what is appropriate or suitable. What we deem suitable is conditioned by our culture, our vision limited by the circumstances of our existence, our imperfect understanding of the past and our ignorance of the future. We are not empowered to decide whether Our Lady should appear once or a hundred times. The initiative is hers under God.

If we are surprised that Jesus speaks so explicitly about the evils in His Church today, who are we, creatures of His mercy, to dictate to Him, the sovereign Lord of heaven and earth? Apart from the fact that St. Peter and Paul laid bare their own failures, one may suggest that we have here a manifestation of divine mercy. It is mercy to those who suffer from the weaknesses in the Church at the present time; it is mercy to those who cause these defects who are given the opportunity to convert and return to friendship with God. In one case it is a guarantee of protection; in the other a call to repentance. As to the choice of a woman for such a mission, again the initiative lies with God. In an age when the claims of women are being pressed insistently within the Church, this particular choice should be welcome.

Are the vivid descriptions of the apostasy in its different aspects an incitement to pessimism? The remainder of this book gives the answer to this question. Jesus pours out abundant light on the sources of hope. He Himself is the first and fundamental one. He is throughout His communications continuously, unfailingly encouraging. He is a limitless ocean of generosity, compassion, support, delicacy; with unrivalled clarity in analysis of evil men and events, He joins limpidity of remedial, restorative advice. He is the physician of souls who in these pages is all Heart. With Him again in clear delineation is His Mother and our Mother, her Heart too a fountain of hope to those who seem to have passed the point of rescue. The entry into the unfolding drama of one whose very name evokes power and victory, St. Michael the Archangel, shows clearly that Jesus does not wish to see us blind to what surrounds us, nor frightened of what may appear menacing.

The third question concerns the purification of which Vassula speaks. We shall see it in the next chapter where we must now study at length with mind and heart Jesus Himself, the centre of all creation, the culmination of all human and angelic life, the one who invites us to intimacy with Him.

Notes:

1. Michel de St. Pierre was president of the national *Pro Fide* association; his books in the seventies - the first some years earlier, forced attention to harsh realities; he was a war hero, a worker for close ties between France and Israel, as his novel *Je reviendrai sur les ailes de l'aigle*, shows;

2. Constitution on the Liturgy, Art. 22, 3;

3. *Inaestimabile donum*, Vatican Council II, ed. A. Flannery, O.P., 93f;

4. English Edition, London, 1985;

5. Como, 1992; Don Bianchi confirmed to me personally that after he had published his book he gave it to a Roman prelate who knew the third secret of Fatima. He asked would the prelate change anything in the light of his certain knowledge. No was the answer. His thesis in the book: the secret concerns the general apostasy in the Church in recent times.;

6. 21 June, 1987, Volume I, page 137;

7. 7 July, 1987, Volume I, page 145;

8. 1 September, 1987, Volume I, page 172;

9. *Ibid.*;

10. *Ibid.*;

11. 28 September, 1987, Volume I, page 192;

12. 12 December, 1987, Volume I, page 246;

13. 21 December 1987, Volume I, page 249;

14. 17 March, 1988, Volume I, page 295;

15. 29 March, 1988, Volume I, page 301;

16. 5 April, 1988, Volume I, page 305;

17. 4 May, 1988, Volume I, page 321; 7 May, 1988, Volume I, page 325;

18. 15 August, 1988, Volume I, page 356; The Two Hearts of Jesus and Mary;

19. 15 August, 1988, Volume I, page 357;

20. 16 August, 1988, Volume I, page 358;

21. 11 October, 1988, Volume I, page 385f;

22. 30 January, 1989, Volume I, page 421f; Pope Paul used the snakes metaphor.;

23. 9 July, 1989, Volume II, page 43f;

24. *Ibid.*;

25. *Ibid.*;

26. 5 August 1989, Volume II, page 56f;

27. 13 September, 1989, Volume II, page 71;

28. 29 September 1989, Volume II, page 83;

29. 10 October, 1989, Volume II, page 90;

30. 12 May, 1990, Volume II, page 175;

31. *Ibid.*;

32. 6 July 1990, Volume II, page 191;

33. *Ibid.;*

34. 5-29 August 1990, Volume I, page 212; the extensive passage depicts the entry of perverse priests into the high places, with disastrous consequences; one of the very severe messages;

35. 22 October 1990, Volume II, page 242;

36. 7 February 1991, Volume II, page 283;

3

INTIMACY WITH JESUS

The Jesus of the gospels invites us, each one of us, to come to him. Again and again through the ages men and women have had to be brought to the truth that Christianity is essentially about Jesus Christ, that the primary task of their lives is to achieve a personal relationship with Him. The task is manifold, for the Christian has to weave into this relationship all that makes the fabric of life in all its phases. He must grow in self-knowledge, as must all human beings aiming at full development of their personality; he must master forces from within his own psyche and from his social, cultural and economic environment which seek to displace Jesus Christ from the centre of his life. Jesus may be obscured by worldly factors, even by the very projects originally undertaken in his name. The forces of evil, temptation which can play on an inherent weakness, human inertia, may conspire to damage Christ-centred integrity.

Jesus Christ has shown Himself conscious of human fragility and fallibility in its quest for Him. The mystic impulse in His Church is one means He uses to bring strength and light where they are needed. Mystic impulse means a focus on persons, adequately endowed, prepared by the Lord Himself to receive and communicate His creative message. This message is always designed to invite and facilitate access to Himself in all His saving resource.

Revelation of the Sacred Heart of Jesus is the supreme instance of the Saviour's generous condescension to human weakness.[1] In the thirteenth century already St. Gertrude the Great was granted this intuition, but as yet it did not spread to the life of the Church. The message, authentically mystic, which was to be of public import, was received by St. Margaret Mary Alacoque in the seventeenth century, succinctly stated in an immortal phrase: "Behold this Heart which has so loved men." It took time for the insight to enter the life of the Church, which had been the very intention of the Saviour.[2] The institution resists the charismatic. As late as the nineteenth century severe restrictions were imposed in regard to a book on the Sacred Heart.

The idea was too powerful to suffer extinction. It became the inspiration of mighty figures in the Catholic community to the extent that one could fix a point in the spiritual growth of saints of the Sacred Heart where this idea effectively touched them, altered their entire outlook. The church authority was totally involved. Leo

XIII following the spreading practice of consecration undertook this very act for the whole human race on 11 June, 1899. His successors in the papacy, Pius XI and Pius XII issued Encyclical Letters on the subject, that of Pius XII, *Haurietis Aquas*[3], something of a classic. Many societies were placed under the immediate patronage of the Sacred Heart. The Society of Jesus one of whose members, St. Claude la Colombière had been the spiritual director of St. Margaret Mary, had a special mission to propagate the ideal. One result was an impressive literature; the more profound effect was a splendid spirituality, widespread. Thus things stood until the strange upheaval within the Catholic Church following Vatican II. "Devotions" characteristically Catholic were if not summarily dismissed, given little pastoral support, marginalised. There was now no apostle of enthronement of the Sacred Heart in homes on the model of Fr. Matteo-Crawley, who travelled the world in the twenties with this mission, blessed by the Pope of the day. Qualifying the various practices centred on this symbol of mystery as "devotions" was to overlook the essence of things. What was implied was really an outlook, an intuition, a way of approaching Jesus, of making Him the centre of life.

Decline there certainly was; as among certain faithful ones there was firm hope of a future revival, a renewal which would of its nature and timeliness be a deepening of the whole spirituality of the Heart of Jesus. The indispensable preliminary was theological. Here two currents of thought met.

Theologians felt the need to base their thinking on the New Testament witness, where they hold divergent views. The great biblical scholar, Ignace de la Potterie, S.J. summarises his own and an opposing view thus:

> "Like other recent theologians (Hans Urs von) Balthasar seems to assume that the text of John 19:31-37 is the most important biblical passage on which devotion to the Sacred Heart is based. These authors give us theological examinations of the importance of the heart in biblical anthropology or in the symbolism of blood and water. It must be noted, however that the word 'heart' is not even mentioned in this text. To be sure, the open side of Jesus, or the blood and water which flowed from it, are extremely rich symbols, but even so they are no more than symbols or signs. Moreover, they are associated with the moment immediately following Jesus' death on the cross. We are told nothing of the living heart of the earthly Jesus, of the interior life of Jesus the man, in the course of His public life. This is where the new developments in Christology can make their precious contribution."

The writer considers especially important analysis of Jesus' consciousness: "To talk of a person's deep consciousness amounts to the same as speaking of what he has in his heart, and this also holds true for the Heart of Jesus."[4] Fr. de la Potterie knows that this is "a formidable problem." So much for the theologians, who will further enrich us.

The other powerful current of thought originates fortunately in the Papacy. John Paul II has added a new dimension to the theology of the Heart of Jesus, classic from the great Encyclical of Pius XII, as a result of his training in phenomenology. He knows the richness of anthropological resonance which the word heart evokes. One of his works before his election to the papal office was *"The Acting Person."* What he said on 28 June 1984 to an audience at the Rome Gemelli Clinic will illustrate his creative thinking, so welcome to those working to recover a mighty tradition of Catholic piety:

"The word evokes not only sentiments proper to the affective sphere, but also all those memories, thoughts, reasonings, plans that make up man's innermost world. The heart in biblical culture, and also in a large part of other cultures, is that essential centre of personality in which man stands before God, as the totality of body and soul, as I who is thinking, willing and loving, as the centre in which the memory of the past opens up to the planning of the future."

"Certainly, the human heart that interests the anatomist, the physiologist, the cardiologist, the surgeon etc.. and their scientific contribution - I am happy to acknowledge in such a place as this - takes on great importance for the serene and harmonious development of man in the course of his earthly existence. But the significance, according to which we now refer to the heart, transcends these partial considerations to reach the sanctuary of personal self-awareness in which is summarized and condensed the concrete essence of man, the centre in which the individual decides on himself, in face of others, the world and God Himself."[5]

Readers of *True Life in God* will find that the Heart of Jesus is a continuous presence in the text. The messages emanate from it; Jesus varies His presentation of the theme from the explicit through so many differing modes of expression to the subtle, the implied, the concept to which one turns as the final satisfying answer. There is too a friendly challenge to the reader's ability to discern or interpret divine pedagogy. Jesus leads His disciple by stages delicately adapted to her spiritual growth into the fullness of the mystery.

Jesus at first assures Vassula of His unchangeable love for her, of His choice to use her despite her unworthiness; He will not cease to guide her; He looks on her as His bride; the charism He has given her will remain with her.

The revelation of the Heart is not long delayed:

"I have come to you to give My message of peace and love. I have chosen a mere child, unfit for My task, helpless and small, without prestige, a nothing, to manifest through you My passionate love and teach those that still do not understand the riches of My Heart. I suffer to watch My teachers so withdrawn from what is heavenly, and the indifference they give to My blessings; for charism is a blessing. How their hearts have become coarse, leading to spiritual deafness and aridity."[6]

The same day He spoke thus to His chosen one:

"I have delivered you from evil, awakening you. I raised you up and lifted you to My Heart, pouring on you many of My works. Accept what I give you, for Wisdom is leading you. Vassula, I love you; little one you are Mine. Daughter, give Me love and give Me rest; let Me rest in your heart; accept Me Vassula, do not deny Me, Vassula. Do you know how many years I was waiting for you to accept Me? Oh how alienated you were from My Heart. Have I ever told you how I really felt then?"

When she answered that she did not remember, Jesus went on:

"I will tell you. You had drifted away from Me, and My Heart was utterly torn with sorrow. Vassula, how then could you resist My appeal, beloved? I have been waiting for you for so many years, Vassula; accept My love; My love heals you."[7]

The importance of this communication is that Jesus identifies His Heart with Himself. He did not say "alienated from Me" but "from My Heart". Two days later He speaks as the pedagogue solicitous to watch her progress attentively and not to demand too much:

"Vassula, it is I, Jesus Christ. I love you. Any messages bearing blames or harsh words, know that it is not coming from Me. I am love, love, love. My Heart is an abyss of love. The guidance I am giving you, is adjusted for you. Regard yourself as a toddler who has started her first steps; no one expects a toddler to walk with confidence and self-assurance. My guidance is for a beginner; I teach you in gradual steps, and every step you take with Me I bless."[8]

When some time later Jesus speaks of Vassula's years of indifference and her sudden turning to Him He says,

"I was at hand's reach; yes, I was so near you; then My Heart could not resist your plea. I came full of joy. Finally, you called Me; I lifted you to

My breast daughter, and I healed your wounds."[9]

But through her He intends to speak to all His children. In a long message in which He speaks of their misery, of Satan "escorting them", He offers hope, but again through His Heart:

"I come, once more, with My Heart in My hand, offering it to you. Will you refuse it?.... My eyes have grown tired watching you slaughtering one another. I care for you, for I am your Father who loves you. Behold I come with all My sovereignty, I who am your God; I come to you offering you My Heart. Here, take it. All of it is yours. My Heart rends and lacerates; feel it; all of it is but one big wound... you have torn the Heart of your God; you have pierced it through again and again."[10]

Reading through the messages of Jesus the one seeking explicit references to His Heart will find them frequent and illuminating, comforting above all. Thus Jesus recalls His agony in Gethsemane and speaks thus:

"Daughter, Judas betrayed Me, but many more like Judas are betraying Me still. I knew instantly that His kiss would spread among many and, for generations to come, this same kiss will be given to Me over and over again, renewing My sorrow, rending My Heart."

Later He went on:

"Love Me, My daughter, in My torments of Gethsemane. I was deceived by one of My own, one of My beloved ones, and today, I still receive indignities, recollecting My agonies of the past. My Heart swelled and filled with bitterness."[11]

Again wishing to ground Vassula in humility He has this message:

"I will prevent you from becoming elated by all My given graces, by reminding you of your wretchedness. I will remind you that all the graces you are receiving from Me are for My own glory. Every grace you receive from Me will be for My own interests and not for your own. So draw from My Heart, and fill up yours. I want My altar to be constantly ablaze. Live for Me, breathe for Me, be My own for all eternity."[12]

The disciple's sufferings Jesus wishes to unite with His:

"Vassula, My Vassula, victim of My soul, victim of My Heart; bear My sufferings and share them with Me. Drink from My cup; feel My scourges.

Beloved of My soul, what will I not do for you out of love? I will allow you
to share My sufferings - I have chosen you to be the victim of My bleeding
Heart, by all the sorrows of which yours is capable."[13]

On this theme of suffering, Jesus thinks and speaks of the Church as a whole:

"See Me as your Redeemer, your Consoler. I come to shine in this dark
world of today as a Light. My house is reigning in confusion; in debates; in
self-interest; in unholiness."

"Peter! Peter! Why are My disciples dispersed in enmity?: Hallowed by
My hand, brother of Mine, I love you from all eternity. My Sacred Heart
is wounded, wounded by thorns that have been driven into it by My own, My
own whom I love. I will show you My wounded Heart; they are piercing
My Sacred Heart all over again."[14]

The Lord then relates all that displeases Him in the conduct of His followers,
"hatred, venomous statements",

"Peter, My eyes have grown weary, watching them accusing one another.
They have laid desolate My lands and have nothing to offer My lambs. Their
ways are not acceptable to Me. I have given them love and peace. I have
never taught them to judge others. Vassula, I rule with kindness. My Sacred
Heart bleeds and lacerates...Child, there has never been absence of love in
My Heart nor in the hearts of My first disciples."[15]

The thought recurs poignantly:

"Behold! Behold Peter, My Sacred Heart once again is being pierced by so
many thorns; thorns that have been driven into Me by those I love! My soul
is once again wounded, they are treading upon our Hearts. Both our Hearts
have been once again crowned with two wreaths of thorns. My side is wide
open and My blood is gushing out. I am at your door now; with Me I carry
My hidden plan of salvation; it is here. This revelation is My voice. I love
you all, with all My Heart; with all My Heart I love you."[16]

The Lord will reassure His servant:

"My Heart is an abyss of love, an abyss of forgiveness." "Lift your mind to
Me, your home, for I am an ocean of tenderness and peace. Draw all of you
from My Sacred Heart to fill up your hearts; I will embellish you. I will
perfect you."

"Rebound My Sacred Heart by believing with a child-like faith. Do not seek why I have chosen you and lifted you to Me - just accept without the whys and the whos. Do not raise any questions - just accept what I have given you. Ah, My child I was behind your doors for years."

When Vassula replied, "Forgive me Lord." Jesus went on:

"I have forgiven you - I am not reproaching you, since this is a past thing, I only wish to show you the joy My Sacred Heart has for I am now with you again. I have formed you to receive Me; so please My Sacred Heart and receive My children - in receiving them, you are receiving Me; I am bringing them all the way to your doorstep - sacrifice your time; they need My peace; they need to be encouraged - encourage them to approach Me intimately, but nevertheless, never forgetting that I am holy."

"Those who love Me will learn to grow in My love so that in their turn they may bring others to Me to love Me. My Sacred Heart is in flames of love and ever so eager to draw all of you in its depths. I thirst for love; all I want from you is love because love is the root of the virtuous tree....(In answer to Vassula's words 'Oh Lord! Some will be persecuted like all other times.') I know My child - some will be persecuted by those whose ears are still closed and reason with their minds and not with their hearts; but by My grace I shall draw many of these too into My Sacred Heart. Little flower, courage, I am beside you and My eyes are upon you, so do not fear."

"In My love and pity I have redeemed you and lifted you up to Me and cradled you in My Sacred Heart."

Whether it is urging Vassula herself to advance in holiness or offering mercy to sinners, it is always the Sacred Heart which is at the centre:

"I know that many of you never cease thinking that I am repeating Myself, but this is because My words do not seem to penetrate you at all. If I do repeat Myself, it is because of your lethargy, because of your deafness, it is because so many of you do not put My words into practice. I come offering you My Heart in My Hand; I come offering you My peace and My love; I come to unite you all back into one single fold; I come to raise this dead era into a living one."[17]

He spoke thus early in June, 1989 and later in the month again spoke of offering His Heart in His hand. Some weeks later He spoke of the "wounds in His Sacred Heart." On 28 July He spoke to Vassula in a personal context:

"Be one with Me. How I the Lord love you. See! My Sacred Heart is open and he who wants to step in is welcome, you are all free to choose. If you choose My Sacred Heart I will fill you. I will let you live in My light, you will absorb from Me. I will nourish you, then I shall ask you if you are willing to share with Me. Like a Spouse and a Bride we will share, and I shall renovate you entirely with My love." "Come and repent" He says, on another occasion, "Fill My Sacred Heart with joy today and set your eyes on Me your Good Shepherd so that you no longer err aimlessly in this desert."[18]

Jesus relates the Eucharist to His Heart:

"Rejection you will never have from Me. Every time you come to receive Me, My Heart rebounds with joy. I have made Myself ever so tiny in the little white host. In taking Me you are accepting Me, and in accepting Me in this way you are acknowledging the truth. I and you are then one, you are in communion with Me, what more delightful than to be together with Me your God? What more pure and holy meeting? I, your God, meeting you My creature. I your Redeemer, and you My redeemed one."[19]

Jesus wished to relieve His servant of any doubt on the reality of His revelation. On 4 February, 1988 she writes: "Sometimes I'm so afraid that all this might be wrong, that maybe I don't see Him but think I see him, yet when it's like this He somehow convinces Me it is all exact to the point. Is it really you Jesus?" In answer He said "I will show you My Heart. Write what you see and feel in My presence." then she could write a little later, "Jesus is two feet away from me, His Holy Face is beauty itself. He asked Me to look at Him. He showed me His Heart, all His breast was lit, shining, glowing out of love." He spoke:

"All is correct, everything you discern is correct. O Vassula, My Vassula, how I love you. Dearest soul, you may come to Me when you wish - you have seen My Heart. When you open our meetings of the day, open them with those prayers My son James has given you. It is I who showed him what to give you."

Later Jesus speaks through Vassula as He often does, to all who will listen:

"My creation, you are Mine, you are My seed. Beloved I am your Saviour - will you return to Me? Will you fall into My arms? I will forgive your sins. Come and eat My Bread, come and taste My Wine. If you repent I will forgive you. Listen to My Heart beats, every beat is a call for a soul."[20]

A fortnight later calling again for repentance Jesus spoke these words:

"Come and learn - I will replace your wickedness by love. Accept My ways, My ways of virtue. Era of unfaithfulness, why have you forgotten My divine ways. Return to Me your Saviour - I have not forsaken you and in spite of all your sins I love you. My Heart is an abyss of love - an abyss of forgiveness."

The sufferings which Christ endures mystically in His Body, which is the Church, are related by Him directly to His Heart:

"In the very sanctuary and depths of My Foundation, My Sacred Heart is bleeding; in My agony I sought to warn them. Arise, daughter! Ecclesia needs you. My house lies in darkness from the apostasy and iniquities, and because of their sins My flock has been scattered. How I cry from My Cross. Ah Peter!! I come to you because I know you remained faithful to Me. Oh, Peter look at My Heart... hear My cries, beloved soul. I, the Lord, find no love, no holiness in those Cains; they are many; they have laid waste My house... Pray Peter and I will lift you up so that your eyes will see this wilderness from above and I will let you penetrate into the wound of My Heart - I will let you see the lance's blade. Your heart will cry out with pain when you will see it. Peter, I will give you the strength and the courage you will need so that you may pull it out."

Again and again Jesus shows that all spirituality, the whole outlook which He wishes Vassula to cultivate must be centred on His Heart:

"I will place all those who love Me into My Heart - My Heart will be their new home. I come from above and from above your new home will descend - this will be My gift and My own new holy Name again will be once more given back to you My beloved ones." "I thirst for love, but you abandon Me in My thirst; I welcome you when I see you weary, to rest you in My Heart, yet when I am weary you reject Me. I open My Heart to you - showing you how you have wounded it - but in your wickedness you are repeating your stabs, piercing Me through and through. I open My arms to welcome you and embrace you, but you turn away, giving Me your backs. Full of tenderness I open My Sacred Heart to warm you, yet when I come to you, you shut your door in My face, leaving Me outside in the cold like a beggar." "Feel how My Sacred Heart is...I am love. I am the supreme source of love, so do not resist Me. Come to Me, plunge in Me, I, Jesus, love you to folly; how could some of you doubt of My love, defiling this pure and holy love? How could so many of you doubt of My holy presence in the host. My Holy Eucharist should not be spilled or treated as though it was not holy. If only you understood fully what I am offering you and whom you are receiving in you, you would be blessing Me without ceasing. Even My angels gazing at you from above desire this Meal you can have, but not they, yet many of you do not seem to perceive its fullness. I am the prisoner of love behind each tabernacle, waiting and hoping to see you come. Approach all you who err still in this wilderness, come to me pure and clean, let Me rejoice in you. So please My Heart further by repenting, recognizing your sins."

Again and again the language of the Heart is interwoven with the thought and expression of Jesus: He calls His disciple "Vassula of My Sacred Heart"; He asks her not to wound His Heart by neglecting Him; He declares "My Sacred Heart is your fortress"; about Our Lady He says "every devotion given to My Mother pleases My Heart." He speaks thus: "I am today beloved ones, asking you to pray fervently and amend for those whom My Heart loves, but have turned against Me." "Creep in the depths of My Sacred Heart and let Me hide you in there, I want you for Myself."

Though Vassula had no knowledge of eastern theology, as has been made clear, nor of any theology, Jesus speaks to her in a way that combines eastern and western traditions: the eastern emphasis, on divinization, on the recovery in redeemed men and women of the divine image in which they were created, and the image of the Heart, embedded in the best of Latin spirituality:

> "I am in your days revealing My Holy Face to you all, yes, My Holy Face shall shine on you My beloved ones. I shall reveal to you My glory, and you who might not know Me yet, I shall come to you too and take your hand in Mine and place it on My Sacred Heart. I shall make you feel My heartbeats and if you would then allow Me, I shall entice your little heart and consume it with My ardent love and make you mine entirely. I shall, if you abandon yourselves to Me, form you into My divine image, I shall give you back your divinity and make you holy as I am holy."[21]

Here certainly is a fusion, a fruitful meeting of eastern and western spirituality, offered to our generation through the medium of a theologically untutored but utterly faithful disciple of the Lord who had no previous knowledge of one or the other. I had no knowledge of this text when I wrote in a brief introduction to Vassula's writings: "I am convinced that we may expect an enriched theology of the heart within the Church from a close, profound fusion of the eastern and western traditions."

Was this in Jesus' mind when He spoke these words to Vassula:

"I love you all the same but many of you do not seem to understand this. Wretched you are all, sinners you are all. Frail you are all, but all of you are My offspring, see Vassula. Have I made any difference? I have come to <u>you</u> and showed <u>you</u> My Sacred Heart. I went in all directions seeking by what means I could make you mine. I showered blessing upon blessing on you to raise you from death and form you since you lacked wisdom. I courted you and in My tenderness I Myself have chosen you to become a witness to a people not your own and of whom many are far from understanding why wisdom has chosen a foreigner among them. I, the Sacred Heart, am determined to show them that I have taken you, a foreigner to them, to share the riches of My Sacred Heart and share My delights and sorrows. Yes, I have come to teach foreigners too of My Sacred Heart's riches, today I have made a new song for them for I am one and the same!"[22]

The reader must study some of the lengthy passages in which detailed spiritual instruction is given to Vassula, with the Heart of Jesus convincingly set before her as the source of her strength and motivation: for example His message on 10 December, 1990. Such language occurs as your Holy One will "place your head on His Sacred Heart, and when you listen to His heart-beats you will no longer resist him"; "I shall hide you in the deepest place of My Sacred Heart;" "I am only waiting to consume your whole being with the flames of My Heart and love;" "I shall arrest your eyes, your thoughts, your desires to become captives of My Heart."

Further extensive quotation is scarcely necessary. Jesus assured Vassula that He intends to disclose still greater wonders from His Heart:

"I still have hidden in My Sacred Heart many things to divulge to you and show you, for the treasures I have within Me are innumerable, but they would be too much for you to take now. Your soul will not be able to take in everything, but little by little I shall unfold to you the treasures of My Sacred Heart and step by step I shall guide you into what looks like a light-house, a mystery of unfathomable riches that have been hidden for generations and centuries. I shall reveal to you, My friend, the rich glory of hope, wisdom and knowledge. Be rooted in Me and you shall bear fruit; remain in Me and you shall live."

Perhaps one final excerpt from Vassula's rich treasury will close the documentation:

"It is I, the Sacred Heart. I come once more to revive this dying flame in your heart, into a consuming fire of tenderness and love. I descend to pour out lavishly all the treasures of My Heart on you, humanity and give light to those who live in darkness and the shadow of death. I come to break in splinters the doors of your dungeons and with My flame melt your chains of sin."

and later in this long message:

"The times are here, those times foretold in scripture, when My enemies will be conferring a title that does not belong on Me and is not Me, a false Christ, a lifeless image, a false god, an idol, subtly hidden under a false ecumenism, the lance's blade which lies deep in My Sacred Heart, and causes so much bleeding. By sword they will force you to eat their defiled food: a portion of rationalism one day and a portion of naturalism the other day and so on, aping the truth, My word, wisdom and the language of My Cross. But fire will come on them from heaven and consume him and his clan; this is sure and will come true. I am telling you all these things, beloved ones, so as to warn you against these false teachers and human doctrines and to tell you that in these coming days of tribulations My Sacred Heart which is on fire will continue to pursue you. As the beggar hoping for alms, I too will be hoping to win your heart before the coming of darkness befalls you. I bless each one of you, leaving My sigh of love sealed on your forehead. I, Jesus Christ, beloved Son of God and Saviour, leave you my peace wholeheartedly. I love you infinitely. Be one."[23]

Where does Vassula's writing on the Sacred Heart fit into the literature, already considerable in volume on this subject? Not with formal treatises or doctrinal essays, but with the records of personal experience. Among the greatest of these are the writings of St. Gertrude the Great (d. 1302) and St. Margaret Mary Alacoque (d. 1690); the latter's autobiography is supplemented by the testimony of her spiritual director, St. Claude la Colombière (d. 1682). Vassula's contribution is different from theirs is, by reason of the circumstances of her life and her mission, highly distinctive.

The saints of the Sacred Heart lived in enclosed religious orders; St. Gertrude was favoured by the Lord almost exclusively for herself and those near to her, during her life or afterwards; St. Margaret Mary had a mission to the Church, in its public life, in its liturgy. But she would act through others, and time would pass before her ideas, which she expressed as coming from the Lord, would take effect. The history of devotion to the Sacred Heart, of its acceptance by Church authorities or rather by their theological advisers is lengthy, complicated, not altogether edifying. The great public acts, institution of the feast and its extension to the whole Church, the papal initiatives in the great act of universal consecration and the publication of Encyclicals, are part of church history. But at a cost in pain to the advocates and proponents of the doctrine and appropriate practice.

Vassula's personal position is very different from that of either saint. She is not a Catholic, but transcribes an experience which is deeply Catholic. This is clear from what has been said about her career. She is not a religious as were the saints. She has, directly from the Heart of Jesus, a public task to be achieved precisely by telling of His communication to her. She has to use all the means available, even the most up-to-date means of communication, cassettes, videos and the fax machine, to make public what takes place in the depths of her soul.

The only spiritual warrant she bears is an unusual one, open avowal of her conversion from a life of religious indifference. Subject to correction this mission and the accompanying credentials are totally singular. The intention behind such things we can guess but without any criterion of certainty. She moves in an atmosphere of freedom, which facilitates her work. She does show respect for everything to do with Catholicism, official or institutional; she shows respect to persons unfailingly and without discrimination.

A still more profound question arises out of the suffering of Jesus, as He describes it to Vassula, suffering that so often goes straight to His Heart. How can Jesus Christ now, according to our faith, seated in glory at the right hand of the Father, still be exposed to pain? The explanation given is Christ's presence in His Mystical Body, which is the Church. The Church grows through its union with the Head and an identity between Christ and the individual member is effected:

> "I have been crucified with Christ; it is no longer I who live, but Christ who lives in me; and the life I live now in the flesh I live by faith in the Son of God, who loved me and gave himself for me." (Gal 2:20)

> "For me to live is Christ and to die is gain." (Phil 1:21)

> "For I was hungry and you gave me no food; I was thirsty and you gave me no drink; I was a stranger and you did not welcome me, naked and you did not clothe me, sick and in prison and you did not visit me... Truly, I say to you, as you did it not to one of the least of these, you did it not to me" (Mt 25:42,43,45)

> "They crucify the Son of God on their own account and hold Him up to contempt." (Heb 6:6)

For this profound reason, Jesus said to Saul, "Saul, Saul why do you persecute Me? ...I am Jesus whom you are persecuting." (Acts 9:4,5) Jesus did not say, "Why do you persecute My bishops, or priests or faithful?" It is in another context, a most striking proof of the authenticity of Vassula's message that she has given this Christ-centred rendering of the problem of evil in the Church. It is one of the insights, utterly rewarding, which she had no means whatsoever of discovering with her own meagre or non-existent stock of Christian ideas. It places her message at the innermost core of the continuing Christ event through history. It is ultimately justified by His lordship of history, His mastery of time, His power to summarize the destiny and fortunes of mankind in his own experience. He is within the process of history, reliving the phases and mysteries of His earthly life, seeking to fashion about and to Him a body made of members alive with His spirit.

Can we capture in a brief character sketch the qualities which make Him so distinctive in His dialogue and discourse with Vassula? People have, with more or less success, attempted the same task on the gospel records.[24] It can never be entirely satisfactory for this Person remains enigmatic, mysterious. He surprises in many ways as we follow Him through Vassula's pages. He is so intensely, consolingly human, sensitive to her needs, thoughtful of her capacity to respond to His wishes, generous, never harsh in one to one situations, so gentle, so prodigal in mercy and compassion, firm and lucid in His comprehensive view of divine and human things, penetrating in His insights on the forces of evil. He is at times very outspoken, as when He is dealing with the apostasy and those responsible for it; He likes figurative language, vipers for the minions of the evil one, "flower" talking to His disciple. He reverts to biblical prototypes, Cains for the unfaithful ministers, Abels for His true friends; He likes biblical figures "two lamps" (Zech 4:11-14) and "two olive trees" (Rev 11:4) for the Two Hearts. What is so touching in the measured, varied sequence of themes all so relevant to our distracted times, is the candid revelation of suffering. The poignancy of the most wonderful Person who ever lived, the Godman prisoner of His own inexhaustible love for His fellow-men, which very love, allied with measureless mercy, makes Him their victim.

Notes:

1.   For theology and history of devotion to the Sacred Heart of Jesus cf. M. O'Carroll, *Verbum Caro, An Encyclopedia on Jesus the Christ*, Collegeville, 1992, article The Sacred Heart, with ample bibl., 158-161;

2.   For St. Margaret Mary Alacoque Cf. M. O'Carroll, *op. cit.*, 107f; for the saint's autobiography, tr. V. Kerns, Westminster, Maryland, 1961, Tan Books, tr. Visitation Sisters;

3.   AAS 48 (1956) 309-353; Cf. M. O'Carroll, *op. cit.*, 62-64;

4.   In *Towards a Civilization of Love: Proceedings of the International Congress on the Heart of Jesus*, Toulouse, July 24-28, 1981, English tr. San Francisco, Milwaukee, 1985, page 48;

5.   *L'Osservatore Romano*, 29 June, 1984; *Insegnamenti*, VII, same date;

6.   30 January, 1987, Volume I, page 24;

7.   *Ibid.*;

8.   1 February, 1987, Volume I, page 25;

9.   12 February, 1987, Volume I, page 32;

10. 21 February, 1987, Volume I, page 43;

11. 17 May, 1987, Volume I, page 102;

12. 19 May, 1987, Volume I, page 108;

13. 8 November, 1987, Volume I, page 222;

14. 13 January, 1988, Volume I, page 264;

15. *Ibid.*;

16. 18 January, 1988, Volume I, page 266f;

17. 1 June, 1989, *True Life in God*, Volume II, page 29;

18. 28 July, 1989, Volume II, page 50;

19. 29 September, 1989, Volume II, page 82;

20. 4 February, 1988, Volume I, page 280;

21. 22 January, 1990, Volume II, page 143;

22. 25 March, 1991, Volume II, page 297;

23. 12 September 1990, Volume II, page 223. Jesus dictated to Vassula many beautiful prayers and formulas of consecration to the Sacred Heart. These appear in a separate publication.;

24. On the character of Jesus, with bibl., cf. *Verbum Caro*, s.v., 33-35;

4

THE HOLY SPIRIT

The Renewal Movement has awakened the consciousness of Catholics to the Holy Spirit. Behind this statement of fact there is a sad history. The Holy Spirit has been neglected in the Latin Church, not of course to the extent that his action was impeded. In 1921 a French writer, Mgr. Landrieux, published a book entitled *Le divin méconnu* translated into English as *The Forgotten Paraclete*, in which he pointed out the need for greater awareness of the Holy Spirit in the life of the Church, a more meaningful attitude towards His presence and His gifts. About the same time the well-known spiritual writer, Dom Columba Marmion, was accustomed to begin his retreat lecture on the Holy Spirit by recalling a suggestive episode in the *Acts of the Apostles*; certain neophytes were asked if they had received the Holy Spirit and replied that, they had not even heard that there was a Holy Spirit. The implication was obvious. (Acts 19:2)

Things remained thus until Vatican II. The Council would bring the Holy Spirit into the focus of Catholic thinking, but not immediately. When the bishops of the Church and the Catholic universities were invited to make suggestions for the conciliar agenda, not one reply mentioned the Holy Spirit. They would have excused this silence on the grounds that there was no need for a doctrinal statement. But John XXIII had given the Council an ecumenical aim; he would later declare that it should have a predominantly pastoral quality. With such an outlook priority should have been given to the Holy Spirit. During the first three sessions of the Council He did not figure very much in the speeches delivered in St. Peter's, nor in the work of the commissions which prepared texts and revised them in the light of suggestions and votes sent back by the assembly.

Before the fourth session something happened which challenged the flow of ideas within the whole conciliar orbit. An article appeared in *The Ecumenical Review*, official organ of the World Council of Churches, over the signature of its editor, a Greek theologian, Nikos Nissiotis, which was severely critical of Council teaching on the very subject which concerns us: the texts issued or being considered would have little impact in the Orthodox churches, as they said nothing significant about the Holy Spirit.[1]

The criticism had been heard in the course of friendly encounters organised by the

Secretariat for Christian Unity; these brought together once a week experts or conciliar representatives and Observers from the non-catholic churches and communions. But the article of Nissiotis called for more serious consideration. Whether as a result of his criticism or not, there seems to have been more attention to the Holy Spirit in the conciliar texts completed and published during the fourth session. This is seen in the *Constitution on Divine Revelation,* and in the *Decrees on the Ministry and Life of Priests* and on the *Missionary Activity of the Church.*

A debate ensued about the teaching of Vatican II on the Holy Spirit: the defence pointed to 258 references to the subject in the documents, to which the reply was that many of these were nominal. Nissiotis used the word "poverty" of the overall treatment. Paul VI had no illusions. He stated frankly that preachers and theologians must now strive to provide a theology of the Holy Spirit which would match the conciliar teaching on Our Lady and the Church. He worked at the task himself, with the collaboration which is normally available to a Pope. Fr. Edward O'Connor of Notre Dame University was able to make a book out of the papal texts and his own valuable commentary: The Pope was especially desirous to offer theological advice to the Renewal Movement and to remove any source of misunderstanding or friction between its members and the Marian movement.[2] A big moment in this policy was Pentecost, 1975. The world congress of the Renewal Movement took place in Rome at the time and so did the International Mariological and Marian congresses. Paul VI named Cardinal Suenens his Legate to the Marian Congress, which had as its theme Mary and the Holy Spirit. In the letter sent to the Cardinal, known also as a patron of the Renewal Movement, the Pope dealt in detail with the Spirit in the various phases of Our Lady's life. Lecturers and listeners had moved freely among the different groups present in Rome and the final assembly at the papal Mass in St. Peter's brought all the participants together.

However it has been John Paul II who, with no lack of appreciation of his predecessor's work, has seen the urgency of the question we are considering and offered the fullest response to it. The Holy Spirit is a persistent theme in his teaching, subject of extensive treatment in separate documents like the Encyclical *Dominum et Vivificantem* issued for the sixteenth centenary of the Council of Constantinople, 1981, and the discourses then occasioned, again the main theme in the weekly catecheses for several months some years ago, exclusive topic in one of the annual letters to Catholic priests from the Pope, taken up in very many other documents and pronouncements, notably, with incisive effect, in the Encyclical *Redemptoris Missio.*[3]

John Paul II deserves the title "Pope of the Holy Spirit." Not only has he published more than any of his predecessors on the subject, he has put forward insights on Our Lady's docility to the Spirit, as she "pondered all these things in her heart" (Lk 2:19,51); to the International Symposium on the Two Hearts he pointed to the role of the Spirit in the "alliance." Especially he has brought to a certain completion two ideas that have increasingly come into the focus of theological thinking: the role of the Spirit in the life of Jesus, and his central influence in the Church's missionary activity. The Pope does not neglect any important aspect of the Spirit's personality or beneficent activity.

The Spirit as indispensable to our understanding of Jesus Christ in His earthly life has been the object of reflection and exposition by theologians of the calibre of Yves M.J. Congar, O.P. and Hans Urs von Balthasar. The theme was magnificently expressed by the Pope in an address on 28 March, 1990, applied in a further essay on spirituality a week later. Since Jesus in speaking to Vassula so often uses the phrase "My Spirit", the papal teaching, being contemporaneous, deserves very close attention. Quotation is needed:

> "If previously we have shown the wonders of the Holy Spirit announced by Jesus and experienced at Pentecost and during the initial journey of the Church in history, the time has come to emphasize the fact that the first and greatest wonder accomplished by the Holy Spirit is Christ Himself. It is towards this wonder that we want to direct your attention.... In accomplishing the mystery of the Incarnation, there was a decisive presence of the Spirit, to the degree that, if we want to grasp and enunciate this mystery more fully it is not enough for us to say that the Word was made flesh; we must also underline - as happens in the Creed - the Spirit's role in forming the humanity of the Son of God in the virginal womb of Mary. A basic truth emerged from examination of the gospel texts: what Christ was, and what He is for us, cannot be understood apart from the Holy Spirit. This means that not only is the Holy Spirit's light necessary for penetrating Christ's mystery, but the influence of the Holy Spirit in the Incarnation of the Word and in the entire life of Christ must be taken into account to explain the Jesus of the Gospel. The Holy Spirit left the mark of His own personality on the face of Christ."[4]

Dealing later with the holiness of Christ the Pope had this to say:

> "The words addressed to Mary during the Annunciation indicated that the Holy Spirit is the source of holiness for the Son who is to be born of her. At the instant in which the Eternal Word becomes man, a unique fullness of human holiness is accomplished in the assumed nature, a fullness which goes beyond that of any other saint, not only of the Old but also the New Covenant. This holiness of the Son of God as man, as Son of Mary, a holiness from the source, rooted in the hypostatic union - is the work of the Holy Spirit, who will continue to act in Christ to the point of crowning His masterpiece in the Easter mystery.... By the power of the Holy Spirit, the

holiness of the Son of Man constitutes the principle and lasting source of holiness in human and world history."[5]

In the fourth session of Vatican II one of the questions which called for reference to the Spirit was the mission of the Church. As a result of the Nissiotis article there was a desire to make the reference overt. A theology of the Spirit's role in mission was adumbrated as time did not allow plenitude in teaching: suggestive but awaiting further development. Paul VI carried the thinking further in his Apostolic Exhortation, *Evangelii Nuntiandi*. In the same line and now totally satisfactory is the magnificent section in *Redemptoris Missio* on the Holy Spirit, principal agent of evangelization.

Papal teaching belongs to the ages. Contemporaries are often willing to leave it to future ages. This has happened in regard to John Paul II's teaching on the Holy Spirit. It must be brought into the lives of the faithful, becoming dynamic, motivating conduct. Those called to such an important task will find the writings of Vassula helpful, illuminating in theory and practice.

Just as the extracts published to illustrate John Paul II's teaching should incite the reader to make further acquaintance with the whole corpus of the Pope's thought, so it must be made clear that what is here quoted from Vassula is but a fraction of what she has written on this theme.

In such communication, in its content, she is in deep harmony with the Orthodox tradition. But not through direct or conscious contact with the great teachers, even with any of our time or century like Sergey Bulgakov. She had no formal initiation in theology; she has stated quite clearly that her religious instruction, her catechetical training, was practically nil. She therefore received the rich doctrine about the Holy Spirit, she became accustomed to think of Him frequently, under the guidance of Jesus entirely because Jesus chose to use her to His own mighty purpose. We cannot say that He did this because she was a member of the Greek Orthodox Church since He has never stated this.

Moreover, in some of the important elements of the instruction Vassula has received from Jesus about the Holy Spirit the reference is painfully to defects in the Latin Church.

It will help to follow the sequence of Jesus' communications. In August, 1988 Jesus' revelation of the Spirit is accompanied by a warning on the evil one.

"I am the Light. I have redeemed you from darkness. Vassula, Satan is desperate and is trying to confuse you and bring you all against each other. Realize how he works - he is trying to confuse you all. He knows how My works save many souls and this is why he wants to thwart My plans and battles against them. I will always be near you. Read Acts II *(the account of Pentecost and St. Peter's explanatory speech with the immediate effects)*. My Spirit is given from above to many but, as always, some would laugh it off - unable to explain His mysteries. I have said again and again that I will pour out My Spirit on all mankind and you shall prophesy. Young men shall see visions. I shall pour out My Spirit. I will display portents in heaven and above, and signs on earth below. Creation! Have you really understood this prophecy? I solemnly ask My teachers who do not believe in Wisdom's works, to look for the hidden sense of proverbs and into the wisdom of all the ancients. They should ask to be filled with the Spirit of Understanding, which will lead them to understand the greatness of My name. Beware of Satan's traps - I have forewarned you of his malice, my Child."[6]

In the following month, in the course of a message Vassula, took down these words:

"I know how weak and miserable you are without me, but I also know that I have in my hands a mere child and a nothing where My Spirit can freely breathe in this space you are giving Me. Allow My Spirit to mould you and form you - all that you learn comes from Wisdom and I am Wisdom."[7]

Later in the same month it was in the context of the spiritual decline that Jesus spoke of the Spirit:

"My house is in ruin today, but the worst is yet to come. The Cains, living in My body and who are the thorns in My head, full of boastfulness, will endeavour to slaughter My Abels - these Abels who understand My Spirit and love Me sincerely; but I tell you truly that their boasts will turn into mourning and My fire will burn these unfaithful servants, for what have they to offer to Me now? They tread upon My Spirit, led by their own desires and bigotry; their unfaithfulness lead them astray and they cannot see clear anymore."[8]

In the same lengthy message occur these words:

"This rationalism made a desert of My Church, bringing it into a ruin where vipers nestled within its depths. For those who defile My name and sit enthroned in earthly glory, satisfying their thirst for money, seeking their own interests and not Mine, I call out in the wilderness you have made, for you to come to Me and repent before the day of purification. I, the Lord, warn you not to suppress My Spirit of truth, who speaks through this weak instrument. I solemnly request My Church to remember the conditions I and My disciples worked in and where our heads rested. Palaces we had none!...

None! Palaces were for kings, not for Me, nor My disciples!"[9]

Passing references to the Spirit are found in the ensuing weeks. In October we have something more elaborate:

"Today, My child, I have ministers in My Church who claim to believe in Me but refuse all My divine works I am offering you in your days and that come from the Holy Spirit. Their aridity is condemning them and in the Day of Judgment I will judge them severely. These people should go back to Scriptures and read how My Spirit works and how I bless the gifts I am giving to the chosen ones - they all come from Me. My child, you and I, I and you, are crossing this wilderness - this deadly wilderness caused by rationalism, lack of faith, lack of love, promiscuity, self-indulgence, vanity and resentment to all that descends from the Holy Spirit. Their obduracy to listen is condemning them - anyone who rejects the works of the Holy Spirit is rejecting Me for the Holy Spirit and I are one and the same... These people are promoting this desert and are making sure that nothing will grow in it; if they see a flower, either they will trample on it and crush it, or will ignore it on purpose and never water it so that it withers and in this way get rid of it. My Cup of Justice is brimming over and already they are sensing the first drops of My justice upon them. All I ask from these people, especially those who serve Me yet refuse the Holy Spirit's works, is to pray, pray, pray for enlightenment and for a stronger faith."[10]

Pope John Paul II once remarked to a friend[11] that we especially need the Holy Spirit in these times, because the evil spirit seems so strong. So much is implicit in the messages just quoted when Jesus speaks of what is evil and relates it directly to rejection of His Spirit. He will continue this theme, when He draws attention to the apostasy spreading through the Church. On 26 October He taught Vassula - this time with the thought of Christian unity in mind - this prayer:

"Pray often to the Holy Spirit this prayer: Come, Holy Spirit, come through the powerful intercession of the Immaculate Heart of Mary, your beloved Bride."[12]

Again some time later when she was praying the Rosary He helped her meditate:

"Enter now into My third mystery when My Holy Spirit descended like tongues of fire. Pray for the coming Pentecost, already your generation feels the pangs of its birth. The night is almost over, dawn is soon to break and when it does, evil who prowled with ease in the night, shall flee at daybreak. Yes, indeed, my Spirit of grace shall be poured out on all mankind and your generation shall be fed directly by Me, you shall be taught and guided by Me and even My saints and angels from above shall meet you at each street-corner."[13]

Soon afterwards He returns to the theme of rejection.

"Today My Holy Spirit of grace is rejected by unbelievers, but they do not know what they are rejecting. It is, as Scripture says, 'the stone rejected by the builders has proved to be the keystone, a stone to stumble over, a rock to bring men down.' These unbelievers stumble over the corner stone because they do not believe in the works of the Holy Spirit. Yes, today My Holy Spirit of grace who descends to show you the Way, the Truth and the Life is indeed the keystone, the corner stone that you do not recognize, and reject altogether."[14]

In the New Year Vassula received a message from Our Lady, which we shall study for another reason. She spoke thus:

"Rejoice that His Holy Spirit is being so lavishly outpoured upon every nation and raising new disciples."[15]

In the years 1990 and 1991 Jesus spoke very frequently to Vassula about the Holy Spirit. He was bringing His pedagogy of the Spirit to a fullness, eventually a splendid climax. Thus on 22 April, 1990, she reminded Jesus of His own words that the Spirit was the keystone, rejected now as He had himself been rejected during His lifetime. Jesus' answer:

"See how former predictions have come true! Indeed I have said that the Advocate, the Holy Spirit, whom the Father will send in My name will teach you everything and remind you of all that I have said to you, but I knew all along that only a remnant would listen and return to Me. On these very ones who would listen to Me, I shall invest with My Holy Spirit of Wisdom and insight; yes, I shall invest them with My spirit of Counsel and knowledge and the flickering light that now is left in this world will become a vivid fire. I repeat that My Holy Spirit of Grace is being sent out to the four corners of the earth to teach you to be holy and raise you up again into divine beings. The earth shall turn into a copy of heaven and thus My will will be done, the prayer I have taught you to pray shall be fulfilled."[16]

To Vassula's further prayer for a second Pentecost Jesus replied with words of confidence, for example

"I am pouring out My Spirit on you, generation to water your desert and to make rivers out of your dry soil... Recognize the times, recognize the gentle breath of My Holy Spirit of grace upon you, I am blowing now on your nations, raising up with My Breath your dead, turning them into a reflection of My image."[17]

In September of that year Jesus, evoked

"Satan and all his empire.. escalading at the peak of their power in My Church and in all nations, together with the false prophet whose footsteps you hear clearer and clearer every day and everywhere. They are armed to the teeth to make war against My Church and all those who obey My Commandments."

Then came the message of consolation:

"I have reserved, beloved children, for your times, this celestial manna given by My Spirit. It is this hidden manna I had reserved for times of wilderness and iniquity; it is the food of the poor and those who are starved, and I promise you they will receive as much as they want to eat and to them I shall confer My new Name; it is this heavenly food I am pouring from heaven; it is the outpouring of My Holy Spirit, filling your interior desert; it is Love speaking to a hostile world; it is Love knocking on every locked door; it is Love calling from the other side of the wall separating us, built up by My enemies; it is Love pleading like a beggar for a return of love.. a smile.. a regret.. a sigh. It is I."

Jesus then promised an outpouring lavishly of "all the Treasures of My Heart on you humanity." Later:

"What will I not do for you? My Spirit is upon you and it will rest on you forever and ever, so open up your hearts and let me fill you with My grace."[18]

In that same month Our Lady gave Vassula a message in the course of which she said:

"I tell you truly that the Kingdom of God is among you and His Holy Spirit of grace is blowing sweetly now on your nations to revive you, so come to the wedding of the Holy Spirit who will wed your lands. Do not reject the Holy Spirit that so manifestly is poured upon you, do not be like the 'builders' who rejected the stone that turned out to be the cornerstone. God wants everyone to be saved. And now this is My solemn warning to all who hear the prophecies of this book: do not suppress the Spirit, the Spirit that now blows on you in the middle and in the peak of your apostasy."[19]

Jesus reminds Vassula of the way His Spirit is offended "persecuted" by those who do not believe in His action in the Church. He also comforts her by assuring her that the Spirit is her guide and counsellor. He strengthens her hope by the promise that "No one can stop this hour of His Holy Spirit." On one occasion He communicated to her the role of the Spirit in the Church so clearly and amply that His words then must surely have a place in anthologies:

"Peace be with you, Vassula. Scriptures never lie. It has been said that in the last days to come, people will keep up the outward appearance of religion but will have neglected the inner power of it. Ah! My beloved, will there be any faith left on My return?"

"The inner power of My Church is My Holy Spirit in it, alive and active, like a heart in a body. My Holy Spirit is the Heart of My Body which is the Church. The inner power of My Church is My Holy Spirit who gives freely and distributes His gifts and its graces so that the Church gets some benefit. The inner power of My Church is My Holy Spirit, the reminder of My Word, revealing nothing new but the same instructions given by the same Spirit. The inner power of My Church is My Holy Spirit that transfigures, uplifts and turns you into real copies of myself. The inner power of My Church is My Holy Spirit, this fire which enlivens you, purifies you and makes out of your spirit columns of fire, ardent braziers of love, living torches of light, to proclaim without fear My Word, becoming witnesses of the Most High and teaching others to look only for heavenly things. The inner power of My Church is My Holy Spirit, the life and breath that keeps you alive and makes your spirit desire Me, calling Me 'Abba.' If you refuse, My child, and suppress the gifts of My Holy Spirit, what services will you be able to do and offer Me? Do not be like corpses that keep up the outward appearance of religion but reject the inner power of it with futile speculations, thus limiting Me in My divinity. Do not stop those who come as children to Me, living a life of devotion to the Holy Spirit - it is I who calls them to the wedding of My Holy Spirit. The secret of holiness is: devotion to Me your God and you can do nothing of yourselves unless My Spirit living in you guides you and teaches you heavenly things. I tell you truly, whoever fears Me will accept My correction - so do not sleep now, for these are the times when one should be awake and vigilant more than ever. These are the times to open your ears and listen to My Spirit and not disregard Him; do not play the sage at the wrong moment by pushing the breath of the Holy Spirit aside and suppressing the inner power that activates My Church. You want to be prudent? Open your eyes then. You want to be prudent? Open your heart and your ears, My friend, not your mind. A prudent person never scorns a warning from the Spirit, only the proud do not know anything about fear. The fear of the Lord is the beginning of Wisdom. You want to be prudent?

Look for the truth that desperately leans over your misery to save you! Look who is bending towards your wretchedness and your wickedness to pull you to Him and lift you from your graves to breathe life into you again! O come! Do not misunderstand Me, I am not forcing you nor am I trying to violate your liberty! I have taken pity on you generation. Do not say that all I had to say has been said. Why limit Me as yourself?"

"I am the reminder of My Word, yes, the inner power of My Church and I am free to send you new portents and do fresh wonders. I am free to rule you generation and pour healing ointment on you from the riches of My Sacred Heart, when I wish and on whom I wish. I am building, yes rebuilding My Church that lies now in ruin. So do not let Me face you generation in the Day of Judgement and be obliged to tell you: you, you were one of My persecutors who pulled down while I used to build. Mercy is at your doors now and My compassion knocks on your doors in your times of tribulations."

"You say yourselves holy? Prove yourselves holy by showing Me your adoration to Me. Prove yourselves holy by showing Me the souls you are converting and bringing to Me, for My Kingdom consists not of spoken words, nor of an outward appearance of religion, but an inner power that only I can give you through My Holy Spirit, if you seek it. Feel My presence and My love I have for each one of you. I, Jesus Christ, am present and bless you all out of the depths of My Sacred Heart, leaving the sigh of love on your forehead. Be one. Ecclesia shall revive."[20]

Pope Pius XII, following on the teaching of his predecessor Leo XIII taught that the Holy Spirit is the soul of the Church. He quotes Leo as follows in his Encyclical *Mystici Corporis Christi*: "It is enough to say that since Christ is the Head of the Church, the Holy Spirit is her soul." Vatican II did not take up the idea, though it recognised that "The inner nature of the Church was now to be made known to us through various images", and noted that these images were "drawn from pastoral life, agriculture, building construction and even from family and married life." The images served a preparatory role in the writings of the prophets."

The Church is a mystery in its existence, manifestation, growth and that it should be described in varying images is testimony to this mystery. It is not the intention of the sacred writers to exhaust its mystery in any one metaphor. It is likewise true that to use the metaphor of the human soul as the Popes did, or to find the word heart on the lips of Jesus speaking to Vassula implies no contradiction. The soul would refer rather, though not exclusively to the essence of the Church, the word "heart" would express more the dynamic life of the Church in the existential order.

To offset the splendid passage, mostly doctrinal in character, we should take the word of Jesus on His programme for us conjointly with His Spirit:

> "Look, look around you, My Holy Spirit comes to meet you and revive you all. Dressed as a beggar, with tears of blood streaming down My cheeks, I descend from My throne, leaning all the way to you, to save your soul from disaster and from famine. For the sake of My Name I shall demonstrate Myself through these very things you do not believe any more. I shall demonstrate My Holy Spirit through marvels, through miracles. I shall demonstrate My power through weakness and wretchedness as never before. I shall come with thousands of myriads of angels to pour on you, generation, My celestial Manna, this hidden Manna (Rev 2:17) and fill your mouth with My food so that your mouth proclaims My Glory. Apostasy challenged My mercy, and rationalism this plague of your era, challenged My power. I am sending before Me, to educate you, the Woman clothed with the sun, the second Eve, to school you and lead you, step by step, into heaven. I am sending you My Holy Spirit in this night to be your companion and Consoler and to remind you of My word. I am sending you a mission of angels of hope to expel your fears. Come and listen all you who are starved. Happy the man I invite to the Wedding of My Holy Spirit; he shall be filled with My celestial food, and though their faults overpower them, My Holy Spirit shall blot them out in his rest on them. Understand, My beloved, that My visit on earth is not to condemn you, but to save you. Who is going to see Me? Who will take notice? Who will recognise the throne descending from the heavens among you? Do not resist My Holy Spirit of grace, I am with you always."

To this sublime passage written, let it be recalled by one with no formal theological training we should add another:

> "The sinners' brood I shall consume by a roaring fire. Your generation will have her wedding with My Holy Spirit, and I shall with My consuming fire change the surface of this earth into a divine, prosperous and new earth, and the world of today will be gone. I shall turn you all with My consuming flame as pure as gold and transparent as glass because your hearts will be Mine and in Mine. I and My Father will be your abode, and you will be our abode. I intend to give you back your divinity, creation, so that My radiant glory will be like a lighted torch inside you. Then like a sentinel guarding a gate, I shall guard you too from anything unclean which may want to come inside you. I shall make out of each one of you a radiant city, I shall renew you entirely for this is the way I shall have you ready to wed My Holy Spirit. My Holy Spirit will make His home in you, transfiguring you to become His Holy City."

The same consoling promise is repeated in a passage such as this:

"You are My Holy City and you, who allowed My Holy Spirit to flow in you like a river, you are My New Jerusalem, the first-fruits, those very ones who had constancy and faith. And like dew coming from My mouth, like raindrops on the grass, you shall put hope in many arid hearts, because all the radiant glory of My Heart shall reflect in you, making you glitter like some precious jewel of crystal clear diamond. I tell you solemnly, many of you who are not born of the Spirit shall receive from above, by My grace, the Spirit of truth. The Spirit of truth shall descend in all His radiant glory out of heaven and make His home in you. My Holy Spirit shall wed you to become His bride, embellishing you by His holiness, and suddenly the heavenly things shall become visible in your hearts and My kingdom unseen yet to the heart shall become visible and crystal-clear in all its glory."

But Jesus does not overlook the reality, that of the indifferent:

"My Holy Spirit is your Guide, your Husband and your Master. I tell you truly that soon I will gather all nations in a circle of love and My Spirit will dwell in you giving sight to the blind, since the light that will be given you is My transcendent light; but how hard it is for those who have accumulated riches, in their spirit to penetrate into My light. How hard it is for the wise to penetrate into the Spirit and perceive its depths... (Jesus recalls His parable of the wedding feast, Mt 22:1-14) "I will come back and they will tremble they will tremble when they will realize who they were rejecting all this time. They renounced My Spirit and allowed themselves to be guided by their own spirit, they renounced My light for their own, they renounced My heavenly knowledge given by Wisdom for a second-rate philosophy and their own rational knowledge. Since they have rejected My Spirit, My light and My knowledge, I shall take away My kingdom from them and give it to a people who can produce its fruit... (Jesus speaks of His choice of the disreputable, out of whom He will make a nation of love "a holy nation and they will glorify Me.") They will be called priests of the Living God, priests of the Amen, and in this priesthood I shall rebuild My Church, in these hearts I shall unite you all and My Body will rest. The hour is here and no one can stop this hour of My Holy Spirit. When you will see the world disintegrating under your feet, when you will look to your left and see tottering kingdoms and cities reduced into a heap of dust, and to your right mountains tumbling, know that these signs are the beginning of the outpouring of My Holy Spirit."

What sets the seal of reassuring intrinsic value on these messages is the conjunction of realism, counsel and firm promise. An enlightened spiritual writer or theologian may set forth truth in the same area, but he cannot speak or write as the one who is totally in control of all that is happening, that will come to pass. This is where the mystic scores; he or she is in contact with the one who combines unerring insight with undisputed power.

One has the same impression while reading a different, singular divine message given by God the Father to Vassula. Here is what He said on 5 October, 1992:

"Today more than ever I am sending you My Holy Spirit to renew you, yet you know how long this generation keeps resisting My Holy Spirit. Tell Me can a body live without a heart? Learn that My Holy Spirit is the breath of My Church, the essence of zeal for Me, your God. My Holy Spirit is the sweet Manna of heaven, nourishing the poor. Happy the man who opens his heart to My Holy Spirit; he will be like a tree along a river yielding new fruit every season, with leaves that never wither but are medicinal. Happy the man who opens his heart to My Holy Spirit. Like a crystal clear stream My Spirit shall flow like a river in his heart renewing him, for wherever the river flows life springs up and joy. Have you not read, the river of life rising from My throne and from the Lamb will flow down in the middle of the city street? My Holy Spirit will take the innocent and make a pact of love and peace with them to become His partner. He will carry them behind the walls of the sanctuary, where lie fathomless riches and mysteries, mysteries that no eye had seen before; and like a Spouse adorning his bride with jewels He too will adorn them with imperial knowledge to delight in throne and sceptre. My Holy Spirit is the zest of your life, the radiant glory of the Living One, the secret revelation of your creation. My Holy Spirit is the flavour of your homilies in My assemblies, and the fulfilment of your times. He is the flaming fire of your heart and the perception of My mysteries. My Holy Spirit is the theme of your praises to Me revealing to your heart that I am who I am, revealing to your spirit that I am your Abba, and that you are My offspring and My seed."

In another touching message the Father warns against false teachers and false prophets:

"I am reminding you to beware of the false teachers and false prophets who induce in your soul desolation and misinterpret the gospels, telling you that the Holy Spirit is not with you to remind you of your foundations, nor of where you come from. They have already made a desolation out of your soul, and dug a vast gulf between you and Me your Father. Do not let them expand this desolation in your soul and mislead you into believing I have left you orphans. These false prophets have made out of My Son, Jesus, a liar, and out of the gospels an echoing cymbal, empty with emptiness. They made out of My Word a gaping grave. So beware of those false teachers who tell you that My Holy Spirit cannot descend to perform in you miracles and wonders. Beware of those who condemn My Holy Spirit who in your days more than anytime reminds you of your foundations. Beware of them who keep up the outward appearance of religion but reject the inner power that is My Holy Spirit."

The message of the heavenly Father ends on a wonderfully consoling note:

"And if anyone of you is calumniated and dejected because you are witnessing to the truth, turn to your Holy Mother. She will console your soul and provide you with courage. If the world inflicts on you impressive wounds, turn to your Holy Mother and She will dress your wounds with her maternal love and affection. As She took care of My beloved Son, your Holy Mother will take care of you too. In your misery and distress She comes flying to you and takes you into her Heart, that same Heart that conceived your Saviour. Your Holy Mother in heaven will teach you to enlarge My kingdom on earth by teaching you to love Me. So let love be the principle of your life. Let love be your root."

Here the eternal Father brings together His Holy Spirit and Our Lady in a way that must satisfy all those who, in recent times, seek deeper insight into the relationship between Mary and the Spirit.

This theme is beautifully developed in a further message given on the 5th October 1992:

"Open your hearts and you shall see My Glory, and like a child needing comfort, My Holy Spirit will comfort you whose love for you surpasses any human love. I, the Creator of the heavens and earth tell you, My Holy Spirit is the Spouse of the Bride, of She who held the Infant Who was to save you and redeem you, and in Whom through His Blood you would gain freedom and forgiveness of your sins. He is the Spouse of the One Whom He found like a garden enclosed, holding the rarest essences of virtues, a sealed fountain, the loveliest of Women, bathed in purity because of her unique perfection. My Spirit came upon Her and covered Her with His shadow and glorified Me making Her the Mother of God, the Mother of all humanity and the Queen of Heaven. Such is the Richness of My Holy Spirit..."[21]

In the following passage He combines the two themes of the Apostasy and the Holy Spirit, and this will concluded this chapter.

"Pray My child, pray for those who offend My Holiness and blaspheme My Holy Spirit calling My Spirit foolish. Have I not said: '....everyone who says a word against the Son of man will be forgiven, but no one who blasphemes against the Holy Spirit will be forgiven.' (Luke 12:10) for the Spirit is not opposed to the Son nor is the Father to the Spirit, since all three of Us agree. Many of you are condemning My Celestial manifestations and persecuting those whom My Spirit speaks through them because you do not believe they come from Me. Daughter, look at the Wounds of My Body... I have little time left now before My Father's Hand strikes this generation. Listen to your Father from whom you are sprung, listen to His Voice.

I went all ways, seeking to gather you and remind you to live holy since I am Holy, but only a remnant of you pay attention when I speak. I have spoken through those you call contemptible. I have spoken through weakness and poverty, but you have made a cult in persecuting My Holy Spirit that guides them, to the point of frenzy!! I have been sending you through them the spirit of Elijah and the spirit of Moses, those two witnesses dressed in sackcloth to prophesy and remind you of My Law, before My great Return. They are to speak to you in My Name and bring you back to the truth and back to your senses but over you spread a heavy darkness and your claims to your knowledge became a battlefield to My Knowledge. The Lie was and is persecuting the Truth but Scriptures never lie. It was said that 'the beast that comes out of the Abyss is going to make war on them and overcome them and kill them.' Indeed your battlefield is drenched now with innocent blood because My Holy Spirit of prophecy has become a plague to those who belong to the world. Their frenzied persecutions and total rejection they have for My mouthpieces are similar to those of Sodom; their stubbornness to open their heart and comply, their refusal to open their ear and listen to My Voice today have gone beyond the stubbornness of Pharaoh in Egypt. Today I am giving you 'things that no eye has seen and no ear has heard,' things beyond the mind of man. All these things that lift your spirit to call Me.: Abba. My Holy Spirit is calling you all to true devotion and to a better knowledge of God Himself, that is why I am continually repeating the same truths given to you. I shall continue calling you until I break through your deafness, generation. I shall not stop calling you in agony, not until I hear from you the word: Abba! The new heavens and new earth are soon upon you."[22]

A final text will show the richness of Jesus' imagery on this most important subject.

"My New Jerusalems! You, who are the first-fruits of My Love, you whom My Holy Spirit seduced by My New Hymn of Love, you whom I wed, go out to the nations and sing to them My New Hymn of Love. Work for Peace, sow the seeds I have given you. Be like trees growing by the banks of the River of Life, let your leaves be a medicinal balm for the wretched and let your branches bear fruit in holiness. Be My breech-menders, restorers of My ruined sanctuaries. Give to those who fell into Satan's impious nets and were fed portions of Rationalism and Naturalism. And My healing Water from My Breast, this stream that flows out of My Sanctuary, will fill you and make you wholesome. No man shall be able to arrest this rivulet. The stream will keep on flowing profusely out of My Heart; it shall flow everywhere, breaking into several parts, separating into other and several rivulets going into all directions and wherever this healing Water flows, Everyone, sick, lame, blind, will be healed."[23]

Notes:

1. The Main Ecclesiological Problems in the Second Vatican Council and the Position of the Non-Roman Churches Facing it, in *The Ecumenical Review* 2(1965) 31-62; id., Critique of Vatican II in *Journal of Ecumenical Studies* 2(1965) 38-40; on the question of article *Vatican II*, 223-226 with sample bibl.;

2. For Paul VI's opinion cf. *La Documentation Catholique*, 1 July 1973, 1635; cf. *Veni Creator Spiritus*, article Paul VI, 179-182 with bibl.; E. O'Connor, C.S.C., *Pope Paul and the Spirit*, Notre Dame, Indiana, 1978; cf. article The Holy Spirit in M. O'Carroll, *Theotokos*, Wilmington, 1983, 329-332;

3. Cf. M. O'Carroll, *Veni Creator Spiritus*, Notre Dame, Indiana, 1978; cf. article the Holy Spirit in M. O'Carroll, *Theotokos*, Wilmington, 1983 329-332;

4. *L'Osservatore Romano*, English ed., March 28, 1990;

5. *L'Osservatore Romano*, English ed., June 11, 1990; cf. *Verbum Caro Spiritus*, article The Holy Spirit and Jesus, 172-174;

6. 20 August, 1988, Volume I, page 364;

7. 6 September, 1988, Volume I, page 369;

8. 27 September, 1988, Volume I, page 377;

9. *Ibid.*, page 378;

10. 11 October 1988, Volume I, page 385f;

11. Bishop John Magee, secretary to the Pope, Master of Ceremonies - Personal communication;

12. 26 October 1989, Volume II, page 96;

13. 4 December, 1989, Volume II, page 117;

14. 23 December, 1989, Volume II, page 127;

15. 10 January 1990, Volume II, page 137;

16. 22 April 1990, Volume II, page 168;

17. *Ibid.*, page 169;

18. 12 September, 1990, Volume II, page 222;

19. 25 September, 1990, Volume II, page 230;

20. 15 April, 1991, Volume II, page 306;
21. 5 October, 1992, Volume III;
22. 23 July, 1991, Volume II, page 336;
23. 2 June, 1991, Volume II, page 320;

5

OUR LADY

The Catholic Church from the years of Cardinal Mercier, the early twenties, to the Second Vatican Council, was in a Marian age. Mercier with all the prestige acquired by his educational achievement in Louvain and his pastoral, patriotic career in wartime Brussels, took up the idea of Mary's universal mediation; he had read St. (still Blessed) Grignion de Montfort's book on *True Devotion to the Blessed Virgin Mary* and had been captivated by it. He obtained a Mass and Office in honour of *Mary, Mediatress of all Graces* from Benedict XV, and from Pius XI the establishment of three theological commissions, Roman, Belgian and Spanish, to study the possibility of solemnly defining the doctrine.[1]

A movement was quickly on foot, in the immediate wake of Mercier, far surpassing his area of influence. Theologians set to work on various aspects of the mystery of Mary, with an abundant, ever-growing literature. Societies sprang up to promote research on a scientific basis. Great names figure in the literary landscape. In Rome an International Marian Academy came into existence and in time initiated congresses which helped to pool resources and research. In the pastoral and apostolic sector missionary societies, lay associations, grew up with the same inspiration. Popular devotion was to find an outlet in pilgrimages at the well-known Marian shrines.

All such things found added stimulus and encouragement at the summit of church authority. Pius XII, Pope from 1939 to 1958, was one of the great Marian pontiffs in history. In 1942 he consecrated the world to the Immaculate Heart of Mary; in 1950 he solemnly defined the dogma of the Assumption; in 1954 he proclaimed the universal queenship of Mary; he declared two Marian years, in 1953/54 for the centenary of the dogma of the Immaculate Conception, in 1957/58 for the centenary of the Lourdes apparitions. He spoke very frequently on Our Lady, addressed by radio regional or local congresses, was noted for a piety which was intensely nourished by faith in the Mother of God. This was worthy of respect because of the Pope's profound theology of the Church, his guidance of the liturgical movement and his charter of freedom to biblical scholars.[2]

Vatican II led to the publication of important texts on Our Lady, especially in chapter VIII of the basic council document. Yet in the decades after the Council practices of Marian piety went into decline throughout the Church; homiletics was sparing about her; despite a specific conciliar ruling recommending the traditional respect for images, statues and pictures were put out of some churches; publishers felt that books on Our Lady involved risk. There were individuals and groups who resisted the trend.

What were its causes? Incidents in the history of the Council could be maliciously misinterpreted. Thus when a vote was taken in October 1963 on the question of having a separate doctrinal Constitution on Our Lady or of dealing with her in a chapter in the Constitution on the church, the second option was chosen, with the narrowest majority of any conciliar vote, less than two per cent, it could be said that the Church was on a back track in Marian piety. The fact that it was officially announced before the vote that doctrine and devotion were not at issue was overlooked. It was known that some of the Observers from the other churches, who did not accept Catholic Marian teaching and practice, thought the vote favoured them.

Again when the actual text was discussed in the Council aula in September 1964 the discordant voices on certain privileges of Our Lady, especially on her right to the title Mediatress, gave the impression of bishops wrangling about the Mother of God; on the very last day of the debate a Cardinal supported by 150 Council Fathers asked to have deleted from the text the word Mediatress, which has been used in the East since the fifth century and in the West from the ninth. It is used in the Council document in a very subdued context, just the statement that she is invoked thus, as well as under other titles.[3]

But the major reason given for reduction in Catholic attitudes to Our Lady was ecumenical. Foremost in the consciousness of certain influential theologians and publicists was Protestant rejection or restriction of familiar Catholic beliefs and practices about the Blessed Virgin Mary. We are in an ecumenical age and less must be said about her - this would be the attitude. No account was taken then of the Orthodox, who have mighty Marian traditions in doctrine and piety, especially in liturgy, wherein they excel, all of which they retain tenaciously. They do not think that truth is negotiable. They would not countenance any tampering with their sacred icons, the most beautiful of which is Our Lady of Vladimir in the Tretiakov Museum in Moscow; nor with their hymns, with the *Akathistos*, the most beautiful ever composed in honour of Our Lady. And the Orthodox, as we shall see in dealing with Russia, are coming back in force.

It would not be accurate to dismiss all Protestants as hostile to the Blessed Virgin Mary. Very many sympathetic works have been published on her from that world in recent times, as Protestants have shown a willingness to initiate and support the Ecumenical Society of the Blessed Virgin Mary, and to participate in dialogue on the biblical witness to her, to speak at Congresses organised by the Pontifical Marian

Academy, or by national Marian societies, the French for example.[4]

Within the Catholic body the tide has turned. Here one must be accurate in presenting the evidence. A speaker at the International Mariological Congress in Huelva in September, 1992, Fr. Ignace de la Potterie, S.J. spoke of a "decade without Mary"; it would probably be situated between 1965 and 1974. The Belgian Jesuit was using hyperbole, but those present knew what he meant.

What caused the recovery? The example of the Popes was potent. Paul VI had never accepted reductionist Marian theses. He personally proclaimed Mary Mother of the Church at the closing of the third session of Vatican II, during which the Marian chapter of the Constitution on the Church had been adopted. Despite criticisms or at least unfriendly murmurings from progressive theologians and journalists, he went to Fatima for the fiftieth anniversary of the apparitions, 13 May, 1967; he issued an Apostolic Exhortation *Signum Magnum* at the time and presented the Golden Rose to the shrine; he also spoke with Sister Lucia, the surviving witness. In the teaching sector the Pope Issued in 1974 a very important Marian document, *Marialis Cultus*, a text composed with strict attention to scientific modern trends, rich in doctrine and spirituality, sensitively embracing liturgical insights.

John Paul II has consolidated the papal position. From the first days of his pontificate he has strongly emphasized ideals and devotional practices centred on the Mother of God. He makes it a point to visit Marian shrines when he travels to foreign countries. In particular he has become involved in the whole movement of thought about Fatima. He attributed his escape from death in the assassination attempt, 13 May, 1981 to Our Lady of Fatima, went on pilgrimage to the shrine in thanksgiving in the following year on the anniversary. In dealing with Russia we shall see how he has acted in regard to the message of Fatima about that country. The Pope declared a special Marian year in 1987/88 and published an Encyclical on our Lady, *Redemptoris Mater*.

As happened so often in past times the Papacy though possibly frowned on by some within the academic establishment, is powerfully supported by the body of the faithful. Movements of Marian piety continue to grow and deepen their influence: the Legion of Mary has remarkable expansion figures to show in the Far East, notably in South Korea; the Messengers of Mary Immaculate, Queen of the Universe are active in many countries; so with notable membership, is the Marian Movement for Priests led by Don Gobbi, as are the Oblates of Our Lady of Ephesus, and in the U.S., Mary's People.[5]

That the faithful follow their own inspiration is especially true of the attendance at Marian shrines. At five major shrines, Aparacedia, Guadalupe, Fatima, Lourdes, Czestochowa the number of pilgrims would now be well over forty million. In the first ten years after the apparition reported in Medjugorje ten million people had gone there from all over the world. Several thousands assemble from time to time at Betania in Venezuela, still more go once a month to San Nicolas in the Argentine.

The word apparition evokes an important factor in the Marian renaissance within the Catholic body, that is among those who practise their religion and those who have returned to practice of it. There have been in recent decades, are currently reported, more apparitions of Our Lady than at any previous time in the history of the Church. In many cases belief in the reality of the apparition creates a focus of prayer, pilgrimage, spiritual renewal.

Are all these reported spiritual phenomena authentic manifestations of the divine? Very many are approved or tolerated officially, others supported by the kind of popular groundswell which I have mentioned. There was one case of fraud exposed on French television, which featured a police intervention. There are others over which hangs some doubt or suspicion. The figure of three hundred has been mentioned by Dom Bernard Billet, O.S.B., a specialist in the matter - that would cover those since the beginning of the century. It would be impossible to quantify numerically those reported at present, as reports increase constantly; it would be very difficult even in a small country like Ireland.[6]

The matter does not, should not, depend on the subjective outlook of an individual church ruler. Specific criteria have been laid down to judge such extraordinary happenings. It is not primarily prudence which is needed; this virtue is needed for all moral conduct, supernatural prudence is required for the whole of the Christian life. It is discernment that is called for, and one must bear in mind that when prudence is lauded what is really meant is caution. The most prudent thing St. Thomas More did was to risk execution - no doubt many at the time thought him imprudent.

The story of a number of recent apparitions is one of a tragic failure in discernment. This is clearly implied in many of the statements made by Jesus, quoted in the previous chapter, on rejection of the Spirit. With failure in discernment there has been, on occasion - I speak of cases which I have personally examined - aggressive behaviour towards visionaries, even sustained cruelty. This is inexcusable on grounds of elementary human rights; it is scandalous conduct on behalf of a minister of Jesus Christ dealing with a member of his flock.

The role of Our Lady in Vassula's life is more fully understood in the light of the brief survey of papal policy and teaching, of all that has happened within the pontificate of John Paul II, and all the movement of special Marian graces. Though Orthodox she is part of the Marian renewal of the Catholic Church. Her conversion dates from the mid-eighties when the recovery programme of the Popes and enlightened apostles of Our Lady was beginning really to take effect, when the best-known apparitions in Europe, the Middle East, Africa, South Korea, the Philippines were becoming widely known; they existed for some time. It was a time also when literature of Our Lady was no longer considered a risk by Catholic publishers. It may be said that Marian theologians had maintained their industry despite the discouraging market signs.

Vassula is in the Orthodox tradition, to which I have briefly referred, as she is in the Orthodox tradition on the theology and spirituality of the Holy Spirit. But in the Marian ideal and practice as in regard to the Holy Spirit all this did not come to her from Orthodox co-religionists. It came to her directly from Jesus. Jesus it was in one spiritual domain and the other, who instructed her as it became a member of the Greek Orthodox church to learn; and mercifully for us He did so in a theological and spiritual idiom wholly congenial and acceptable to the Latin church. It was a delicacy on His behalf, an act of condescension towards her and towards her Catholic constituency, which is worldwide.

Nor must it be thought that she has formed a coterie with other visionaries. She follows her own way, has had contact once or twice with others who receive favours from the Lord, but adheres to her own mission essentially. So committed is she to the task of Christian unity, as we shall see, that she joins with those to whom the Lord has assigned this mission, Myrna of Sophanieh in Damascus, for example. As we shall she see, Vassula does identify with Catholics in forms of prayer. She was instructed by the Lord to learn the Rosary, and to say the powerful prayer of petition, the *Memorare*.

We may begin some reflections on messages given to Vassula about Our Lady with this remark made by Jesus to her as she wept on one occasion in difficulty - it was a moment of spiritual frustration.

"Reserve your tears" Jesus said to her "for the time you will hear offenses being said on account of My Mother."[7] The words are of interest, for those who were campaigning, are still campaigning, for reductionist attitudes, theological and devotional, in regard to Our Lady, often claim that they are acting out of respect for the unique position of her divine Son. Newman admitted, in his time, that he rethought his whole outlook on Our Lady when he recognised by study of the facts, that he had been misled in the matter. He had been persuaded that devotion to Our Lady lessened respect for the Lord, the incarnate Son of God. He found, to his surprise, that it was in areas where devotion to her had remained strong that belief in His divinity endured; elsewhere, to his alarm, it had declined.

Another aspect of the same sad deterioration is seen in a reported conversation between Cardinal Suenens and the great German theologian, Fr. Karl Rahner.

Cardinal Suenens asked why there had been a decline in Marian piety. "Jesus Christ has been turned into an ideology" was in substance the reply "and an ideology has not a mother."

Some days after the Lord's words to Vassula, now on 8 October 1987, she addressed him thus:

> "Lord, I wish to repair every offence said about our Blessed Mother. I cannot bear to hear offences said from your creatures about her, especially priests. I would see my head roll and defend her."

Jesus' reply ought to induce a change of heart in those opposed to His Mother. We have had reports of anti-Marian writings and discourses from Catholics, even and especially at times from priests. We have naturally wished to believe that there was exaggeration in these alleged negative statements; it is also possible that things were worse than we heard or read. Let Jesus then be heard:

> "Vassula, I will let you understand how love suffers, hearing these offences. Vassula, let it be known that I, the Lord, honour My Mother; let it be known to those who offend her, that she is the Queen of Heaven, and that on her head, I, the Lord, placed a crown, a crown of twelve stars. She reigns, beloved, and this is written in My word. I honour My Mother, and as I honour her, you should honour her. I love you. Both My Mother and I bless you."[8]

Here Jesus confirms, by His affirmation, the truth proclaimed by Pius XII on 1 November, 1954, with accompanying delegations in Rome from Marian centres across the world, the universal queenship of Mary. Theologians and historians of Marian spirituality and piety had prepared for the event by research of the most impeccable kind. Vatican II takes up the truth in these words:

> "Finally, preserved free from all guilt of original sin, the Immaculate Virgin was taken up body and soul into heavenly glory upon the completion of her earthly sojourn. She was exalted by the Lord as Queen of all, in order that she might be the more thoroughly conformed to her Son, the Lord of lords (cf. Rev 19:16) and the conqueror of sin and death."

Vassula questioned the Lord:

> "Lord, the (Protestant) pastor denied her as our Holy Mother that we should venerate, and when I told him that you said it from the Cross, he said that you meant it only for John, and that nowhere in the Bible is it written that she is our Mother too and that we are her children."

Let us hear the words of Jesus:

> "But again I tell you daughter, that My Mother is your Mother too; you are
> her children; it is written in My word, and I am telling it again for those who
> do not know. Scripture says..." (Vassula queried 'Where, Lord?') "in the
> Book of Revelation, that when Satan failed in his pursuit of My Mother, he
> was enraged with her and went away to make war on the rest of her children,
> that is, all who obey the commandments and bear witness for Me (Rev
> 12:17)."[9]

Here we enter an important debate. It is the instinct, the deep sentiment, of the
faithful that Mary is their Mother. But when theologians come to justify this truth
from Sacred Scripture and Tradition (rightly understood) divergent opinions are
manifest. The early Fathers of the Church did not so interpret John 19:26-27,
"Woman behold your son. Behold your Mother." Among modern writers Newman
- in his famous *Letter to Pusey* - did so read the text; the modern Popes did likewise.
In the vast research on the subject conducted by Marian theologians over recent
decades, opened to discussion in sessions of the Marian study societies, the search
has been for a sure biblical foundation for the spiritual motherhood. Many would
settle for the Rev 12:17 text. They would include the wider function in the Fiat at
the Incarnation.

The dialogue just reported took place on 8 October 1987. Two days later Vassula
took up the subject again:

> "Oh, Jesus, I never knew that Christians do not believe, do not venerate St.
> Mary. I never knew how they felt about her. I never knew there was such
> tremendous difference between Christians; I didn't know it is so bad."

Jesus replied: "Oh Vassula, it is worse than you think." "Would they then venerate
our Blessed Mother if they are united?" she continued. "Child, they will" is Jesus'
reply. When Vassula asked him, "Do I understand that 'they will' means 'it will
be'? Jesus answered "I will bend them; I will bend their knees, and they will
venerate and honour My Mother."[10]

Jesus had told Vassula to reserve her tears for His Mother. He came back to this
plea:

> "Reserve your tears, for there will be none left when your ears shall hear the
> infamies said about My Mother."

On 12 December 1987 He pointed to the source of this baneful error:

"(Satan) blinded them, leading them when blinded into another path and in their delusion they not only disregard My Mother as Queen of Heaven, but disregard My Peter too and the authority I Myself have given him upon all My lambs."[11]

Those who in deepest error thought that Our Lady could be an obstacle to Christian unity will be enlightened by Jesus' words on 22 December, 1987:

"Vassula, the time has come to unite My Church. Come together again beloved, come and rebuild these ancient ruins; rebuild my old foundation, a foundation established by My own hand. Honour My Mother as I, who am the Word and above all, honour her. Would I not then desire that you, who are dust and ashes, recognize her as Queen of Heaven - honouring her? My grief today is to see how little My creation knows of her importance. Most of my devout ones who are under the name Luther and who have isolated themselves entirely, must return to Peter."

Vassula queried: "Lord! will they be shocked?" To which Jesus replied:

"Vassula I will bend their knee to venerate My Mother; it is I, the Lord who is speaking. I will bend them! and when they do, I will let My light shine on them and raise them. I will strengthen your stems and you shall be like an irrigated garden, like a spring of waters whose waters never run dry. I will rebuild My foundation."[12]

On 7 September 1987 Jesus invited Vassula to listen to His Mother speaking to her personally:

"Vassula, *pethi mou* (Greek, 'my child'), do not fear; I am with you. My Son Jesus expressly limited you with the proofs and signs you were asking Him to give you, but He has His reasons. He has though given you the grace to believe; He has instructed you with wisdom. Vassula, you have indeed believed blindly."

"Have I?" asked Vassula.

"You have;" was the mother answer "otherwise you would not have had this fervour in coming to us and writing, letting yourself be used at His will. Having done this, beloved, proves that you believe blindly, and God delights in this; your faith is great. Jesus wants, by this, to teach others too to have faith and believe blindly in His heavenly works. Be innocent; be like children in whom God delights."

"What if they don't, St. Mary?" asked Vassula, who noticed that now Our Lady's voice suddenly changed tone and became very grave.

"Your sufferings will be great; you will be like a mirror reflecting Jesus' image; His sufferings will reflect." "You mean Jesus will suffer if they show disbelief and contempt?" "Precisely; Jesus will suffer; upon you will show His sufferings." "But since He has laid His plan before, why couldn't He have made them so that there won't be any contradiction?" "Child this is the way men tend to think; do not forget His teachings; Jesus wants that His works are acknowledged with grace." "Jesus told me that He would not stand by if He sees someone wanting to hurt me." "He has indeed said it, and I tell you this daughter, I will not stand by either! I love you and I will not see them hurt you."

Vassula felt very emotional,

"I am a coward"; she said "but I will cling to you and Jesus."

"Daughter, I will tell you something more. God has laid His justice upon men; His cup is now full. Listen to me carefully; beyond these words lie many more. Glorify God. Vassula, I am your holy Mother; daughter, rely on me; weary not of striving; remember, Jesus was abandoned by everyone on the way to be crucified; He bore His Cross alone."

"Yes, Mother, I will not ask anything more than what He gives" was the faithful reply.

"Vassula, let me answer your question withheld in you. If they do not believe again, God's wrath will grow, augmenting His cup of Justice; it will be the vision God has given you. Pray and amend, for the end of times is near."

Our Lady here refers to a vision given Vassula on 1 September, eight days previously, in which she saw a reddened sky and heard Jesus speak of thundering with His justice against His creation which has become "in its decadence, a replica of what Sodom was." His eyes have grown "weary of watching hypocrisy, atheism, immorality." He has given "signs hundreds of times and what have they done? Times have not changed; many of My sacerdotal souls are just the same replicas of the Pharisees."[13]

There was now a bond of direct communication between Vassula and Our Lady. Before following some of the insights that will come from the Mother, we may profit by delaying on a theme which much occupied Jesus and His Mother in their dialogue with their messenger, Garabandal. As a preliminary it may be said that very soon after her conversation Vassula felt a kinship, a facility in prayer at Marian shrines; this has continued to the present time. In the New World, in Canada at Cap de la Madeleine, in Mexico, twice at Guadalupe, she has felt at home in such places, rejoices in their atmosphere. She has been to Knock in Ireland, to Lourdes of course, twice to Fatima, to Czestochowa in Poland.

Garabandal, for the unitiated, was the focus of attention in the early sixties because of apparitions of St. Michael and Our Lady which were reported from this remote village in the hills above Santander. The visionaries, three young girls, spoke of things to come, a special divine intervention, and they spoke of apostasy among the clergy - priests would lose their faith in the Eucharist. The children were seen receiving Holy Communion miraculously from the Archangel Michael. The apostasy and the breakdown of faith we have seen as times unfolded.

But what of the visionaries? They were discredited on their own avowal. They retracted their assertions under examination by an episcopal commission. So all was over? Those who thought so had one surprise after another. They learned that one member of the commission had resigned, dissatisfied with procedure; they then learned that he was named bishop of the diocese; and still stranger to their ears, that he, in this office, had ordered a fresh investigation of the apparitions. They also learned that Conchita, a child of twelve years, had been grilled for seven hours continuously, that she had been bullied into signing the letter of retraction. She had been excommunicated for daring to say that priests would behave as we now full well know they have well and truly behaved: badly behaved that is.

When will those in positions of church authority learn?

Garabandal would strengthen the sympathy, a kind of affinity with Catholic things which was growing in Vassula's heart. She had no knowledge of the apparitions and the strange sequel when, on 4 September, 1987 she received this message:

> "Daughter, write down the word Garabandal. Vassula when I stirred you from your sleep it was not just to wake you up; it was also to be able to use you, beloved. Purifying you was not just to cleanse you, it was so that you feel My presence and be in My presence. Using you was not just to use you writing My messages and desires; it was so that I write down My blessings for My little children of Garabandal. I come to have My message glorified. Altar, keep this flame ablaze; by My power I will restore My Church. Love Me, do not falter; lean on me and rest; I will help you advance. The hour is near. Pray with me."[14]

Jesus then invited her to join Him in a very beautiful prayer to the Father. Next day He took up the theme again:

"Vassula, do not fear; write the word 'Garabandal'. Garabandal is the sequel of other signs. Garabandal's apparitions are authentic. Believe all you who have not seen. Believe; believe. Daughter, I have used you to be able to manifest Myself through you. My Mother had appeared to My chosen souls; out of their mouths the truth was said, but many of My sacerdotal souls declared them as uncertain, and some of them denied them altogether. I have manifested Myself through you to lift this doubt of Garabandal. Garabandal's apparitions are authentic; and My children have indeed seen My Mother and heard her messages.

"Vassula, a harder trial will come upon you, making My Cross heavier on your shoulders and augmenting My cup of justice. I have forewarned the world."

Vassula replied: "My God, very few probably know of this happening." then Jesus went on:

"True, many do not know, because of the doubts and fears my sacerdotal souls bear. By doubting, they deny my heavenly works; they have forgotten that I am omnipotent. Hardened at heart they have lost their spirituality; blinded, they seek without light and without wisdom. All My works have always been given to mere children, and never to the learned. My works appear unorthodox in their eyes, but it is because they compare themselves to Me. I have since the beginning of times, never abandoned you."

Vassula then understood that the signs given are to remind us of Jesus' presence among us, encouraging us. Jesus continued:

"Vassula, do you remember the Pharisees?" She replied: "Yes, Lord" Thereon He spoke thus: "They at one time accused Me of preaching against Moses' Law. What difference is there today? I had been accused of promiscuity and going against their Law; Garabandal's accusations and uncertainty is not far from this. Let Me tell you, those who defy Garbandal's apparitions and messages are those who wound Me; they are the thorns of My body; I have told you some time ago that I will lead you with heavenly force right into the very depths of My bleeding body. I said that I will point out to you with My finger those who wound Me. I am Jesus Christ, beloved Son of God. Vassula, fear not, for I am before you."[15]

That was in December 1987. Over a year later, in March 1989 she was in Lourdes, where she also felt quite at home. She went to the grotto and then to the crypt, the first church built after the apparitions. There she had a locution, which was now becoming and would remain the leit-motif of her spiritual existence, "In the end, our Hearts will prevail." She had spoken at a meeting in Biarritz. From there she decided to go to Garabandal. It was not an easy journey with oncoming night, and at times, though accompanied by a guide, they were almost lost in rain and fog. But God's presence was palpable to her:

> "No, He will not abandon us now. I had only to abandon myself completely to Him and trust Him fully; I felt all over again this intimacy He taught me and shares with me. I called Him, Abba. Yes Abba is taking care of me with great love."

Entering the church where Mass was still being celebrated, Vassula found herself facing a statue of the Sacred Heart of Jesus, and to His right was "our Blessed Mother with open arms. I heard her say, 'Thank you for coming to me.' Delighted, I answered, 'Thank you for bringing me here.'"

Jesus did assure her that it was He who had brought her to Garabandal. In what He said occur these words:

> "Let these words be known from both My Mother and I, 'In spite of the thorns covering Our Hearts by our enemies, Our Hearts will prevail in the end.'"

Then Our Lady speaks:

> "Jesus and I are with you, my child. We bless all of you, come."

Two days later back in Switzerland Vassula heard this message:

> "My rose, behold how I guide you. Have you not noticed how I laid smooth your path? I have carried you to Garbandal to fulfil My desire. I had asked you to sanctify Garabandal. I have lifted you there and now you have done it. My ways are not your ways. I have taught you to abandon yourself entirely to Me, to leave space for the Spirit to breathe in you, see."[16]

Our Lady too spoke to Vassula about Garabandal:

> "Daughter, beloved, sanctify Garabandal; I have appeared in Garabandal, giving my message. My Message was not properly diffused; many sacerdotals have denied my apparitions, thus refusing us a place in their

heart, but I have not forgotten my beloved children. There were times when they themselves doubted and, falling into confusion, denied my apparitions; this was given as a similitude. It is to show my children how and what a confusion reigns in the church of today. I have promised that I will confirm my apparitions of Garabandal. The hours are fleeing and my messages were not diffused properly - neither has my holiness been honoured."[17]

These words prompt two comments. Jesus and Mary appear to deal with Vassula as if she were a Catholic. They seem to assume that they have so formed her that her spiritual reflex is Catholic. A point to ponder deeply, momentarily put back for further reflection.

Secondly attention to these texts should relieve Catholics of a curious misconception which has attendant dangers, which if overtly formulated may increase the difficulty Protestants have about our devotion to the Mother of God. They think that Our Lady acts on her own, that she has almost taken over the Church and its day to day running, that the Holy Trinity, and even her divine Son have released her from the very essential reality of her existence, her presence within the Triune God, as "preferred daughter of the Father, Mother of god the Son, sanctuary of the Holy Spirit." (Vatican II) In all that Mary, our Mother does on our behalf she acts on a mission from the father, as Mediatress with her divine Son, the eternal Word of God, in the power of the Holy Spirit. With the Holy Spirit she has, by reason of the Incarnation, a relationship which Popes and Doctors have striven to express satisfactorily; a number have invoked the concept of spouse - of course it must be remembered that the Holy Spirit is God.

Jesus' involvement with everything Mary does, with her apparitions especially, is evident in a message which Vassula received about Fatima and Garabandal:

"Fatima's shrine cries out for the sanctification of Garabandal. I have taught you to read the Signs of the Times - are you looking for those Signs? How can you not tell the Signs? Have you no perception? Why are your minds closed? Why do you refuse to see? Why do you refuse to hear? Have you forgotten My words? Why repeat your mistakes? Beloved why all these venomous attacks on the message of Garabandal given by your Holy Mother, who is the Ark of Alliance of My word to you? The opposition My sacerdotals have towards Garabandal's apparitions and messages are all manoeuvres from Satan. Once again, as in Fatima, he is trying to prevent My message from becoming universal. Have you not understood that Satan, knowing the value of my salvation plan given through My Mother at Garbandal to mere children, is trying once again to erase My plan thus leaving you all in darkness to fall? Satan is re-doubling his efforts more than ever now to triumph over your Holy Mother; manoeuvring My Church to deny these apparitions which are the sequel of Fatima's message of salvation. Satan in his fury is trying to prevent you to feed upon Me. My salvation plan is clear - I came to redeem My children. Recognize My voice - do not be surprised at the kind of instruments I use."

Some days after this Jesus spoke these words:

"Blessed are the simple in heart. Blessed are those who will pray the Rosary on the day of Garabandal's sanctification and whose knees are bent and who hail my Mother."[18]

Vassula expressed her love for St. Mary and asked for her help when she heard these words:

"You will get support from me and I will help you."

On 26 January 1988 began a series of communications from Our Lady of considerable import. Jesus spoke thus to Vassula: "Vassula, will you work with your Holy Mother? We are inseparable." When she replied "Yes, Jesus." He went on "I love you; I am always near her; your Holy Mother will teach you now." Vassula had the clear impression that the Son and Mother were there. "They are always together."

Then Our Lady spoke:

"Daughter, I have been always with you. I am protecting you and helping you. I will be helping you till the end."

Vassula then understood by locution that they should go over Apocalypse 12.

"Come, I will explain. When Satan lost, he swore to pursue the rest of My children and make war on them; he swore to devour them in his raging fury because he knows that his days are numbered and because of this, he wants to drag with him as many souls as he could. Yes, he is the dragon and with his tail he tries to sweep along God's creation into destruction. Vassula, my child, as he is vanity itself, he accuses the Almighty's works, wanting to prove to God that He has failed His creation and that our children are made to follow his evil ways. Vassula, I will tell you something, something that all those who love me will rejoice in, this year will be for my glory. No, you do not quite understand: My Immaculate Heart will prevail. I shall draw many souls back to Jesus..."

"Like I have appeared at Lourdes and at Fatima I have likewise appeared at Garbandal giving a similar message. Garbandal is the sequel of Fatima's message, but once again Satan has thrown dust in the eyes of the ecclesiastical authorities to confuse them. He has sown his seeds in their heart so that they deny my apparitions and prevent my message from becoming universal. Vassula, our Hearts are bleeding, wounded by thorns which have been driven into them. How I weep on you children. I love you. My wounded Heart lacerates to see you being swept by the dragon's tail." (St. Mary was very much in pain.)[19]

Our Lady spoke words of encouragement such as these:

"If you only knew how I love you all; I want to embrace you all and draw you all near my Heart."

When she knew that Vassula was thinking of the doubts and scepticism her message might provoke in ecclesiastical authorities this was her message:

"Child why do you forget how Jesus had it while on earth in the flesh? He was persecuted, ridiculed and disbelieved in by the Pharisees. Today, daughter, they disbelieve in many of God's heavenly works. Your era, daughter, has fallen as low as Sodom was. Jesus warned that your oppressors will be many, but I am shielding you from the worst that could have come. Come, Vassula, do not forget the event of God's holiest place - I am telling you this to remind you that God has placed you in His Sacred Heart."

The dialogue continued intimately and finally Vassula felt the Heart of Mary and that she knew was wounded as was Jesus. This prompted Our Lady's response:

"Yes wounded I am for the repeated error the ecclesiastical authorities are doing by rejecting my message of Garabandal. Garabandal is the amplification of Fatima's message."[20]

Our Lady uses fully the language of the heart, in speaking of Jesus and of herself. We shall study separately the important theme of the two Hearts united in a saving alliance. Our Lady speaks of Jesus

"He goes with His Heart in His hand from door to door, hoping, longing for that soul to hear Him."

Mary enjoins the law of love on Vassula, as of obedience to Jesus. She also says:

"I pray. I pray for the salvation of souls. I shield you from evil - I am your shield. Like any mother who would shield her child from being harmed I shield you from Satan and from his impious nets. I pray for souls to return to Jesus; I gather them, blessing them, blessing them. True, they do not see me, but many do feel me."

We may anticipate quotation in the next chapter with one excerpt from Our Lady's messages in this first month of 1988, especially as Garabandal is still high on her spiritual agenda:

"Please my Son furthermore by offering Him all your love and devotion for My Immaculate Heart. Please my Son furthermore by offering Him souls so that He may redeem them. Please me by offering me your vows of fidelity; this you will do by following Jesus. Be His reflection. Be faithful to Him. I will pray for you - I will intercede for you. Betrothed of Jesus, both Our Hearts are encircled with a wreath of thorns. My message at Garabandal was ignored. Let my beloved son, John Paul II, come to me and feel my Immaculate Heart and Jesus' divine Heart. Let him feel how Our Hearts rend and lacerate. They are one big wound. They have torn the Heart of their God, and they have torn my Immaculate Heart of a Mother. I want you to be praying for all those who will reject you. My child how you will have to suffer."

Next day Our Lady gave this assurance:

"Vassula, do not get discouraged when trials come, keep praying, come to me, bless those who will persecute you, pray for your oppressors, repay evil with love - in the end my Immaculate Heart will prevail."[21]

Henceforth as readers of *True Life in God* will know, messages of spiritual substance from Our Lady appear regularly in the text. I may limit quotation to two singularly rich on a theme of great relevance to the Church today, Mary and the Spirit:

"I want, if you allow me, to make you a reflection of the eternal Light so that when you meet God you would look like an untarnished mirror of God's active power and an image of His holiness and His goodness. Today I invite you all to pray with fervour for the renewal of the church, for the second coming of the Lord, for the second Pentecost. This is why Jesus and I come today in various countries to prepare you all for this coming. Pray and lead a life of adoration, pray for the conversion of souls so that everyone may be ready for the Lord's return."

The reader will not miss in this passage the clear advertence to the doctrine of the image, dear to eastern theologians. The reference to the "second Pentecost" would have heartened Pope John XXIII, who hoped that his Council, Vatican II, would herald a second Pentecost. Why his hope was not fulfilled is a complicated story, in which, as we have seen, neglect of the Spirit by the Council Fathers as an element in the assessment is not to be omitted. Let us conclude Vassula's testimony with this quotation:

"Am I to remind you that the Lord is tenderness and compassion, slow to anger and rich in graciousness? Jesus was the stone rejected by the builders that became the keystone. I tell you truly that the Kingdom of God is among you and His Holy Spirit of grace is blowing sweetly now on your nations to revive you, so come and see the Wedding of the Holy Spirit who will wed your lands. Do not reject the Holy Spirit that so manifestly is poured upon you, do not be like the 'builders' who rejected the stone that turned to be the cornerstone. God wants everyone to be saved. And now this is My solemn warning to all who hear the prophecies of this book: do not suppress the Spirit, the Spirit that now blows on you in the middle and in the peak of your apostasy. Do not say later on, on Judgement Day, 'I had never heard, I had not known.' Jesus and I are revealing things beforehand, before they happen, so that you cannot say when you meet God face to face, 'I was unaware.' The citadel of the proud shall fall and the devils shall be cast out from within her womb. May you be blessed; may you all be blessed for hearing me. I am your beloved Mother, the Theotokos who loves you all."

Anyone who has visited, as I have, the special room where icons are kept in Zagorsk, may have seen over sixty beautiful examples of this religious art form. He will also have noticed in a remote corner and image of the Immaculate Heart of Mary. It seems alien within this world. Yet, as we shall see in dealing with Russia, the power of the Immaculate Heart of Mary has been decisive. It may serve to recall very briefly emergence of the idea and devotion centred on the Heart of Mary in the Latin church. It is a pure glory of this communion. Though the first prayer addressed explicitly to the Heart of Mary is from Ekbert of Schönau (d. 1184) the Jewish idea of the heart as the centre of personality would have possibly influenced the Fathers of the Church who spoke of Mary's *Fiat* as coming from her heart; it involved her whole being. The great mystic of Helfta, St. Gertrude the Great (d. 1302) as some of her contemporaries, knew of the Heart of Mary in association with the Heart of Jesus, on which she was fully enlightened. But as yet all was within the spiritual domain.

Important developments would come later. The seventeenth century in France was capital. St. Jean Eudes (d. 1680) celebrated the first Mass in honour of the Heart of Mary in 1648 and he composed the first substantial work on the theme, *The*

Admirable Heart of Mary, which appeared the year after his death. Pope Pius XII marked the tercentenary of the liturgical celebration by a special message. We move forward to the French Revolution and the initiative of Pierre Joseph de Clorivière, founder of the first religious society taking the title Daughters of the Heart of Mary. Thereafter during the nineteenth century the concept of Mary's Heart would be creative in many religious sectors, Religious congregations like that founded by Pere Condrin in honour of the two Hearts, the society of the Holy Heart of Mary founded by the convert Jew, Francis Libermann, the sons of the Heart of Mary due to St. Anthony Mary Claret, the Miraculous Medal which had the two Hearts in its design, all showed that from within the body of the faithful there was an unmistakable stirring of faith within the People of God: all oriented towards Mary under the sign of her Heart. The two greatest theologians of the nineteenth century, M.J. Scheeben and John Henry Newman saw the theological propriety of the Heart of Mary linked with the Heart of Jesus. Newman composed a beautiful litany in honour of the Immaculate Heart of Mary. A great archconfraternity - of the Immaculate Heart of Mary, Refuge of Sinners, took its origin in the church of Our Lady of Victories in Paris. In answer to a heavenly inspiration the parish priest, Abbe Desgenettes, had consecrated his parish to Our Lady under this title and seen it transformed miraculously.

With such a deep supernatural current within the Church Vassula's mission is henceforth linked. Her message will meet a response in any sector where there is a strong sense of the Immaculate Heart of Mary. It will have a still more saving and sanctifying effect when it is assimilated in contemplation of a sublime mystery, that of the Hearts of the Son and the Mother.

Our Lady's close relationship with her divine Son is also shown in a passage where He speaks of sending His Mother as our teacher.[22] In another passage He lists important, meaningful titles such as Door to Heaven, Queen of Peace, Arc of the Alliance, Woman of the Apocalypse, and Second Eve.[23] He holds out wonderful consolation:

> "The Queen provides you with courage and comes and dresses your wounds with her maternal love and affection. Your Mother is caring for you My child like she has cared for Me. In your misery and distress she comes flying to you and takes you into her room. (Vassula took this to refer to her heart) That same room of her that conceived Me."[24]

Finally, those who have to engage in the battle of righteousness for truth and honour will be heartened by these words.

> "Remember that I shall defend you as a lioness defends her little cubs.", words from Our Lady herself.[25]

Notes:

1. Cf. M O'Carroll, *Theotokos, A theological Encyclopedia of the Blessed Virgin Mary*, Wilmington, 2nd ed., 1983, articles Mediation, Mercier, Cardinal, 238-246;

2. *Op. cit.*, article Pius XII, 290;

3. Op. cit., article Vatican II, 351-56;

4. *Op. cit.*, article Ecumenism, 127-130;

5. No attempt here is made to give a detailed survey of present day Marian associations or groups. Prayer groups due to the apparitions of Our Lady at Medjugorje are in scores of thousands: 6,000 in three Australian cities, Melbourne, Brisbane, Sydney;

6. The most reliable author on this subject is Fr. René Laurentin, who has published more than eighty volumes on Marian apparitions, past and present; cf. *Presentday Apparitions of Our Lady*, Dublin, 1991;

7. 5 October, 1987, Volume I, page 198;

8. 8 October, 1987, Volume I, page 200;

9. *Ibid.;*

10. 10 October, 1987, Volume I, page 201;

11. 12 December, 1987, Volume I, page 246;

12. 22 December, 1987, Volume I, page 250;

13. 7 September, 1987, Volume I, page 176f; 1 September, 1987, Volume I, page 172;

14. 4 September, 1987, Volume I, page 174;

15. *Ibid.,* page 175;

16. 24, 26 March, 1989, Volume II, page 5f;

17. 4 December, 1987, Volume I, page 241;

18. 28 December, 1987, Volume I, page 253;

19. 26 January, 1988, Volume I, page 271;

20. *Ibid.*, page 272;

21. 31 January, 1922, Volume I, page 275;

22. 8 June, 1990, Volume II, page 182;

23. 10 October, 1990, Volume II, page 234f;

24. 4 December, 1990, Volume II, page 253;

25. 1 June, 1989, Volume II, page 30;

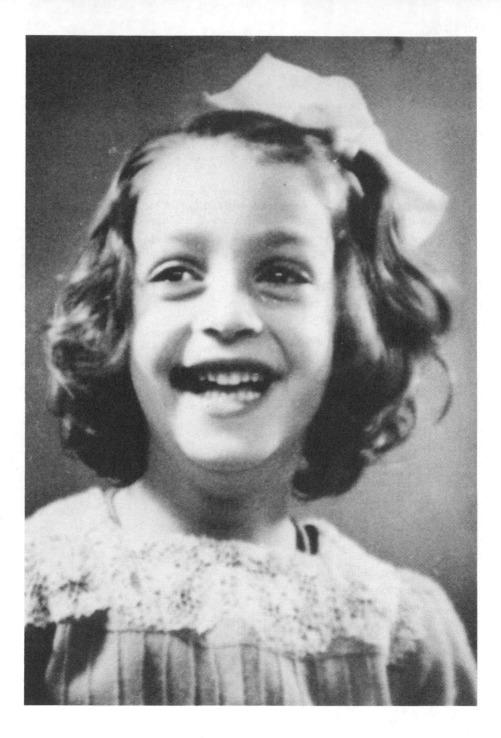

Heliopolis (Cairo), Egypt, 1947. Vassula, aged 5.

Mozambique. Vassula with youngest son, Fabian.

Vassula with husband, Per.

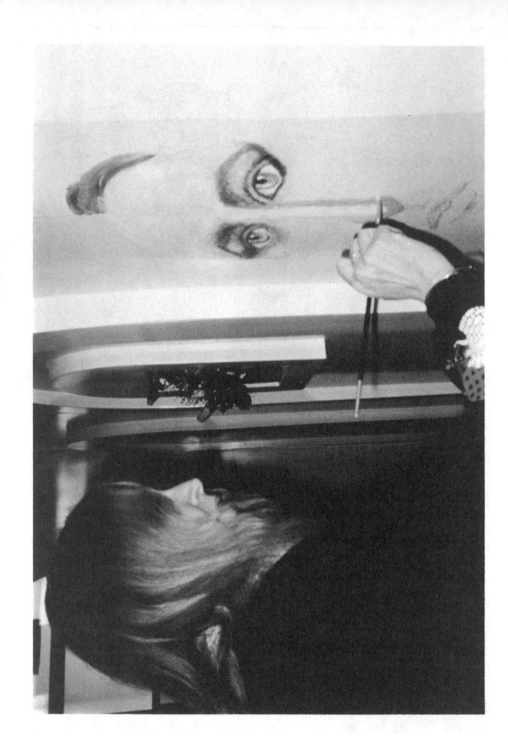

Los Angeles 1993. Vassula's painting of the Holy
Shroud portrait on a private chapel wall.

Pully, Switzerland 1992. Vassula with Abbé Rene Laurentin.

Bangladesh 1986. Vassula on canoe in search of a priest to discern writings.

Red Square, Moscow, October 1992. Vassula with author as pilgrims on peace tour.

New York, 1991.   Private visit to Conchita of
Garabandal.

Besançon 1991. Vassula with Myrna of Damascus - both
invited to speak on unity at Besançon.

6

THE TWO HEARTS

Here we meet a further confirmation of Vassula's mission within the Catholic Church. She has ample illumination on the Sacred Heart of Jesus, equally explicit and enlightening ideas about the Immaculate Heart of Mary. To those with knowledge of important devotional trends within the Catholic Church in recent decades it will come as a welcome surprise that she has had direct, continuous instruction on the divine dispensation which comprehends a union of the two Hearts as a special, plenary source of spiritual rescue and relief for our time.

We may begin with John Paul II in an attempt to sketch a necessary background. We have seen that he has a profound insight into the theology of the Heart, that his training in phenomenology has enriched his stock of ideas in this area. He was led by his prayer and reflection to advocate piety and spirituality centred on the Hearts of Jesus and Mary.

During the summer of 1985 the Pope spoke several times of the Hearts of Jesus and Mary. He used one memorable phrase, "the Alliance of the Two Hearts." This happy formulation of a profound mystery evoked a splendid response from certain key figures in the Philippine Catholic Church, Cardinal Sin, Archbishop of Manila, Fr. Catalino Arevalo, S.J., of Manila Ateneo, member of the International Theological Commission, adviser to the Philippine hierarchy, and Howard Dee, at the time appointed Ambassador of his country to the Holy See, one of the most remarkable laymen in the Catholic Church.[1]

This distinguished trio had the idea of an international symposium on the theme of the Two Hearts. A steering committee was named and it had the assistance of the Pontifical Marian Academy, especially of its president, Fr. Paolo Melada, O.F.M., while the Blue Army, the World Apostolate of Fatima, was generous in helping with expenses; Fr. Arthur Calkins, an American research worker in Marian theology, acted as secretary and co-ordinator.

A meeting in Rome in 1985 agreed on a list of contributors, and all but one of those named accepted the invitation. The exception was Hans Urs von Balthasar, whose health condition forbade the journey. He named an excellent substitute, Fr. Christoph von Schönborn, O.P., then at the University of Fribourg (Switzerland), later Secretary to the Commission on the Universal Catechism, now Auxiliary Bishop of Vienna (he is an Austrian nobleman). The participants in the symposium, which was held in Fatima in September the following year were: Sacred Scripture, Fr. Ignace de la Potterie, S.J., of the Rome Biblical Institute; Patrology, Fr. Domiciano Fernandez, C.M.I., one of the foremost Claretian theologians; the Middle Ages, Fr. Theodore Koehler, S.M., director of the International Marian Research Institute, Dayton, Ohio, long-time member of the French Society for Marian Studies, prolific in contributions to this body and elsewhere; the seventeenth century, Fr. Arthur Calkins, specialist in the Mariology of the recent Popes; the nineteenth and twentieth centuries, Fr. Michael O'Carroll, C.S.Sp.; the Church's Magisterium Fr. René Laurentin; the Liturgy, Dom Anskar Chupungo, O.S.B., rector of the Anselmo University, Rome; mystical theology, Fr. Candido Pozo, S.J., member of the International Theological Commission, author of important works on the theology of Mary, well known as a teacher in Spain; doctrinal synthesis, Christoph von Schönborn, O.P.[2]

Each of the contributors had qualifications in academic work or publication, most in both. Seven nations were represented. Cardinal Sin received an official letter from the Pope conveying good wishes and blessing to the symposium. In the course of this letter the Holy Father wrote:

"Your symposium will provide biblical scholars and theologians with the valuable opportunity for reflecting on devotion to the Sacred Heart of Jesus and the Immaculate Heart of Mary in the perspective of Sacred Scripture and Tradition. Much research has already been done on devotion to the Sacred Heart of Jesus, but it is your aim to focus attention on the Immaculate Heart of Mary and the inter-relation of love between the Hearts of the Son of God and His Mother. Your reflection will also endeavour to explain the Christian's participation in these mysteries and thereby render a worthwhile service to the whole Church by clarifying the importance of devotion to the Hearts of Jesus and Mary.

"We can say that just as the mystery of Redemption began in the womb of the Virgin Mary, so did that splendid union of the Hearts of Christ and His Mother. From the very moment when the Word was made flesh beneath the Heart of Mary, there has existed under the influence of the Holy Spirit, an enduring relationship of love between them. The Heart of the Mother has always followed the redemptive mission of her Son. As Jesus hung on the Cross in completion of His salvific work, Simeon's prophecy foretelling the definitive alliance of the Hearts of the Son and of the Mother was fulfilled: 'And a sword will pierce your own soul too.' (Lk 2:35) Indeed the centurion's lance that pierced the side of Christ also penetrated the Heart of His sorrowful Mother and sealed it in sacrificial love.

"Since the Hearts of Jesus and Mary are joined forever in love, we know that
to be loved by the Son is also to be loved by His Mother. At the foot of the
Cross, Mary was proclaimed our Mother, and her Immaculate Heart now
continues to enfold us with the same maternal love with which she loved her
Son."[3]

On 22 September of that year the symposium members were received in Rome by
the Holy Father. On the conclusion of their labours they wished to present to him
the full text of the proceedings. They requested in a Votum, with due deference, that
he take account of their findings to issue a statement for the benefit of the whole
Church on the theme which he had made particularly his own. His address that day
is so important that it is reproduced in full in the present work.[4]

In December of the year after the symposium a public congress held in Manila helped
to diffuse its manifold message among the faithful. When the full proceedings of the
symposium are published the sureness, depth and mysterious potential of the doctrine
and ideal will be apparent. The faithful have known that the Angel of Peace spoke
explicitly three times to the children at Fatima in 1916 of the Two Hearts, a prelude
to the apparitions of the following year; they know too that earlier the design of the
Miraculous Medal showed the Two Hearts.

What the Fatima symposium accomplished was to uncover and disclose the deep
theological structure and framework which gave support and validity to these
manifestations of piety. To do this there had to be a change from previous
theological thinking, a loosening of the Graeco-Roman mental categories which ruled
heretofore, which remain helpful but are not exhaustive in face of the Christian
mystery. In passing it is interesting to note that a theological giant like Newman who
was not trained in the scholastic tradition where Graeco-Roman conceptualization was
dominant, saw the importance of the Two Hearts.

John Paul II in his address to the symposium members said,

"My esteemed friends, I encourage you to continue your scholarly efforts to
promote among the People of God a better understanding of devotion to the
Hearts of the Son and of His Mother." The Pope did not think, nor did any
of his listeners, that the Lord was preparing a very powerful, persuasive,
persevering collaborator in the accomplishment of this task.

For the intuition, rather revelation, of the united Hearts of Jesus and Mary, forms
an integral element in the message contained in the writings of Vassula. It has
become central to her apostolate, the mainspring of her hope, comfort and
refreshment in the labours and trials which her mission increasingly entails.

Those who reflect on the significance of her lifework may see the hand of Providence clearly in a remarkable convergence of the Teaching Authority of the Church, the reflection and research of theologians and an authentic exercise of mystical power. Vassula, be it noted, had no knowledge whatsoever of how the Pope and the theologians were thinking.

As for the revelation to Vassula of the Sacred Heart of Jesus and the Immaculate Heart of Mary the intuition that they constitute a sacred, saving alliance is entirely new in Orthodox spirituality or developed theology. Vast perspectives are thus open to those seeking Christian unity, spiritual assimilation to Jesus Christ, "the Image of the invisible God", to those searching for a valid theology of women in Christ, even - be it said with total reverence - to those in awe of a wonder that challenges genetic science.

"One of the first messages to come of the Alliance of the Two Hearts," Vassula writes, "was on 25 January 1988." Here are the words she then recorded:

"Vassula, I wish you to draw two Hearts. Yes, near each other, in fact united. Encircle them with one wreath of thorns. Yes, my Mother's Immaculate Heart is united to Mine. I desire from each one of you the devotion her Immaculate Heart deserves. You see, daughter, how Our divine Hearts are covered by thorns from men who only show us ingratitude, sacrilege, lack of love; it is the whole of their sins. Vassula, I who am the Word, love and respect her; I desire you to approach My Mother and honour her as I honour her. I desire that every knee bends, honouring her; I desire you to pray the Rosary and hail your Holy Mother. I want you to repair your sins; asking her to teach you. Be vigilant, daughter. Come I have revealed to you how My Mother's Heart is united with My divine Heart, encircled by one wreath of thorns. I will remind you of My presence. I love you."[5]

Earlier in the same month Jesus had intimated the truth He was now explicitly stating: He spoke thus, as if addressing the Pope personally:

"Behold! Behold Peter. My Sacred Heart once again is being pierced by so many thorns; thorns that have been driven in Me by those I love! My soul is once again wounded, they are treading upon Our Hearts. Both Our Hearts have been once again crowned with two wreaths of thorns. My side is wide open, and My blood is gushing out. I am at your door now; with Me I carry My hidden plan of salvation; it is here. This revelation is My voice. I love you all with all My Heart; with all My Heart I love you."[6]

In the same year, 30 January 1988, it was Our Lady who took up the theme, as we have already seen in the previous chapter.

Some years on she spoke words which set the mysterious union of the Hearts in a theocentric perspective:

> "Write, My daughter: blessed of My soul, beloved of My Heart; today I ask each one of you to apply your heart to walk with God. God is your strength, your life and your happiness, no man can live without God. Jesus is the true Vine and you the branches. A branch cut off from the Vine dries and withers immediately, it is then no use but to be thrown on the fire. Walk with the light and do not be afraid of abandoning yourselves entirely to Him, give yourselves to God and your hearts shall be filled with joy. Understand, beloved children that God in these days is coming to save you and untangle you from Satan's nets and bring you back to His Sacred Heart. Our Two Hearts are united in spite of the arguments and the denials of the world for this truth, for they have not all accepted this truth, but use this truth instead to combat one another. Our Two Hearts are united and thirst together for your salvation, children. Come and hear us this time; make peace with God, be reconciled. Lift your face to God and ask him to fill your heart with His light. Learn to love God as your Father, He who loves you more than anyone can imagine, and without ceasing sends you from His Heart His flowing peace, like a river to assuage the interior desert of your soul."[7]

Our Lady spoke here as one intimately associated with the salvation and sanctification of mankind. Her Jewish mentality would not be alien to the rich significance which the word heart assumes in this context: the whole thrust of her powerful personality, enlivened by divine grace. On Christmas Eve, 1991 Jesus too set forth the whole subject comprehensively. Many important strands of thought are interwoven in this message, which shows the depth of meaning, the cosmic import of the specific revelation on the Two Hearts. The entire text will repay attention and reflection:

> "Tremendous reparations have to be done to cicatrize the wounds of this earth; wounds and cuts made by wickedness and sin; delight the eyes of your Saviour and expand; that My message becomes so ample, so vast, testifying itself that wickedness, apathy and atheism will be seized and will repent. Child! cling to the hem of My clothes and stretch even more now, from one corner of the earth to the other. Enter into My sanctuaries, if they welcome you into My sanctuaries; if men forbid you, do not let this afflict you nor bring you sorrow, do not despair; your oppressors will look back on these scenes in the day of the Purification and will weep, remembering their rejection; they will realize how they were rejecting Our Divine Hearts, not you, Our Two Hearts that prophesied.

"Daughter, follow my blood-stained footprints and pronounce My Holy Name in any gathering. The time has come that you should not hesitate any more. Plant vineyards everywhere and anywhere you can, make gardens out of deserts. I have blessed My messages to prosper and take root, so courage, daughter."

Vassula felt a "sword of fire" pierce her and she cried out, "Lord I miss you." Jesus continued:

"You miss Me because you saw My Glory... write: Citadel after citadel is being besieged by the rebel. I come today and offer all mankind My peace but very few listen. Today I come with peace-terms and a message of love, but the peace I am offering is blasphemed by the earth and the love I am giving them is mocked and jeered on this eve of My birth. Mankind is celebrating these days without My Holy Name. My Holy Name has been abolished and they take the day of My birth as a great holiday of leisure, worshipping idols. Satan has entered into the hearts of My children, finding them weak and asleep. I have warned the world. Fatima's message speaks: that in My day I shall make the sun go down at noon and darken the earth in broad daylight; I will allow the Dragon to bite this sinful generation and hurl a fire the world has never seen before or will ever come to see again to burn her innumerable crimes. You will ask: 'will all the inhabitants perish, the good with the bad?' I tell you: the living will envy the dead; out of two men one will be taken; some will ask 'where are Elijah and Moses who are to come?' I tell you, you evil generation: We have not been speaking in parables all these years; Elijah and Moses have come already and you have not recognized them but treated them as you pleased. You have not listened to our Two Hearts, the Immaculate Heart of My Mother and My Sacred Heart, you faithless generation... Our Two Hearts have not been speaking to you in parables nor in riddles. All Our words were light and Our Hearts like two lamps are shining near each other, so bright that everyone may see, but you have not understood. Our Hearts, like two olive trees, one to the right and one to the left, were for so many years trying to revive you. Like two olive branches pouring oil to heal your sick generation and cicatrize your wounds, but your generation treated Our Two Hearts as they pleased; Our Two Hearts are anointed and are living. They are like a sharp sword, double-edged, prophesying, but the rebellious spirit in this generation is re-crucifying My Word, the double-edged sword and is rejecting our Two Hearts who speak to you today; just like Sodom's and Egypt's rejection of My messengers. This era's stubbornness has surpassed Pharaoh's because their claims to their knowledge have become a battlefield, indeed Our Two Hearts have become a plague to the people of the world but soon, very soon now, My voice will be heard again. I shall visit you by thunder and fire.

Justice is at hand and Our Two Hearts you have combated shall prevail in the end and the kingdom of the world will become My Kingdom. This is all very close now.

"Open your eyes and look around you; I am giving you all the signs of the times, and you who are labouring to bring to the surface the devotion of the Alliance of the Two Hearts, do not lose courage; the Book of Apocalypse speaks as well as the Book of Zechariah of this truth. Do not fear, spread this devotion with trust and with courage."[8]

To see the full import of this luminous pronouncement, one must recall the great theological truth of the primacy of Christ in creation. That Jesus Christ, the incarnate Son of God is pre-eminent among those whom acting with the Father and the Holy Spirit, He brought out of nothing, that is in all creation is indisputable. This is His primacy of perfection. But theologians, there are, whom I follow, who hold that He enjoyed primacy absolute and universal. This means that in the all-wise counsels of the Holy Trinity the Incarnation was first decreed and then creation decreed to receive Him.

This is more than an answer to the hypothetical question, if man had not sinned would God have become man? It is a sweeping and yet intimate view of the very meaning of the universe in relation to its Creator. The beauty, the majesty, the magnificent resource, microcosmic and macrocosmic of our universe, is only fully understandable in the light of the One who from all eternity was destined to enter it as its ultimate crowned Lord and Master, its very justification, the guarantor of its meaning in structure and evolution, Alpha and Omega.

In the light of this reality the Two Hearts as a source of spiritual rescue and supernatural renewal lead us to the threshold of divine mystery, challenging a response far deeper and more meaningful than sentiment, however noble this may be. That the ideal should be proposed, now made clear and complete, beyond the partial disclosure at one time or another in the past, further prompts a thoughtful, fully committed response.

Jesus, revealing His Heart, has the commanding vision of the Lord of history. Associating with the revelation the Heart of His Mother, He shows us patently how, majestic and transcendent as God, He still enters the lowly, risky process of human change, toil, struggle, endurance, suffering. The Two Hearts are complementary, mutually pedagogic for us, for each tells us about the other, an inexhaustible treasury which dignifies and elevates that which appears so intrinsically human. At the centre of the world are Two Hearts beating as one.

Did Vassula advert to such a cosmic vision when she took down Jesus' message?

When for instance she wrote such words as these:

> "I Myself have filled your mouth with My Wisdom, so that you may learn and not fall into error. I have given you My instructions so that you may find your defence in them. Listen now and understand; set our Two Hearts like a seal on your heart. The Immaculate Heart of your Mother shall be your defence and My own Sacred Heart your home. With this sign sealed on your Heart, the foxes that make havoc of My vineyards that are now in fruit, shall be caught. You My little ones are Our vineyard of Our Two Hearts."[9]

These words were addressed, through Vassula, to members of a prayer group formed with the help of her family, on the island of Rhodes, with Orthodox membership. The prayer group had the title "of the Two Hearts." Hidden strands of history could have met there, for the primacy of Jesus Christ, shared with the Blessed Mother had been elaborately defended by fourteenth century Orthodox theologians. They are generally known as the Palamite school, from their leader, St. Gregory Palamas; closely one with him in thought were Nicholas Cabasilas and Theophanes of Nicaea who expounded the view that Mary was with Jesus, and dependent on him, our universal Mediatress with God.

Again and again Vassula was instructed on the resistance offered by the forces of evil to the divine plan of salvation, originating in the love and mercy of the Father, to be accomplished by Jesus through His Spirit. Often the promise of victory will be in the words, "Our Two Hearts will prevail." It is all beautifully expressed in this prayer;

> "Father, blessed be your name, since your beloved Son Jesus Christ came to the world not to condemn it, but to save the world, have mercy on us, look at your Son's holy wounds, that are wide open now and remember the price He has paid for us to redeem all of us. Remember His sacred wounds and the Two Hearts you yourself united in love, and who suffered together, this one of the Immaculate Conception and that of your beloved Son. Father remember His promise now and send us the Advocate in full force, the Holy Spirit of truth, to remind the world of the truth and of your Son's docility, humbleness, obedience and great love. Father, the time has come, when the reign of division cries out for peace and unity. The time has come that your Son's wounded body cries out for righteousness, that of which the world has not known yet, but through the Immaculate Heart of Mary and the Sacred Heart of Jesus, give us, precious Father this peace in our hearts and fulfil the Scriptures by fulfilling your beloved Son's prayer to you that we may all be one, one in the divine Holy Trinity so that we worship and praise you, all around one tabernacle. Amen"

Perhaps one should here ponder words of mysterious hope spoken to Vassula on 2 March 1991,

"Very soon now, My friend, I shall be with you all again and My priestly prayer to the Father will be fulfilled. You shall be one like us in the Holy Trinity. I still have hidden in My Sacred Heart many things to divulge to you and show you, for the treasures I have within Me are innumerable, but they would be too much for you to take now. Your soul will not be able to take in everything, but little by little I shall unfold to you the treasures of my Sacred Heart and step by step I shall guide you into what looks like a light-house, a mystery of unfathomable riches that have been hidden for generations and centuries. I shall reveal to you, My friend, the rich glory of hope, wisdom and knowledge. Be rooted in Me and you shall bear fruit; remain in Me and you shall live."[10]

There are some brief very meaningful words of counsel from Jesus.

"Listen now and understand; set Our Two Hearts like a seal on your heart. The Immaculate Heart of My Mother shall be your defence and My own Sacred Heart your home. With this sign sealed on your heart the foxes that make havoc of My vineyards that are now in fruit shall be caught. You My little ones, are the vineyards of Our Two Hearts."

Another similar recommendation:

"You want to glorify Me? Then love Me and adore Me, the door to heaven are your prayers to Me. I want prayers from your heart, so I tell you, pray, pray, pray. Remember that your Mother's Heart and Mine are united in love; so you, you whom My Heart loves, come to us and I shall offer you your rest in My Sacred Heart and protection will be offered in your Mother's Heart. I am the Resurrection and I shall resurrect many more of you as I resurrected you. I am mercy and out of My boundless mercy I let My Heart be touched. Love and Mercy is at your very doors, now."

Hope in the Two Hearts is again and again inculcated by Jesus:

"You need not fear, in the end our Hearts will prevail. I will show everyone how I can save. Scriptures have to be accomplished. You see it is written that the beast that comes out of the Abyss is going to make war on the two Lamps that stand before the Lord of the world, those two witnesses who represent My body and are My body."

Again speaking of the divisions made in His Church and the suffering they cause him Jesus says:

"I am not alone to swallow My tears, your Holy Mother is sharing My grief since her Immaculate Heart is united in love to My Sacred Heart."

Jesus wishes the ideal to spread:

"Be firm about the Two Hearts united in love; I have spoken in many hearts already about this truth, a truth that many will reject but in the end Our Two Hearts will prevail. Such is the world; today they reject, but tomorrow they will honour this truth; I Jesus love you all. Have no other but Me in your heart. Have Me as first. Have My peace."[11]

We are presently at the outset of what may be styled an immense spiritual adventure: the search for total doctrinal and experiential knowledge of the two greatest human beings in history at a point of their immediate creative encounter, a union of their spiritual dynamism, divine intrinsically on one side, divinized completely on the other. Not only knowledge but a possible ascension from the pitiful human condition in which our universal lot is cast as to a fountain of healing, ennobling to the point of transformation, creative in ways unknown and impossible to any spiritual force lesser than theirs. The Hearts of Jesus and Mary are not mere pleasant symbols decorating the Christian scene to render it picturesque or attractive. The Hearts of Jesus and Mary are united in a divinely willed alliance which surpasses the very central indispensable energy of the whole universe.

This is the vital pulse of humankind. It was partially revealed, heretofore known in a fragmentary way and beneficial. In its plenitude for which we hope from divine condescension, it will provide essential sustenance to all who assimilate it into their lives.

The mystery of the Two Hearts is grounded in the reality of the Incarnation. "The Word became flesh." He did so by the power of the Holy Spirit but only in answer to a movement from the very centre of a human personality, a movement which committed every cell of her psychic and physical entity, every moment of her time, her eternity.

As has been stated we may very well be impeded in reflection on this reality by Graeco-Roman mental categories as by Roman legalism. Here we meet the One who transcends time and taking it into His being removes it moment by moment from its perishable frame. Every moment in the life of the Godman is imperishable. With each such moment we may be united when He has brought us into Him, eventually perfectly when every obstacle to this union, every failure in the spiritual fabric designed to effect the union, are removed, when we are free from sin. With one human being the Godman had total success.

Success in personal contact with her, which He seeks to renew with all others received into Him. For God made man does not look at us globally, but singly, personally. He sees each first then all, not as we do, all first then each laboriously. In this direct salutary approach to each one He acts from His Heart. All that He is finds expression, by His deliberate choice, through His Heart. To this, in these end times, He calls His Mother to speak the same language, to express her whole being through her Heart.

What provides a basis for their union? The fact that His Heart came into existence from a free act of her will given concrete reality by the movement of her Heart; the fact that since she was a virgin Mother, the only physical source of His human nature, His Heart was uniquely of her flesh, which opens natural mysteries of genetics; the fact that she had a maternal office to give, during nine months, sustenance to His Heart as a baby in the womb, nurture during His infancy, education in His childhood years. The bond of her Heart with His could not be rivalled or equalled by anyone else. Not even by the great St. Joseph, first among the saints.

These are but suggestions, indications which will doubtless be superseded, on our approach to a unique subject of theological and spiritual reflection. In making them one's aim is to eliminate anything superficial, spurious, superstitious, from what is henceforth for each of us a question of life and death. All human misery, all human hope of rescue meet at this blessed partnership of love, concern, renewal, restoration. Two Hearts united hold within their union the fortunes, the destiny of mankind.

Is there recognition of this awesome reality, this splendid vision of hope incomparable? Increasingly the sure voice of the People of God proclaims its urgency. We have seen whence came the first inspiration, who prompted the first steps in the mighty adventure, the Philippine Catholics. They still maintain their enlightened effort in diffusion of the ideal. Striking examples of their zeal were the International Youth Congress on the Alliance of the Two Hearts organised in a large Moscow Hotel in October 1992, and the Congress which followed it in Akita, Japan some weeks later. There have been other such theological meetings; there are very many prayer groups throughout the Church occupied with continuing reflection on the theme; there are centres in several countries which help in providing resources to further conviction and practice. Our hope is that there will be growth and increasing enthusiasm. From the Two Hearts united in the Spirit will surely come positive inspiration and strength.

Notes:

1. Pending the publication of the Proceedings of the symposium the two source books are: *The Alliance of the Hearts of Jesus and Mary*, Texts and Documents of the International Pastoral Conference 27 November - 3 December 1987, Manila 1988; *Mankind's Final Destiny* by Howard Dee, Manila 1993;

2. Fr. von Schönborn was a member of the International Theological Commission;

3. Text reproduced in *The Alliance of the Hearts of Jesus and Mary*, page 351f;

4. Appendix I;

5. 25 January, 1988, Volume I, page 269;

6. 18 January, 1988, Volume I, page 266;

7. 13 June, 1991, Volume II, page 324;

8. 31 December, 1991, Volume II, page 406f;

9. 2 August, 1991, Volume II, page 340;

10. Prayer to the Father 25 March, 1991; 4 March 1991, Volume II, page 289;

11. 8 December, 1991, Volume II, page 405; on 24-25 March, 1993 the Philippine Catholics with U.S. colleagues organized a seminar in Washington D.C. composed of the United Marian associations on the theme the Grand Alliance of the Two Hearts; they planned an international Asian meeting in Manila in the month of June 1993 and a further one in Fatima next October;

7

CHRISTIAN UNITY

On 23 January, 1992 Vassula addressed a special meeting organised at the headquarters of the World Council of Churches in Geneva. Among a select audience were representatives of the highest rank in this body.[1] Vassula read from the messages which she has received from Jesus on the theme of unity. When she asked beforehand if she should read the most severe of these divine communications, or omit them and read some less rigorous, her sponsors opted for the first that she mentioned. She was heard with great respect and spoken to with great confidence afterwards over lunch.

The event may have been unique in the history of the WCC. Not less remarkable was an encounter which took place in Russia, in the city of Moscow, in October of the same year. Vassula was a member of the International Peace Pilgrimage organised by the 101 Foundation in the United States. The pilgrimage had reached Fatima for the seventy fifth anniversary of the last great apparition, 13 October, 1917 - 13 October, 1992; the route had been from Our Lady of Victories in Paris and Lourdes. Vassula having completed a session in Oporto joined the pilgrims as they honoured Our Lady in her great Portuguese shrine. It was her first visit to Fatima where she would also come in February of the present year to spread her message of peace, love and mercy.

From Fatima the International Peace pilgrimage went on to Prague, where the priests and bishops concelebrated Mass in the cathedral, where some of the pilgrims went to honour the Infant Jesus in His hallowed shrine.

Then it was Moscow. Here sensational events jostled with each other. The statue of Our Lady of Fatima was borne from the plane to the airport terminal with an honour guard of bishops and priests. On the intervening Sunday this statue was crowned publicly in Red Square at ten o'clock in the morning and then, for the benefit of the young people attending the congress on the Alliance of the Two Hearts, at twelve o'clock at night. On this occasion some of those present reported extraordinary signs.

These facts which may appear a digression are a necessary background to another ecumenical experience in the life of Vassula. An initiative taken by the organisers of the Peace Pilgrimage was to commission an icon of Our Lady of Fatima by an expert iconographer, Patricia Delehaunty Moran, in the hope that they would be permitted to present it to the Patriarch of Moscow. An appointment was sought with the Patriarch on the Saturday evening of our stay in the capital city. He received Fr. Kenneth Roberts, a well known English priest on the American mission; David Manuel, a Protestant; and Vassula. He expressed his willingness to receive the icon. If he could not be present next day in the cathedral for the ceremony his delegate, the Archbishop would receive the icon in his name.

It was a moving ceremony. After the Divine Liturgy the Archbishop met the pilgrims in presence of the congregation. He explained the significance of the ceremony. He expressed thanks for the prayers offered for so many years to Our Lady of Fatima on their behalf; and he offered to each of the pilgrims a replica of the icon of Our Lady of Khazan. The original is in Fatima awaiting its return to Moscow. The Archbishop accepted also a chalice "of unity" offered to him by Vassula, David and myself.

Vassula was also invited to a meeting of Orthodox theologians with a view to sharing in their ecumenical concern. This initiated her to the intimate world of the Russian Orthodox. For reasons which will be made clear later it touched at the centre of her lifework, her mission.

Integral to that mission is the cause of Christian unity. It is the desire, the hope, the cherished aim of many followers of Christ. But it seems delayed to the point that some are tempted to think it impossible of achievement. The first institutional action towards the goal of unity was the decision of two important inter-faith associations, *Life and Work* and *Faith and Order* to merge into one body. The first steps had been taken at their 1937 conferences in Oxford and Edinburgh respectively. Further progress was made at a conference at Utrecht in the following year. But formal decision and inauguration was delayed by the war. The World Council of Churches came into existence on 23 August, 1948 at Amsterdam. The body was strengthened later by the adherence of the International Missionary Council.

The attitude of Catholic authorities to the problem of Christian Unity was expressed mostly in appeals to the separated brethren to return to the true Church. Pius XII did go a step further in setting up a commission named *Unitas*, to promote unity which published a review with the same name. Its effect throughout the body of the Church was very slight.

There had been individual initiatives in the decades between World War One and Vatican II. The Malines Conversations between a Catholic group led by the prestigious Cardinal Mercier and Anglicans led by Lord Halifax are well known. Others were not so well known, like Fr. Paul Couturier (d. 1953) promoter of the

Octave of Prayer for Christian Unity, a development of the Church Unity Octave, which had been founded by two Anglicans in 1908, Dom Lambert Beauduin, O.S.B. (d. 1960) founder of the liturgical and ecumenical centre at Chevetogne, Bishop Marius Beson of Fribourg (d. 1944) author of two remarkable ecumenical works, *La route aplanie* and *Après quatre cents ans*, the first bishop in Europe who instructed his priests to use the designation "separated brothers" and no other, Fr. Yves M.J. Congar, O.P., (b. 1905-) a theologian of Christian unity of gigantic stature, who would live to see his insights and aspirations recognized at Vatican II, Catholics supported movements working for Christian unity or advocating inter-faith co-operation like *Una Sancta* in Germany, the wartime *Sword of the Spirit* in Britain. An unexpected success was the Mercier Society launched in Dublin in the early forties by Irish Catholics and members of the different Christian communions, unexpected in the cultural quality of membership and the theological level of the exchanges.

Within the Catholic Church these ecumenically minded individuals and groups met with a minimum of official support. They were isolated and where vulnerable. Were made to feel so; prelates of the stature of Mercier and Besson were automatically immune from pressure; they still rallied little lasting support.

John XXIII is the landmark. He is so because he summoned a General Council of the Church and gave it an ecumenical aim and orientation; because he gave concrete form to his intuition by establishing the *Secretariat for Christian Unity*, a permanent structure which was to outlive the Council; and because he ensured that the whole subject would be dealt with in a conciliar document, known as the *Decree on Ecumenism*.

From all this great hopes arose. Now thirty years on we are entitled to ask whether these hopes have been fulfilled. We should not wish to minimize the importance of the high-level encounters and theological discussions which have been reported in the intervening decades since the Council. Eastern Patriarchs have met the Pope, as has the Anglican Archbishop of Canterbury - out of the first encounter between Paul VI and Michael Ramsey came the Anglican Roman Catholic International Commission (ARCIC) reports from which we study from time to time. Yet the Catholic Church remains as it was with no additions in any corporate sense; Protestants remain Protestants and Orthodox are still solidly Orthodox. So where is the progress? Does agreement between theologians or happy meetings between high-level ecclesiastics constitute Christian unity?

Perhaps we should here look at the messages recorded by Vassula. A first important one was a vision of three bars erect, rigid; and she had, at the same time, a message "to unite, you must all bend; you must be willing to bend by softening."[2] Vassula was anxious but Jesus reassured her: "Beloved, come; leave your fears and hear Me.

Wait upon your God. I want to unite My Church. I have trained you to receive Me. Beloved, courage."[3]

That was on 2 June, 1987. On 17 June Jesus again made the same firm statement "Daughter, I desire unity in My Church. Unity." On 7 July Jesus after speaking of those who deny His divinity, His infinite wealth, promoting paganism, multiplying His "scourgers", deriding Him, invites Vassula to join with Him in this prayer:

"Father of mercy, unite your sheep, bring them together again. Let them realize their aridity, forgive them. Mould them into what you desire them to be, remind them of your ways. May all glory be in your holy name, for ever and ever. Amen."[4]

In October of that year Jesus foretold the future:

"Vassula, I always reach My goals. Come, I will tell you. One day My kingdom on earth will be as it is in heaven. My Church will be united and blessed, for all My devoted ones will understand one another. Exalted by My hand, purified by My blood, My Church will be one."[5]

He was equally firm some days later:

"Vassula, the day will come, and that day is very near when My Church will speak one language; but before this glorious day there will be tremendous upheavals, partly because of man's vanity, sin and lack of love, and partly because My Body is torn apart. Let Me tell you once more that My Body I will glorify and unite. Flower, love will unite you all. Write down this too; stay small so that all authority will come from Me. Let it be known that My wishes are inflexible, they stand firmer than ever."[6]

On 27 October of the same year Jesus spoke of Orthodox, Catholics, Protestants. He initiated the dialogue by saying:

"I desire, and this desire comes from the very depths of My Heart, that the apparitions of Garabandal be sanctified and honoured by the Holy See. Vassula, will you gratify Me and tell My Holy See what I have come to ask you?"

When she demurred wondering how she would undertake such a mission, recalling too what a Catholic theologian had done in her regard when He learned that she was Orthodox - he had lost interest, Jesus reassured her:

"But Vassula, of course you do not belong to them, you belong to Me - I am your Creator and Holy Father, you belong under My Authority."

Vassula replied: "Lord, yes we are under your authority but it is organised and there is a system of belonging in one of the Christian communities, so I was told."

Jesus replied:

"All are the same in My eyes. I have never wanted My Body parted, it is you who have dismembered Me. You have decided upon My Body. You lamed Me."

Vassula exclaimed: "Oh God.." To this Jesus replied:

"Daughter, have I not told you to reserve your tears for My Mother."

"Yes, Lord" replied Vassula "but you seemed so hurt; I'm only human."

Jesus spoke these words:

"Vassula, this is because we are sharing My cup. My cup tastes bitter. Tell the Holy See that it is I who sends you to them. Hear Me, if they ask in which community you belong tell them that you belong to Me and that you are under My authority."

Vassula replies:

"Lord, I do not like to argue but can't I tell them that I am an Orthodox?"

Then Jesus spoke as follows:

"Orthodox! Catholics! Protestants! You all belong to Me, you are all one in My eyes. I do not make any distinction, so then why fear? As for My well-beloved Pope John Paul - he will not make any distinction. Vassula, tell him this: 'Beloved, I the Lord am standing at your door, knocking, will you hear Me calling, will you open the door? If you do, I will enter your house and share your meal, side by side with you. Prove victorious and I will allow you to share My throne.' Hear Me: listen to what the Spirit is saying to the Churches."[7]

For those who think that this savours of religious indifferentism there is abundant assurance in what Jesus says on false ecumenism, on the duty to accept the faith, especially as we shall see, on the imperative of unity under the authority of Peter's successor. Jesus also points out that changes must take place in belief, notably in regard to Our Lady, and to the Eucharist, the "perpetual sacrifice." When Vassula heard the words "All are the same" and "You all belong to me," she understood that Jesus spoke of all as his children, made in his image, defaced by sin, which is restored in them by him. Jesus reserved the right to judge each single person on his conscience. He does not give us the right to change his truth. Pope John Paul II, it is well known, invited representatives of the world religions to pray with him at Assisi, home of St. Francis God's instrument of peace.

The inner cause of disunity is given by the Lord three days later: "Suppose Lord they bend" said Vassula (the Lord had just said that people are afraid of mockery, afraid of their superiors, putting "the honour of men before the honour that comes from Me.")

His answer to her plea:

"I would uplift My justice that lies heavily upon them but they still hurl venomous arrows at one another, afflicting My Body. There will always be disharmony reigning among them because love is missing. Vassula, had they followed My command to love one another as much as I love them and humbled themselves, My Body would reign in harmony. Have they ever humbled themselves, washing each others feet? Have I not given you this as an example so that you may copy what I have done? Bend! Bend to be able to unite! Soul, the time has come where My beloved servant John Paul should hear Me. I have indeed heard his cries; his cries have reached heaven; his cries resound in the entire universe; his cries have reached My ears! Let me tell you that in a short time there will be one flock and one shepherd. I will lead all My sheep, even those that are not of this fold. Love will unite you, but before this there will be tremendous tribulations. The entire heavens will shake. Be vigilant, daughter, hand over My instructions; they are all within My sacred writings. By forwarding My message you will understand."[8]

Vassula then turned to Our Lady, saying that she did not have the power to take such a mission. She was comforted with these words:

"Vassula, do not fear, your incapacity infatuates Jesus - stay small. (Vassula: "St. Mary, suppose they don't listen") Little one, this divine revelation will be His last warning. If they do not want to listen or understand I will allow His hand to fall on them and strike them. Vassula, all you have to do is to love Him. Be vigilant because Satan is furious and will try all sorts of traps. Do not fear. I am guarding you."

On 30 November of that year Jesus just affirmed this:

"I Am. I, Jesus guarantee to you all that My Church will be one, united. Beloved, be faithful to me, trust Me and be confident."[9]

Jesus shows with some insistence where He sees the principle of unity:

"Peter! Peter! Why, why are My disciples dispersed in enmity? Hallowed by My hand, brother of Mine, I love you from all eternity. My Sacred Heart is wounded, wounded by thorns that have been driven into it by My own, My own whom I love. I will show you My wounded Heart; they are piercing My Sacred Heart all over again. My blood is gushing out; they are recrucifying Me; they are not sincere. My Body aches with lack of love; My lips are parched with lack of love. I am thirsty, beloved... they have forgotten My ways, they have forgotten that I am humble, meek and full of love. All I ask from you is love; love one another as much as I love you. Why combat in My Church? Why these disputes in My presence? Why this hatred? Why these venomous statements? Where is their holiness? Why are they neglecting My garden? They are dispersing My lambs more than ever and the few that remain will also vanish from the fold because they have deserted them. Peter, My eyes have grown weary, watching them accusing one another. They have laid desolate My lands and have nothing to offer My lambs. Their ways are not acceptable to Me. I have given them love and peace; I have never taught them to judge others."[10]

Some time later:

"O Peter, My Peter! Lead, beloved of My soul, My flock into integrity! Peter? Look at Me; look beloved into My face; honour Me your Lord. Love and loyalty now meet; righteousness and peace is at your very doors now. I rescue all those who cling on Me - I am your refuge. Look around you Peter, have you seen? Have you not noticed? My eyes have grown weary watching the Cains slaughter My Abels, for I have given them ears but they refuse to hear; I have given them eyes but they refuse to see; their hearts have grown coarse - they seek their glory and not Mine. O Peter how weary I am... Love is missing. Glorify Me Peter! Glorify me beloved."[11]

Another grave warning:

"I Am. Pray for the renewal of My Church. Pray for those who oppose Peter; pray for those who are trying to silence Peter. The days are numbered and My soul is submerged in sorrow; My Sacred Heart is imbued with bitterness; My soul is yearning for them to realize their error. Those that oppose Peter are opposing My Church; they are opposing My law; they are opposing Me their Lord and God; they are condemning Peter of My Lambs, thus condemning My law. Blinded by Vanity himself they do not see clear anymore that by condemning Peter they are not following the law but instead become judges of My own law! O listen to what the Spirit says to the Church! Return, come back beloved one (presumed by Vassula to be Bishop Lefebvre). It is I, the Lord who have selected Peter; Peter who today bears the name John Paul II. I am telling you, beloved one, My Sacred Heart has chosen him. Come back, reconcile for My sake beloved. I the Lord will forgive your sins and will purify you. Return. Return all of you to Peter, for it is I your God who have chosen him. It is I who have given him a disciple's tongue and through Me he is able to reply to the weary... Today I, the Lord, will add one more commandment. Write: 'Bend! Bend to be able to reconcile and unite; humble yourselves to unite.'"[12]

In October 1989 Jesus returned to the theme of the "three iron bars":

"My Vassula, draw three iron bars with a head on top; these represent the Roman Catholics, the Orthodox and the Protestants. I want them to bend and unite but these iron bars are still very stiff and cannot bend on their own, so I shall have to come to them with My fire and with the power of My flame upon them they shall turn soft to bend and mould into one solid iron bar, and My Glory will fill the whole earth. Pray often to the Holy Spirit this prayer: 'Come Holy Spirit, come through the powerful intercession of the Immaculate Heart of Mary your beloved Bride. Amen.' With this prayer My Holy Spirit will haste and come upon you. Pray for the effusion of My Holy Spirit to come upon you."[13]

In October 1991 Jesus gave Vassula important messages on unity. He commissioned her as His apostle, His envoy of unity:

"Daughter, for My sake, take My cross of unity and carry it across the world. Go from country to country and tell those who speak of unity, yet never cease to think the contrary and continue to live the contrary, that their division has separated My Heart from theirs. Shout and eventually My voice shall break through their deafness. I am with you in this desolation so do not fear... Whenever My enemies pierce you, rejoice and offer all your wounds to Me and I shall soothe you immediately. Every time you lift your eyes looking for Me, My Heart, rich in mercy will not resist you. You are My child whom I adopted raised and fed, so do not fear men, they cannot destroy you. Soon I shall set you free. In the meantime go around with My cross of unity and glorify Me. Be the defender of the truth and of the one Church

I Myself have established. Go to every nation and present yourself to them. Tell them that I want peace and one Church under My Holy Name - tell them that he who maintains to be just, yet remains divided, will eat from the fruit he has sown and will perish. Tell them how I abhor insincere hearts; their solemnities and their discourses weary Me. Their judgement appears indeed great and impressive to men but not to Me; I cannot congratulate a dying Church nearing putrefaction. Tell those who want to hear that: unless they lower their voices, they will never hear Mine. Should they lower their voices then they will begin to hear Mine and thus do My will. I am one, yet each of them made a Christ of their own. I am the Head of the Body, yet all I see are their heads, not Mine. Tell them to lower their heads and they will see Mine, tell them to lower themselves so that I may be able to lift them to Me."[14]

Jesus points out the fruits of those in power:

."Do not" He says to Vassula "be like those who persist in differentiating themselves under My Holy Name. Do not be like those who pretend that unity is appealing to them and remain dead to their word, achieving nothing but a resentment from the Father. Both the Father and I abhor their arguments, contrary to what they think. Yet nothing retains Me from crying out to these men of power: 'Descend! Descend from your thrones and may these scales on your eyes fall to see what a desolation you have made of My house! You have robbed My sanctuary and all that was within it! You shattered the shepherd's staff not only in half but in splinters!, but today open your eyes and see. Keep your eyes open and you will get to know poverty, sackcloth and barefootedness, keep your eyes open and with one look get to know My Heart... If you say you love Me and call yourself under My Holy Name, then for the sake of My Holy Name and for the sake of My love, unify My Churches.'"[15]

Jesus makes another impassioned plea for unity with such words as these:

"Unite! Assemble! Invoke My name together. Consecrate My Body and Blood together! Do not persecute the Way. Humble yourselves and bend to be able to unite and glorify Me. You speak of the Spirit, but do not act in the Spirit..."[16]

Jesus is as always essentially encouraging:

"Tell them that the Heart of the Lord is love and that the Heart of the law is based on love. Tell My people that I do not want administrators in My house, they will not be justified in My day because it is these very ones who have industrialized My house. I have sent you My Spirit to live in your hearts, this is why the Spirit that lives in you will show you that My Church will be rebuilt inside your hearts and you will acknowledge each other as your brother in your heart. Will I, brother, one more season go through the pain I have been going through year after year, or will you give Me rest this time? Am I going to drink one more season the cup of your division, or will you rest My Body and unify, for My sake, the Feast of Easter? In unifying the date of Easter, you will alleviate My pain brother and you will rejoice in Me and I in you and I will have the sight of many restored. 'My beloved, my Creator! He who is my husband has revealed to us things that no human hand could have performed', this is what you will cry out once your sight is restored in My name, and I will come to you. I solemnly tell you: summon, assemble all of you and listen this time to your Shepherd. I will lead you in the way that you must go. Send My message to the ends of the earth. Courage, daughter, smile when I smile. I am with you to guide your steps to heaven."[17]

The ecumenical teaching conveyed in Vassula's writings is not theoretical, though the theoretical basis is not wanting. It is existential, poignantly real, accessible in praxis. We can all behave humbly in dealing with those separated from us in their communion. The change needed to unify Easter involves practically nothing - the trouble is that one cannot say that it involves no one. It is personalities that create many obstacles; it was personalities that made the rifts at the beginning.

The importance of the Eucharist in Christian unity is stressed by Jesus:

"Prove yourselves in your Makers eyes by bending; prove yourselves in your Makers eyes by unifying the date of Easter. Prove yourselves to Me by breaking bread together; robe yourselves in majesty and splendour with humility and not with an outward of appearance of religion and piety, repent! once you lived in humility, simplicity and unbounded love with rich food covering your table. Yes, the greatness of My Church exceeded everything and every living creature because the Eucharist made the life of My Church. If My Church today lacks brightness, it is because many of My Churches have abolished My perpetual sacrifice."[18]

Our Lady has shown her concern for Christian unity:

"Treason barricades unity among brothers, insincerity of heart induces God's Cup to augment. They wrenched the Body of My Son, divided It, mutilated It and paralysed It. I am reminding you all that through Him, all of you have in the One Spirit your way to come to the Father, yet you remain divided under My Son's Name. You speak of unity and peace and yet stretch a net for those who practice it. God cannot be deceived nor is He convinced by your arguments. The Kingdom of God is not just words on the lips, the Kingdom of God is love, peace, unity and faith in the heart. It is the Lord's Church united in One inside your heart. The Keys to Unity are: Love and Humility. Jesus never urged you to divide yourselves, this division in His Church was no desire of His. I implore My children to unite in heart and voice and rebuild My Son's primitive Church in their heart."[19]

Jesus prays to His Father for unity:

"Holy Father, keep those you have given Me true to Your Name so that they may be one like Us. May they all be one. Father, Righteous One, remind them of My docility, My humility, My sincerity and My great Love, so that they may end My Agony, this Agony which is the cause of so much bleeding in My Body."[20]

And again:

"Am I, Father to drink one more season of the Cup of their division or will they at least unify the Feast of Easter alleviating part of My pain and sorrow? Will this reign of Darkness last much longer? They have severed My Body and have forgotten that it is My Head which strengthens and holds, the whole body together. O Father! Reconcile them and remind them that by My death on the Cross I have given them My Peace."[21]

In December 1992 during the Octave of Prayer for Unity, Vassula spoke on the subject in Sacramento, California.

"I want your voice to thunder this time in January! I want your voice to thunder as loud as ever! You will speak on My behalf. Let the whole world hear - the days are now counted, there is not much time left and grace that enfolded mankind shall come abruptly and all of a sudden at its end... this will be done so that the world realizes how great was My Mercy and My Goodness that had flowed down from above year after year....

"Tell those who work for unity to look up at the skies - see how far they are from the earth? This is how far their hearts are from one another, this is how far they are apart. When will they all pass a decree by unanimous vote to celebrate the feast of Easter all in one date? I am weary of hearing their noble language, perhaps it is suitable and eloquent for them but to Me it sounds like a stroke on a gong because it is empty with emptiness. I have come to talk to them - first, out of concern, then out of pity, but no one yet to this day has lowered his voice to hear My Voice. Alas for you, who say you are at My service yet prevent My Kingdom from finding unity and stability! But it is not you who will bring My Kingdom together... For you do not understand anything and never will... If you, in spite of My heavenly calls, did not sound the depths of My Heart, how would you unravel the arguments of My Mind, how can you fathom the Riches of My Sacred Heart? I have not spoken in parables, nor have I spoken in riddles, I have taken plain words to speak to you."[22]

Notes:

1. Some works on the ecumenical movement: A. Cardinal Bea, S.J., *The Unity of Christians*, London 1963; *id.*, *Unity in Freedom*, London, 1964; T. Stansky and J. Sheerin, *Doing the Truth in Charity*, New York, 1982; K. MacNamara, ed. *Ecumenical Conversations*, New York, 1984;

2. 2 June, 1987, Volume I, page 124;

3. *Ibid.*, page 125;

4. 17 June, 1987, 7 July, 1987, Volume I, pages 135, 145;

5. 16 October, 1987, Volume I, page 207;

6. 18 October, 1987, Volume I, page 208;

7. 27 October, 1987, Volume I, page 217f;

8. 30 October, 1987, Volume I, page 218f;

9. 30 November, 1987, Volume I, page 237;

10. 13 January, 1988, Volume I, page 264;

11. 2 March, 1988, Volume I, page 286;

12. 21 June, 1988, Volume I, page 341;

13. 26 October, 1989, Volume II, page 96;

14. 7 October, 1991, Volume II, page 372;

15. 13 October, 1991, Volume II, page 375;

16. 14 October, 1991, Volume II, page 378;

17. *Ibid.*, 379f. Many references occur to the Successor of Peter, more than in any other writing from the Orthodox Communion. I, 305, 313, 321, 325, 288, 335 - utterly unique.

18. 25 November, 1991, Volume II, page 401;

19. 23 September, 1991, Volume II, page 365;

20. 10 March, 1990, Volume II, page 158;

21. 25 October, 1991, Volume II, page 387f;

22. 21 December, 1992, Volume III;

8

RUSSIA

We open here a vast subject. Some background is necessary. Among the many sayings attributed to Napoleon one will introduce the subject: "A hundred years from now Europe will be either republican or Cossack." It was not a wild conjecture, as things worked out, if one does not take the "hundred years" too literally. We are for decades conscious of a Russian presence in the world, and especially in part of Europe, in a way that scarcely seemed possible in the early nineteenth century. A man and a book seem to initiate the movement: Karl Marx and *Das Kapital*. The Czarist regime in Russia would have possibly collapsed to give way to some other governing personnel. That the rulers of the country from the year of the revolution in 1917 were the Soviets, that their system was allegedly based on the proletariat or working class, was a typical case of text-book procedure.

Das Kapital was the text-book, understood in the light of the other prime document, *The Communist Manifesto*. It has been said that if when Napoleon approached Jena during a series of spectacular military victories, he were to lose the battle but in some way cause the death of Hegel, then teaching at the university, he would have changed the course of history. For through Karl Marx Hegel's ideas were to infiltrate the mind of half the world. Stamped with the marxist mould certainly, but the intellectual ancestry is there.

It would be intriguing to ponder in Marx the politico-literary phenomenon: how did an apparently remote theorist, Marx, who spent so much of his life in the library of the British Museum, succeed in capturing the minds of activists, political leaders, social reformers and militarists? His oft-quoted remark that religion is the opium of the people has been adjusted to record one of his singular triumphs: Marxism is the opium of the intellectuals. They were blind to the fact that marxist economic theory, which they lauded, has been the ruin of Russia and its satellites. Alexander Solzhenitsyn saw that long ago. Much is explainable through the personality and career of the heir to the revolution, Dugashvili, alias Joseph Stalin, one of the worst tyrants in history.

The Russian revolution took place in 1917. When its chief architect, Lenin, died in 1922, Stalin assumed the leadership and in time became a dictator with power unequalled in history. After the war he took over eastern Europe. Within the political system, sustained by the Red Army and the secret police, dissent was destroyed; atheism was a chief active ingredient of the ideology, which prompted war on religion. In the early ruthless years all but a subservient shell was eliminated, with a heavy toll of martyrdom and incarceration. Through the Komintern Russia was then seeking worldwide diffusion of its ideology and what else could be exported. These ideas were supposedly dropped during the war. But with Stalin's victory in the treaty of Yalta, the post-war settlement was his to dictate, and his ambition was insatiable. By some miracle western Europe was saved in the critical year, 1947. But behind the Iron Curtain his will was imposed with iron-clad efficiency. Across the world spies, fellow travellers, in some countries communist parties bowed to his diktat.

The Catholic Church suffered heavily in the stalinist years. Its fortunes were varied, that is in point of survival. The Poles were the most successful, through the influence of a wise, strong, patriotic leader, Cardinal Wyzshinski. They were a majority religion and some instinct seemed to tell them that if they practised in large numbers they had a degree of immunity, "You cannot put the whole town in jail." The Pax movement, prepared to work with and for the regime and favoured accordingly had no members among the clergy, as it had in other European countries.[1]

The story of religious change in the eastern European countries is within recent memory. Looming over all is the big question of Russia itself: when will its conversion take place? Has it begun? We have evidence of different kinds to weigh. But first we must look at an important source of Catholic hope and prayer, one which is not free from controversy: Fatima. The publicized events in that remote spot in the Portuguese countryside occurred in 1917. They were preceded by a vision indeterminate in meaning in 1915 and by three visions of an angel, the Angel of Peace, the Angel of Portugal in 1916. These are considered in another chapter of the present book. They were a prelude to the apparitions of the following year; the visionaries were the same three children, Lucia dos Santos and her cousins, Francisco and Jacinta Marto, aged eight, seven and six respectively at the outset.

What is relevant to Russia is a message received by Lucia on 13 June, 1917 - the series of apparitions had begun on 13 May. Our Lady said to her: "You have seen hell, where the souls of poor sinners go. In order to save them, God wishes to establish in the world devotion to my Immaculate Heart. If you do what I tell you many souls will be saved, there will be peace. The war will end. But if men do not cease offending God, another and more terrible war will break out during he Pontificate of Pius XII (I follow the text certified as from Lucia by Bishop of Leiria-Fatima - others give Pius XI).

"When you see a night lit up by an unknown light, know that it is the sign God gives that He is about to punish the world for its crimes by means of war, hunger and persecution of the Church and the Holy Father. In order to prevent this, I shall come to ask for the consecration of Russia to my Immaculate Heart, and the communion of reparation on the first Saturdays. If my wishes are fulfilled, Russia will be converted and there will be peace. If not, Russia will spread her errors throughout the world, promoting wars and persecution of the Church. The good will be martyred, the Holy Father will have much to suffer, and whole nations will be annihilated. But in the end my Immaculate Heart will triumph. The Holy Father will consecrate Russia to me, and it will be converted, and a time of peace will be conceded to the world."

In June, 1929 Lucia, now a religious in Tuy, was given the instruction:

"The moment has come when God asks the Holy Father, in union with all the bishops of the world, to make the consecration of Russia to my Heart, promising to save it by this means."[2]

Pius XI was informed, but did nothing. Pius XII received a lengthy letter from Sister Lucia in 1940. He did not act until 1942; we shall see how. Note that the words she heard on 13 June, 1917 were four months before the Russian Revolution.

Let me interrupt the sequence of events and pronouncements at the level of the Papacy to review the communications received from Jesus by Vassula on the subject of Russia. On 4 January, 1988 Jesus spoke to her thus: "Vassula. O Vassula! I have one of my beloved daughters lying dead! A sister of yours!" "Who's lying dead, Lord?" she replied. "My well-beloved daughter Russia. Come! Come and I will show her to you. Look!"

Thereon Vassula was taken to the edge of a desert and shown a body lying dead in "the middle of the wilderness.. Abandoned even at her death, she had died all alone with no one near her to console her." Vassula burst into tears of pity at the sight. Then Jesus spoke to her: "O do not weep; I will resurrect her Vassula; I will resurrect her for My glory; I will revive her as I have revived Lazarus." Again Vassula cried out, "O God, You give me so much pain." Then came this lengthy divine analysis of Russia's plight and future hope:

"The pain you feel is nothing compared to mine. I love her Vassula have pity on her too. I will not leave her dead and exposed to the scorching winds. Vassula, love your sister; pity her, go to her, love her. Love her, for she is so unloved by everyone! Vassula, she had abandoned Me and turned against Me. She turned against Me when she grew and when it was her time for love, I called her to share My cloak but instead she walked away. Feeling mature, she believed she would be able to feed herself on her own. She turned her back to Me and walked away, like an unfaithful wife she fled. My beloved, do you know what it is like losing a daughter? My heart lacerated, wept. Like this was not enough, she proudly and without the slightest remorse declared openly war against Me, her Father and against all the martyr saints. She believed in Me no more, she stopped worshipping Me, hoping in Me and loving Me. She seemed to have forgotten the love we once shared. I had given her sons and daughters but in her fury she slaughtered My children and handed them over to Satan as one offers a burnt offering. Then, as though this was not enough, she turned to Satan and made a pact with him to be faithful to him and worship him instead, if he would offer her all that she desired. Satan agreed with the condition to leave him free. Satan then disconnected her entirely from Me; she let him cut our bonds - he made her trust him. Treacherous as he is, he led My daughter into marshlands first, where she would have to lean on him, from fear of sinking into quicksands. She asked him to allow her to lean entirely on him. Vassula, like Jerusalem at one time who fled from My house, My house of Holiness, to become a daughter of no morals, offering her children, one after another as a sacrifice, Russia, My daughter, thought it wise to do the same. She took My holy presents and offered them to Satan, who turned them all into weapons. Satan blinded her with his glory and in her blindness removed her from the marshlands and placed her into the wilderness to thirst and die. I saw her walking naked and struggling in her own blood; I called her but she would not listen. I called her again, but she would not hear My call; instead she provoked Me, calling her younger sisters to support her morals - if they refused she forced them with her sword. Have I not said, 'he who will raise the sword shall perish by the sword'? I rationed her bread so that she would need My Bread but she preferred to starve rather than eat from Me. Exhausted and hungered, she sent her younger sister to continue her wicked works in secret because her vanity was inspired by Vanity himself who is Satan. Her lands bore not enough to feed her; she became as one would say 'a dependent' on My enemy."[3]

Jesus promised to continue this communication next day, when this dialogue took place:

"Do not weep Vassula, I told you, I will resurrect her."

She had read the passage about Russia lying dead and wept bitterly, "I love her, Lord, I feel pity for her Lord. I love her." "Love her as I love her, she is My daughter too - your sister." "Lord" Vassula replied "will you go over to her and resurrect her? Will she return to you, O Lord?" "I will go to her and resurrect her and carry her to My House. I want all My children to love her - we will all surround her with love." Then when she reminded Him of His promise the previous day:

"I will continue. When Russia became a dependant of Satan because her land was barren, he offered her the deadly fruit he keeps in store for those I love. It kills in stages - the more one eats of it the more one needs it. It's deadly - killing slowly. he nourished her with his fruit and killed her; she died with this fruit still clenched in her hand. Vassula, trust Me, I will resurrect her. Daughter, be still, do not worry, leave Me free and I will accomplish My works."[4]

On 1 February it was Our Lady who spoke to Vassula about Russia:

"Vassula I have so many times asked for the consecration of my daughter Russia. I have implored her consecration. Today Vassula is the day she has seen the light - she will be commemorating her millenary anniversary. Vassula your sister is dead but the Lord is near her now and will resurrect her and Love will love the unloved and she will cry up to him: 'you are my God and Saviour!' With this cry the demons shall take flight; fearing demons will flee for this nation will become one and God's most devout servant. Healed and resurrected by God's strength, her stature of holiness will attract all her neighbours by her devotion to the Almighty. Russia will be the symbol of God's glory, of God's mercy and love. Her hymns and chants that are so sweet in our ears, with her graceful movements, will rise up to heaven like incense. Love will resurrect her, as He resurrected her a thousand years ago."[5]

Then Jesus spoke to Vassula:

"I am the Lord - the Resurrection. When I will resurrect Russia, she will restore My gifts, she will embellish My House again with love and I will unite her again to me. I will offer her My Bread and My Wine and she will not refuse My Food. She will accept My offer and she will eat My Bread and drink My Wine renewing herself, praising Me. I will clothe her with My Glory, I will adorn her majestically, I will irrigate her from My own springs, I will replenish her stores, My eyes are upon her. Ah Vassula! Just wait and see. Daughter, how I long to see Peter, My Peter, visit your sister..."[6]

When Vassula begged "Encourage him Lord to go, Lord open his path if this is your will" Jesus replied "Come, I am working in many hearts Vassula. Pray to attain My Father's favour. I will restore My Church. Woe to the unfaithful."[7]

Vassula's comments on this encounter are stimulating. She had an intuition that Jesus had much hidden which will be unveiled. "He sounded happy, excited" she said.

On 11 March Jesus returned to the theme:

"Pray beloved for Russia's conversion. Russia will be resurrected by My divine hand and at this peak of holiness (while My hand will be posed upon her, warming her cold heart, reviving her), she will arise from the stillness of death and her world of darkness into My world of peace and light. With a loud cry she will manifest her joy, beholding her Saviour at her side. I will lift her to Me and My flame of love will inflame her heart, purifying her and leaving her in total rapture before Me, her God. O Russia! My Russia! How I the Lord love you. How I wept to see you dead. I shed so many bitter and sorrowful tears upon you beloved when I lost you and all Heaven was mourning for you. Why, why, My beloved had you rejected Me, piercing My Heart full of love and tenderness..?"[8]

That same day Our Lady intervened again:

"Peace upon you my child, I am your Holy Mother. Pray for your sister, for the Lord is by her side today and soon His divine hand will touch her cold and dead heart. O creation! The Lord will revive your sister so unloved. Be alert daughter, for her time of glory is near. Petro! My so beloved Petro? Yes Vassula, for years I have been pleading (with) you to consecrate Russia. Now the Lord and all the Martyr Saints have heard your pleas and cries; all your sacrifices were not in vain beloved all your tears were not shed for nothing - those tears were a balm for Jesus' wounded Heart. Praise the Lord Petro - Jesus is at your very doors, knocking. Peace upon you. Peace upon you all. I love you all."[9]

In the following year, 13 November, Jesus returned to the subject of Russia, optimistically:

"Peace be with you, My child. Evangelize with love for Love. Ecclesia shall revive because I, the Lord shall overthrow all the imposters who have placed themselves in high seats within her. Daughter, remove these thorns that pierce My head, thorns that cause so much bleeding, do not fear them daughter for I am beside you and I tell you truly that with My power and My great mercy I shall overthrow each one of these.

You see my child, all heaven was too long in mourning for your sister-so-unloved, for years we are swallowing our bitter tears. O Russia! Mere creature of flesh! Evil coiled in your very womb, creature of mere dust and ashes. I the Most High shall resurrect you for I am the Resurrection. I shall nurse you back to life and I shall with My finger upon you, transfigure you into a glorious nation as I was transfigured. You shall be majestically dressed in dazzling white robes and all heaven shall thrust away its mourning garments and heaven's bitter tears shall turn into joyful tears. All heaven will celebrate your Resurrection and all the martyr-saints, who prayed without ceasing by the feet of your Holy Mother for her intercession, shall in this day too, together with My Mother and her innumerable holy angels, all descend in your childrens' homes and make their home together with them. I then shall feed them My Body and offer them My Blood to drink. Russia will eat Me and drink Me with great love, praising Me. My Russia shall be the living example of your times for generations to come, because of her great conversion. Your sister so unloved by many shall renounce all her evil behaviour and shall call Me her God with all her might.

Vassula, can you hear? Listen, listen to your sister's childrens' laments, her children are lamenting and there is wailing. It is My Russia's children who are weeping, all heaven plainly hears their grieving. Heaven is deeply moved by their distress and I, who have never ceased loving her, now am near her dead body. My hand upon her cold heart and her bones will flower again from her tomb and her name shall be well spoken of for I shall adorn her and her sons and daughters.."[10]

On Christmas Eve that year Jesus spoke thus:

"Let the nations realize that it is I, the Lord, who come to free these captives from prison and lift them to Me; it is I who reduced your enemies into everlasting shame and this is not all, I shall, with you sister Russia, sign a covenant of peace and love and her crimes shall be forgotten by Me and I shall make her My Bride again and out of her heart shall come this song: 'I will keep my love for Him always, and my covenant with my God shall stand.' My soul is thirsting for this glorious moment. I mean to show My splendour and My glory to every nation under these skies, through your sister Russia. I shall dress her with My beauty and with My integrity and I shall parade her to your brothers so that they may see My beauty and My integrity through her and in her. Daughter, the wedding of your sister's conversion is soon to come. I have said that I am He who descends in your era's misery to console the oppressed and free her captives from prison and those who live in darkness from the dungeon. It is I your Saviour who comes to rescue you from the red dragon's claws; it is I, your Jesus My doves who comes to break your cages and free you. It is I, your Holy One, who never abandoned you and I tell you truly your gates shall not be closed to Me. Vassula, I shall overthrow with disgrace and humiliation all these evil powers, these powers who knocked down My house and made out of it gaping graves. My light shall resurrect your sister Russia and all her neighbouring countries. I shall break all your cages and set you free. Learn that salvation and liberation comes from Me alone. Pray for your sister, pray for her neighbours."[11]

Vassula had a special thought for Romania and spoke to Jesus of the innocent people who suffered unto the shedding of blood. Jesus replied:

"Be assured that I have with Me all the martyr-saints of your season, victims of Satan's fury. I have with Me all those who perished as victims. I tell you that his fury was such that knowing that he was losing his grip he intended to annihilate every single flower of Mine."[12]

We move forward to another exchange of opinion between Vassula and Jesus on the subject of Russia. On 3 September 1991 she addressed him thus:

"Lord, Father and Master of our lives, do not abandon us now nor in the days of distress. Lord, Father and Master of our lives, help Russia to grow in your Spirit. You have pierced the Red Dragon through that besieged her. Lord, Father and Master of our lives, rescue us from the Rebel that still remains among us."

Her words drew this response:

"Ah, my child, I shall teach you all by My purifying fire, wait and you shall see. Hear Me now and write, My child: Not long ago most of the nations of the world never believed that the enemy, the Red Dragon, would lose its power in Russia so suddenly. Vassula, if your sister Russia rebelled against Me, it came through the sins of the world and its crimes. Tyranny comes from below."

Vassula then asked, "But how did her children feel, those martyrs who belonged to you?" Jesus replied:

"How can I describe what her children suffered, to what can I compare them, daughter? All Heaven mourned for her children. Her sons laid helpless, but who was there around them to mourn for them? Was there anyone strong enough among them to pierce the Dragon through? not when their skins were shrunken against their bones. Her children were begging for bread, oppressed by the enemy they collapsed under their burden. If they left in secrecy to take refuge in My arms, they would be punished severely, they were not allowed to show their zeal for Me. Their pursuers were swifter than vipers eyeing each step they took, and had they any suspicions that the Book of Life would be hidden under their mattress, My children would be harassed, tracked, then captured. Ah daughter, my eyes wept ceaselessly to see this nation reduced to silence by the sword, priests and prophets were made prisoners and were forced to dwell in darkness. Many of them were slaughtered pitilessly before My very eyes. This nation who at one time honoured Me and praised Me openly, radiant as sapphire, a citadel of delights, was reduced to a waterless country of drought by the sins and crimes of the world. I tell you, My daughter Russia, your sister, has not yet shown you what she will accomplish in My name. The Day of Festival has yet to come and how I wish it were here already. Pray, pray for this glorious day."[13]

On 30 January, 1992 Vassula had a vision of Russia, which Jesus told her to write. He reassured her:

"Do not weep, she will recover. Weep bitterly rather for those who have gone away from Me. I will rebuild her. Weep for the one who is dead. I will embellish her, Vassula."

Then Vassula described what she saw:

"O God, I have seen her misery! What I have seen is this: A woman approached me, young, not very beautiful but neither ugly. Her name: Russia. She came over to me and I noticed from her clothing that she was poor. She opened her mouth to talk to me and I saw then that half of her teeth were missing and that made her very ugly, but I knew that a woman, so young, would do something if half of her teeth were gone, unless extreme poverty covered her. Russia, in spite of her poverty and misery was courageous and on her feet. She showed me with what she would earn her bread, an old-fashioned instrument. Russia was telling me that she will work on it, to be able to earn what will keep her alive. I was torn inside me with sadness. Then another woman came, she was also Russia, she too had most of her teeth missing. Then two more women came, all of whose teeth were missing, and showing extreme poverty. Then suddenly a young man enters, he was the husband of Russia. I noticed that he was well-built, healthy, tall and very good-looking. I thought: how could he stand someone like Russia, with no beauty in her and repulsive for lack of teeth... While I was thinking all these things, Russia's husband approached her tenderly and put his arm around her shoulders and I saw in his eyes infinite tenderness, love and fidelity for ever and ever. I saw that he would never abandon her in spite of her unattractiveness. I recognized you, my Lord."

This is Jesus' reply:

> "No, I shall not abandon her, nor does she repulse Me. I am Her Father and her Spouse and My name is 'Faithful and True'. I shall dress her up again, giving her fine clothes, and her heart will be the ornament of a sweet and gentle disposition. I have never ceased to rain a downpour of blessings on her, I shall never deprive her of my love. Ah, Vassula, be patient as I am patient. Lean now on me."[14]

We should look at recent history to see how these messages reflect reality. Papal action my be noted. On 31 October, 1942 Pius XII consecrated the world to the Immaculate Heart of Mary. He referred to Russia not by name but to the land where there was not a house that did not honour Our Lady's icon "though now perhaps hidden and put away for better days." Ten years later in the Encyclical *Sacro Vergente Anno* (7 July 1952) he consecrated and dedicated "in a very special way all the peoples of Russia to this Immaculate Heart." On 21 November, 1964 Paul VI, in his address for the conclusion of the third session of Vatican II proclaimed Mary Mother of the Church and associated himself with Pius XII's initial act of consecration: Council teaching on Our Lady had been formulated during the third session. Many bishops would have wished for something more from the Pope. It was an ideal situation for a collegial act of consecration. Paul VI possibly thought that not all the bishops would have supported him. Some of them, not noted Marian theologians, had adopted reductionist attitudes in the conciliar debate on Our Lady: many of them did not even accept the title Mediatress, campaigned up the last day to have it eliminated from the text, despite its validity established by unimpeachable scholarship.

The term collegial needs explanation; it is henceforth crucial. It means joint action by the Church's hierarchy in union with the Pope. John Paul II is the Pope involved. Prior to the attack on him life on 13 May, 1981 he did not publicly manifest interest in Fatima; his Marian spirituality, which is profound and intense, was oriented towards Our Lady of Czestochowa, her image prominent in his residence in Cracow. But the Fatima coincidence with 13 May marked him. He was convinced that Our Lady saved his life and went to Fatima on the exact anniversary, 13 May 1982 to thank her; he did likewise on the tenth anniversary, 13 May, 1991.

On the first visit the Pope gave a lengthy address dealing explicitly with consecration to the Immaculate Heart of Mary. Soon after Sister Lucia stated bluntly in letters, particularly one to her niece, that Our Lady's request had not been met. On 25 March, 1984 the Pope in Rome, before a statue brought on his orders from Fatima, recited a lengthy formula of consecration. This time he had informed the world's hierarchy months before. He used such language as this:

"In a special way we entrust and consecrate to you those individuals and nations which particularly need to be thus entrusted and consecrated." "The power of this consecration lasts for all time and embraces all individuals, peoples, nations."

The Pope did not name Russia. But when the Bishop of Fatima thanked him for consecrating the world to the Immaculate Heart of Mary, the Pope said "and Russia." When, soon after, the Apostolic Nuncio to Portugal asked Sister Lucia if Our Lady's request had now been rightly answered, she replied affirmatively, adding "God will keep his word." Copies of letters from Lucia saying the same thing are widely distributed. Mgr. Luciano Guerra, Rector of the Fatima sanctuary, sent me some in answer to my query on the substantive matter.

This has not ended controversy, especially in North America. Critics have objected that Sister Lucia's letters are typed and it is known that she does not type - I had to face this objection personally. Better leave these debates and turn to the reality inside Russia.

An important factor in the change has been the personality of Mikhail Gorbachev, who in March 1985 had effective control of the USSR. His campaign to institute *perestroika* (restructuring) and *glasnost* (openness) is well known as is his encounter with the leaders of the Russian Orthodox Church. The world was stunned when Gorbachev, now president of the Soviet Union, lineal successor to Stalin, went on an official visit to John Paul II in the Vatican. He invited the Pope to Russia, promised diplomatic relations with the Holy See and a charter of religious liberty in Russia: which has been enacted.

Visitors to the country report signs of change favourable to religious revival. Foremost among these witnesses is Tatiana Goritcheva. Her story is required reading for those interested in the Christian revival inside Russia. A university lecturer, she was converted from the life-style of her peers to active Christianity. This led her to join the underground feminist movement, *Maria*, so entitled from its inspiration in Our Lady, thus proclaimed. With her associates she was harassed and eventually given a choice, prison or exile. In exile she revealed much of the incipient revival of Christian practice despite so many obstacles. With the recent changes she has gone back, moved freely about the country, found heartening signs of a thirst for God.

A symbolic incident took place on 13 October, 1991. During the coup against Gorbachev in August when Boris Yeltsin raised the standard of defiance against the rebellious clique, he needed help by way of a radio link with the people. It was provided by a Belgian Catholic radio crew who were in Moscow. After his success he asked them how he could thank them: "By allowing a transmission of the religious service from Fatima to your country on 13 October." The request was granted and it was done.

ADDENDUM: I give here some comments which Vassula made after reading the text of this chapter. She quotes from a message received on 25 October 1992:

"Russia is like an open field ready to be sown. Her soil is ready to receive any seed... nobody will be allowed to lay down any other foundation than My very own foundation."

In the same message we read:

"It is I, God, who designed Russia for My glory, and it is through her that light will shine out of her darkness. It is through her light that your generation's heart will be enlightened with the knowledge of My glory. I shall pour out My Spirit on the house that I had given her and I will display My holiness in her to honour My name."

He repeats what he had said elsewhere that Russia will lead other nations into piety and holiness.

"No one will gloat over her for I will lift her to become the head (spiritually) of many nations. In her poverty I will rebuild My kingdom; ah Vassula just wait and see!"

Vassula interprets this to mean that as Russia will be the one who will glorify God most, and the answer to our query as to what would give God most glory in Christ's Church, is the unity of his Church. "It is the last thing he had asked from the Father" she writes, "'That they may all be one even as thou my Father art in me and I in thee, that they also may be in us so that the world may believe that thou has sent me' (Jn 17:21). It is obvious that after her full conversion Russia will be the first one to take the step into unity. When the Churches are united the second part of Christ's prayer too will be accomplished. The whole world will be converted, and it will be beginning of Rev. 21, New Heavens and New Earth."

Vassula recalls the word of Jesus spoken on 4 January 1988, "Vassula love your sister, pity her, go to her, love her." She was sent to Russia in October 1992, 18-20. Again she notes the words of Jesus on 13 November 1989, "I shall nurse you back to life and I shall with My finger upon you transfigure you into a glorious nation as I was transfigured." The importance here for Vassula is that Russia's transfiguration from communism to liberty took place on the third day of the Orthodox feast of the Transfiguration, the attempted coup against Gorbachev occurring on the 19, 20, 21 August, 1991. She also thinks that Our Lady's words recorded on 11 March, 1988 seem to confirm that the consecration was made by John Paul II as she had wished. Vassula in footnotes to Volume I, page 291 writes: "Suddenly St. Mary turned her head towards John Paul II, as if he was present; in pronouncing his name her voice was very sweet but sad, full of a special love for him." and again St. Mary had tried to keep back her tears, but could not. She said these words ('My so beloved Petro') breaking into tears, she wept very much, shedding many tears and I started to weep too with her. I felt that our Holy Mother had a weakness for Petro."

ADDENDUM II: There is considerable evidence, in correspondence from Sister Lucia, and in reported conversations, notably with the Apostolic Nuncio to Portugal, that in her role as Our Lady's intermediary, she is firmly of the opinion that the consecration of Russia sought by Our Lady has been made. A recent testimony of importance is reported by Howard Dee in his book, *Mankind's Final Destiny* (Manila, 1993) The former Ambassador accompanied Mrs. Cory Aquino when she visited Sister Lucia in the Carmel of Coimbra - the former president was on her way to Fatima for the seventy fifth anniversary celebrations on 13 October, 1992. Ambassador Dee put this question to Sister Lucia: "Can I ask a question relating to the consecration to the Immaculate Heart of Mary?" "Of course you can" she replied "and I will answer if I can also." The question: "Can we attribute the collapse of communism in eastern Europe to the consecration made by Pope John Paul II in 1984?"

Sister Lucia replied:

> "The consecration made by Pope John Paul II was valid... There was no need that the bishops do it together in one place; what matters is the union of the intentions with the Holy Father and that the bishops do it in union with their faithful in their dioceses. That the consecration was valid is proved by what happened afterwards in Russia, the peaceful change and the collapse of communism. In the formula of the consecration there was a veiled mention of Russia. That was enough; you do not need to tell God everything. He knew what was in the heart of the Pope and he accepted the consecration."

Lucia then gave her opinion that God works in the minds of those who may not believe in Him. She cited the momentous decision of Gorbachev to come to Rome and to achieve reconciliation with the Pope. "The great thing" she added "Is that the changes came about with acceptance of all the other communist leaders, without anyone resorting to the horrors of war." Vassula believes that the fall of communism is the *sign* of Russia's conversion. In addition to the statute of religious liberty which Gorbachev promised to John Paul II and which is already enacted, there is the immensely symbolic opening to worship of the three churches within the Kremlin, hitherto preserved as museums, the churches of the Annunciation, of the Assumption and of St. Michael. When one thinks of what the Kremlin has meant in anti-religious history!

Notes:

1. For documentation on the situation of the Church in Russia and countries controlled by Stalin cf. A. Galter, *The Red Book of the Persecuted Church*, London, 1957; for recent history cf. P. Walters ed. *World and Christianity* - Eastern Europe, Keston College, Eastbourne, 1988; for Poland cf. M. O'Carroll, *Poland and John Paul II*, Dublin 1979; for very recent events, cf. T. Tindal-Robertson, *Fatima, Russia and John Paul II*, Augustine Press, 1992;

2. Literature on Fatima is abundant. Two volumes of Fr. Joaquin Alonso's monumental, 20 volume work have appeared; cf. W. Walsh *Our Lady of Fatima*, 1946 etc... bibl. M. O'Carroll, *The Heart of Mary in two Revolutions*, 1987, Mariological Congress; *Fatima in Lucia's own Words*, intr. Dr. Alonso, Fatima, 1976;

3. 4 January, 1988, Volume I, pages 256-258;

4. 5 January, 1988, Volume I, page 258;

5. 1 February, 1988, Volume I, page 276f;

6. *Ibid.*;

7. *Ibid.*;

8. 11 March, 1988, Volume I, page 291;

9. *Ibid.*; Footnotes in Vassula's text are: "Suddenly St. Mary turned her head towards John Paul II as if he was present; in pronouncing his name her voice was very sweet and sad, full of a special love for him. St. Mary had to keep back her tears but could not. She said these words breaking into tears; she wept very much shedding many tears and I started to weep with her. I felt that our Holy Mother had a weakness for Petro. The word 'you' after 'I have been bleeding' was John Paul II.";

10. 13-14 November, 1989, Volume II, page 105;

11. 25 December, 1989, Volume II, page 129;

12. *Ibid.*;

13. 3 September, 1991, Volume II, page 352f;

14. 30 January, 1992, Volume II, page 416f;

9

ST. MICHAEL

For many Christians belief in angels means prayer to their Guardian Angel and to St Michael. A whole generation of Catholics were brought up on a daily prayer to St Michael the Archangel.[1] Since the days of Pope Leo XIII the well-known prayer was recited each day after Holy Mass. It was eliminated in the liturgical reforms which followed Vatican II. This is the prayer which Jesus told Vassula that she was to recite on certain occasions, adding that presently it is a need.

The whole reality of angels has been called into question by some modern Catholic theorists. It must be firmly proclaimed in the light of explicit Old and New Testament witness, and of the unvarying testimony of tradition in the east and the west. Many factors contribute to encourage a vital attitude to St. Michael at the present time. There is the sense of evil apparently triumphant, certainly very menacing; there is improved knowledge of the Archangel's role in church history; there are reports of his apparitions, notably at Garabandal, which will have a decisive effect in the future of the Church.

The iconography of St Michael, and his sanctuaries are splendid. Jacob Eppstein's three quarter relief statue designed for the new cathedral of St. Michael in Coventry is much admired - as is the same sculptor's wonderful statue of Mother and Child in Cavendish Square, London. Monte Gargano cannot fail to impress the pilgrim whose faith leads him to the height. Guido Reni's triumphant conqueror in the Capuchin church on the Via Veneto will delight those who love colour flamboyant. Mount St. Michael off Cornwall is not so well known, nor is the Collège St. Michel in Fribourg, Switzerland, brainchild of St. Peter Canisius, noted for his piety to the Archangel - as were so many other saints, Louis Marie Grignion de Montfort, Francis of Assisi, Francis de Sales and, above all, the young girl whose life and mission were identified with the Archangel's love for her country, Joan of Arc. Rightly is he honoured in so many French churches. Nowhere in the world has he, the lover of high places, chosen a spot where towering natural grandeur unites so harmoniously with artistic genius as the Mont St. Michel. The story of its restoration in the present century is a tissue of the miraculous. A pious Frenchman favoured with angelic visitations, M. Martin, one day saw St. Michael who complained that his great shrine had fallen into disrepair. M. Martin must go to *La Croix*, the French Catholic daily, and ask to have a request for funds to aid the work of restoration inserted in their columns. Timorous the good man did as he was told only to receive all-out editorial support. The result was munificent and the sanctuary - a thousand years old - was restored. Then the good M. Martin had a second visit from St. Michael. He must go to M. Frémiet, an outstanding Paris sculptor - totally unknown to him until then - and ask for drawings of a statue to surmount the spire of the church. Frémiet reacted as had Eppstein when Sir Basil Spence had succeeded in cajoling the conservative Anglican Governors of Coventry cathedral to accept him: he almost danced with joy, for this is a sculptor's dream. In due course he supplied the drawings, and St. Michael came one day, looked them over and chose the one he wanted. I have seen it in photograph, in replica and, through binoculars, on the spot. It is just beyond praise, one of the greatest pieces of sculpture in the world.[2]

It is fascinating and utterly comforting to read through the messages of this mighty protector of God's people as they are unfolded to Vassula, God's instrument for conversion, renewal, sanctification. She was instructed by the Lord to recite daily the traditional prayer to the Archangel. On 10 September, 1988 while she was doing so she suddenly knew that St. Michael was present to her. She heard the words "Glory be to God! Glory be to God" and exclaimed "St. Michael?" "Vassula" the Prince of Angels replied "I will tell you this: all this revelation comes from the mouth of the Most High - be certain of His mercy." She replied "Thank you St. Michael."[3]

On 1 March of the following year St. Michael came with a message for a meeting which she was to attend:

"Vassula, Glory be to God! Praised be the Lord! The Lord's mercy is boundless, the Lord's grace is upon you. Awake! Awake! Come back to the Lord all those who have abandoned the truth. Return and repent! Pray for the conversion of your brethren. Take heed upon the Lord's warnings. Peace, peace, make peace with God! I, Saint Michael, am near you, to defend you. Pray without ceasing - your prayers are needed more than ever these days of Lent. I bless you in the name of the Father and of the Son and of the Holy Spirit. Amen."[4]

On 4 July, 1989 St. Michael gave a more lengthy message:

"I am St. Michael. I am your St. Michael to whom you pray for protection and for defending you against the evil one. Have no fear, your hardships will be redressed by this prayer. Allow the Spirit of love to expand his calls of grace, listen to the Spirit of grace, listen to the Spirit for his mercy is great; do not suffocate those who receive the Holy One's messages like your ancestors by saying to the seers 'see no visions' and to the prophets 'do not prophesy to us for we are in the truth.' Instead lift up your eyes and look around, all are assembling and coming back to God, your sons far away and your daughters being tenderly carried, for the Lord has announced this 'though night dominates your era, My Light shall pierce it and will cover this earth and all nations shall come to Me and My flock I will gather again into one holy Fold under My holy Name.' Pray, O children of the Lord, and allow the Lord to redress this people by accepting what comes out of the babe's mouth and the lowly. Have no fear, salvation is near and at your very gates. I bless you in the name of the Father and of the Son and of the Holy Spirit. Amen. Allow the Lord to use you, Vassula, yearn for the Lord. Love Him for He is most compassionate."[5]

On 19 January, 1991 Vassula received this message from the Archangel:

"Peace be with you. I, Saint Michael, ask you to consecrate your days and nights to petitions, fasting and prayer. Soon, all things that have been hidden to you shall be revealed, may it be the Lord's will that you shall find His mercy in His day. If only you who have hardened your heart would listen to Him today, if only you would only open your heart to hear His voice... open your hearts not your minds... Everything goes in accordance with the Scriptures. Soon many will start bending their knee to God, and many tongues that have not uttered a prayer shall start praying. Be united, you who are God's people, in your convictions and in your love, be united in prayer. I bless you all in the name of the Father, and of the Son and of the Holy Spirit. Rest in the Lord's Heart, Vassula, be the sign of His love. Have my peace. Saint Michael."[6]

On the feast of St. Michael, 29 September, 1991 he greeted Vassula thus: "I love you child of God, trust me."[7]

Through these messages St. Michael's direct involvement in the whole process of salvation is clearly assumed. His knowledge of future events is manifest. His role as defender, protector, is emphasized. His intrinsic power is stated in the Old and New Testaments, Daniel 12:1 where he is called "great prince who stands over your people", but especially in Revelation 12:7 where he leads the triumphant angelic hosts against the dragon and his spirits. Significantly in view of what we have seen about the widespread apostasy at the present time and the one who foments it, the Archangel of power is the one who along with Jesus and Mary comes to give messages to Vassula, and those who listen to her messages.

In August, 1992 Vassula as is her custom annually was in the neighbourhood of Greece. She went to the small island named Parnormiti, to pray to St. Michael in a monastery named for him which has a miraculous icon of the Archangel. She had in the morning before leaving for the island a dream vision of Jesus who seemed to appear palpably to her and give her a message. Then He told her to listen to His Archangel who spoke to her as follows:

"Child of God, do not fear, stand firm when they persecute you, you are not alone. Give your True Shepherd all your problems and He will guide and lead you; and the Mighty One has His Hand on you; listen when He speaks for He has great plans on you; He is the living God and there is no one above Him; I shall help everyone who is willing to overcome the Evil One and in the Father through the Father I will undo the work of the devil; let anyone who wants to boast, boast of the Lord! Praised be the Lord; remain in His Heart and remember, He has truly spoken to you, God's Archangel Michael."[8]

Notes:

1. Cf. article Angels, in M. O'Carroll, *Veni Creator Spiritus,* Wilmington, 1987; G. Davidson, *A Dictionary of Angels*, New York, London, 1967; J. Danielou, *Les Anges et leur mission d'apres les Pères de l'Eglise*, Collection Irenikon, 1952; *St. Michael and the Angels*, Tan Books, Rockford, Illinois, 1977;

2. Information supplied to me by the French art historian Count Paul Biver, a friend of M. Martin;

3. 10 September, 1988, Volume I, page 371;

4. 1 March, 1989, Volume I, page 431;

5. 4 July, 1989, Volume II, page 39;

6. 19 January, 1991, Volume II, page 273;

7. 29 September, 1991, Volume II, page 368;

8. 27 August, 1992, Volume III;

10

GOD THE FATHER

The attack on the divinity of Jesus Christ calls for a renewed reflection on His divine sonship, that is on God the Father.[1] As we saw in dealing with the Holy Spirit, there is a failure to realize that the Father exists as a Person and that a personal relationship with Him is possible. Perhaps we should say that this relationship is obligatory. It is the hope of all believing Christians to spend eternity with Almighty God. God is a Trinity of Persons, and with each of the Holy Trinity we shall have to commune, we shall rejoice to commune. It is almost a matter of theological common-sense that we should make some effort to do so as a preparation for eternity.

In the early centuries there were two somewhat different, though complementary approaches to profound, sustained reflection on the Godhead. The eastern Fathers of the Church took as a starting point consideration of each divine Person, whereas the Latin Fathers began with the Trinity in itself; this is exemplified in the lengthy treatises of St. Hilary of Poitiers (d. 367) and St. Augustine (d. 430). It must be admitted that with the passage of time, emphasis has understandably been very much on the Word made flesh, on Jesus Christ true God and true man, revealed and known to us in the New Testament. Such thought as has been given to the Holy Spirit would also invoke the same source. For His advent into human affairs, into the life of the Church was a moment of manifest power, highlighted by signs of a kind to mark consciousness collective and personal.

We are presently becoming aware of the need to develop a theology of God the Father. Preparing a contributory essay in honour of Professor Heinrich Beck of Bamberg University on the theme "God the Father, our Father" I was agreeably surprised to note an interest and search manifested in quite a large literature that has grown up in recent decades. Systematic theologians, biblical scholars, spiritual writers, catechetical instructors have felt drawn to the theme. A great theologian like the Belgian Professor in the Gregorian University, Rome, Jean Galot, S.J. a specialist in Christology with wide-ranging interests, set the problem in focus. F.X. Durwell, C.SS.R., whose book on the Resurrection opened up a vast new perspective (one anticipated by Newman in his Protestant days) has within the last six years followed his book on the Holy Spirit with a powerfully suggestive study of *Le Père: Dieu et son mystère*. The international review *Concilium*, founded to continue the theological concerns stirred by Vatican II, representative of a particular trend devoted a whole issue to the subject; so did the catechetical review *Lumiere et Vie*. The prestigious encyclopedia, *Le Dictionnaire de Spiritualité* commissioned articles by two authors, each valuable. It must be admitted that some works appearing with the word Father in their titles are more concerned with the mystery of the godhead, not with the theoretical or devotional aspects of the personality of God the Father.

Jean Galot sees important reasons why a profound and productive reflection on the theme of God the Father should be undertaken at the present time. Jesus' own consciousness of His divine sonship needs to be clarified and defended against proponents of a reductionist Christology. This implies clarification of the personality of God the Father. Secondly the irruption of feminist theology into the whole programme of biblical and traditional teaching calls for careful explanation of the concept of divine fatherhood. Thirdly, paternity is under attack in the relationship which is at the basis of the human family, nowadays so often troubled, needing support from the intimate life of God Himself.

The idea of God as Father goes back to Old Testament times: "Is He not your father, who created you, who made you and established you?" (Deut 32:6); "Have we not all one father? Has not one God created us?" (Mal 2:10); "As a father pities his children, so the Lord pities those who fear Him. For He knows our frame; He remembers that we are dust."(Ps 103:13f)

There are important differences in the Old Testament from the Near Eastern mythologies. There is never reference to God as direct physical ancestor, one who begets. The divine fatherhood is, moreover, towards Israel as God's special elect: "And you shall say to Pharoah, 'Thus says the Lord, Israel is My first-born son, and I say to you, Let My son go that he may serve Me; if you refuse to let him go, behold I will slay your first-born son'" (Ex 4:22,23); "I am a father to Israel, and Ephraim is My first-born." (Jer 31:9).

The restriction in the idea of fatherhood to the people is strong in attitudes of prayer. "To date" writes the great biblical scholar, Joachim Jeremias "nobody has produced a single instance in Palestinian Judaism where God is addressed as 'my Father' by an individual person." The Gottingen professor explains the apparent exception in Sirach 23 - it is a Greek mistranslation "O Lord Father and Ruler of my life" for "O God of my father", which correction has been made by a manuscript finding in the present century.

The advent of God's Son on earth would change entirely the focus of the word and idea of Father. The New Testament unfolds the mystery steadily and fully. Jesus speaks constantly of the Father, not often of God. In Matthew alone He speaks of "My Father" six times. In the many references to the Father in John He affirms His exclusive share in the Father's love, and His uniquely privileged knowledge of Him. He and the Father are one; to see Him is to see the Father; He is in the Father and the Father is in Him. God the Father is spoken of as the Father of our Lord Jesus Christ several times by St. Paul.

Jesus effected a total innovation in doctrine and prayer centred on the Father, His *Abba*. This is of interest nowadays when there is such attention, with abounding literature, to His Jewishness. He was the fullness of Israel. But from within the Jewish thought-processes and intellectual legacy He extracted a nomenclature which served as a vehicle for a wholly new idea, that in God He had a Father. St. Irenaeus thought that the God of Abraham, Isaac and Jacob was the Father. It was not made explicit, could be so only when the Son became man. In the capital passages in Matthew and John, Jesus using the language of the Old Testament, expands its meaning to utterly unforeseen theological dimensions - He would do likewise with the *Ruah* term in regard to the Holy Spirit.

In Matthew 5:35 and 6:26-32 Jesus accommodates His thinking to the mentality of His audience; it is "your Father who is in heaven." But in the Hymn of Jubilation He confronts His listeners with the sublime reality: "At that time Jesus declared, 'I thank thee Father, Lord of heaven and earth, that thou hast hidden these things from the wise and understanding and revealed them to babes; yes, Father, for such was thy gracious will. All things have been delivered to Me by My Father; and no one knows the Son except the Father, and no one knows the Father except the Son and any one to whom the Son chooses to reveal him." (Mt 11:25-27) In the parallel passage in Luke the evangelist, true to his fondness for the Spirit in the life of Jesus gives this preface: "In that same hour He rejoiced in the Holy Spirit and said" (Lk 10:21)

This plenary revelation was, with Jesus' revelation of the Spirit, to afford the basis of Trinitarian doctrine. We have everything to gain by constant reflection on the teaching of Jesus. In the messages given by Him to Vassula we reach a summit when we study the revelation He makes of the Father, when we meet the words spoken to her by the Father. Here is the answer to the question raised by a great theologian, Fr. Karl Rahner, on the failure of Catholics to make the Holy Trinity relevant to their lives. Jesus fully understood means that we advert fully and consciously to His Father whom He gives us as our Father. Jesus cannot be understood save in His mission from the Father. It is not to God primarily that He introduces us but to the Father. His revelation of Himself is intrinsically linked with the revelation of the Father.

Have we neglected the Father? Should we not then listen to one who speaks with such cogency about Him? Even a cursory look at the writings thus far published in her name will show the reader a most remarkable series of prayers addressed to God the Father. Vassula was told by the Father, "You are Mine. I created you. I love you. You are My seed." She began very soon to learn the prayers to the Father from Jesus. These prayers now constitute a unique treasury of Christian piety - using that word in its very best sense. Let us take the very first:

"Help me Father and lead me to your pastures of repose, where everlasting pure water flows. Be my light to show me the way; with you, by your side will I walk; with you illuminating me, will I talk. Father, beloved, remain within me to give me peace, to feel your love..."[2]

Another which Jesus taught Vassula was for those in perdition:

"O Holy Father, by your power and with your mercy I implore you, gather all your sheep; forgive them and let them return to your beloved home; look upon them as your children, and with your hand bless them. Amen."[3]

At intervals there follow very moving examples of which we may choose these as typical:

"My Father, lead me wherever your will wishes me to go. Allow me to live in your light and warm my heart, that it may glow, giving warmth on those who approach me. Blessed be your name for giving me all these graces, in spite of my nothingness. Blessed be your name for the good you have done to me, and the mercy you have shown me, lifting me near Your Heart. Amen."[4]

"Beloved Father, purify me with your Son's blood; Father, purify me with your Son's body, beloved Father, hold away the evil spirit that now tempts me. Amen."[5]

"O heavenly Father, Father of love, come to us, delivering us from evil. Father, love us and allow us to abide in your light. Do as your Heart desires. May your name be glorified. Amen."[6]

Very often in such prayers Jesus invites Vassula to pray with him. In one instance he invited her thus:

"Come now, let us join in prayer, a prayer to the Father for unity: 'Father, I come to you, and ask you to enlighten My sheep. Enlighten them to find peace and love in unity. Amen."[7]

"Heavenly Father, may I glorify you; redeem your children from evil; may they be in your light, may their hearts open and with your mercy receive them. Amen."[8]

The Father speaks directly to Vassula. He intervened in a Trinitarian dialogue with her. Jesus is addressing her:

"Your laments and your supplications suddenly broke the deathly stillness surrounding you and your terrified cries pierced the heavens, reaching the Holy Trinity's ears.. 'My child!' The Father's voice full of joy resounded through all heaven."

After this the Son spoke and He was followed by a message from the Holy Spirit.

In December 1992, the Father gave Vassula lengthy messages. Before a meeting in Australia He spoke thus to her:

"Tell them that I am the most tender Father; tell them how I lean to reach them now. Love and loyalty now descend to embrace all of you, to renew you, to revive you and lift you up from the lethargy that covers this earth; do not say I am too far to reach, unmoved by your misery and unresponsive to your calls; if the flames lick up your countries and fires devour the people of the earth it is all due to the great apostasy that seized nation after nation infiltrating in the heart of My law; this apostasy beggared you and made you believe you are fatherless..how I pity you! O generation, for how long must I wait? My warnings and My calls echo the earth and though My grief is acute and My justice now brimming over, I can still relent and I can accept the homage you would offer Me; I am ready to forgive you through the blood shed by My Son and through His sacrifice, if you take My words to heart. I who created you out of love ask you: will I hear from you your cry of repentance? Daughter, glorify Me and reveal My face with love to everyone."

In another lengthy message at that time the Father, despite the failure of response to His appeals, could say:

"Yes I am pouring out My Holy Spirit now to remind you of your true foundations and that all of you are My seed; but today My seed is filled with dead words..I am the Holy One who held you first; for how long will your soul resist those eyes who saw you first? and for how long will your soul deny My distressed calls? Many of you are still fondling the Abomination of Desolation in the most profound domain of your soul; can you not see how the viper repeatedly is deceiving you in the same way he deceived Adam and

Eve? Satan is suggesting to you, untiringly and subtly, to cut off all your heavenly bonds that bond you to Me, your Father in heaven; he mesmerized the memory of your soul to make you believe you are fatherless, thus creating a gulf between you and Me, your God; Satan wants to separate you from Me and cut off your umbilical cord that unites you to Me in which rivers of life flow into you, generation you have still not set your minds for Me. When will you decide to return to Me? Do you want to pass this era's threshold by blazing fire, by brimstone and devouring flame? How could your soul trade My glory for a worthless imitation that the evil one offers you daily? Ask Me for your daily bread and I shall give it to you. Why are you all so willing to listen to the viper? You and I know that Satan is the father of lies, then why are you still listening to him? I, your Creator, am your Father and I am calling you back to Me; believe in My distressed calls; will your soul continue to befriend the rebel, or will you deign to come down from your throne and repent? It is for you to decide - there is not much time left. I am reminding you to beware of the false teachers and the false prophets who induce in your soul desolation, and misinterpret the Gospels, telling you that the Holy Spirit is not with you to remind you of your foundations nor of where you came from; they have already made a desolation out of your soul and dug a vast gulf between you and Me, your Father; do not let them expand this desolation in your soul and mislead you into believing I have left you orphans. These false prophets have made out of My Son, Jesus, a liar and out of the Gospels an echoing cymbal, empty with emptiness; they made out of My Word a gaping grave; so beware of those false teachers, who tell you that My Holy Spirit cannot descend to perform in you miracles and wonders; beware of them who condemn My Holy Spirit who in your days more than anytime, reminds you of your foundations; beware of them who keep up the outward appearance of religion but reject the inner power of it, the inner power that is My Holy Spirit; and if anyone of you is calumniated and dejected because you are witnessing to the truth, turn to your Holy Mother. She will console your soul and provide you with courage; if the world inflicts on you impressive wounds, turn to your Mother and she will dress your wounds with her maternal love and affection; like she took care of My beloved Son, your Holy Mother will take care of you too; in your misery and distress she comes flying to you and takes you into her Heart, that same Heart who conceived your Saviour; your Holy Mother in heaven will teach you to enlarge My kingdom on earth by teaching you to love Me. So let love be the principle of your life; let love be your root. Allow Me, your Father, to bond you to Me; allow Me to touch your soul; come to Me and thrust yourself into My arms. What greater bliss than being held by those hands that created you? Place your ear on My mouth, that mouth that breathed in you through your nostrils life, and from the dust of the soil I revived you to conquer the earth; I touched you and

asked you to listen to My Word since then; come, you must set your heart
right, renounce the iniquities that stain your soul and with all your heart
hallow My Name."

Like one of the passages quoted in the chapter on the Holy Spirit this text must
surely find a place in the anthologies of spiritualite. It will meet the criteria of the
expert theologian and strike a sure chord in the depths of every Christian heart.

We many end this chapter with a prayer to the Father which is particularly dear to
Vassula:

"Father, blessed be Your Name since Your Beloved Son Jesus Christ came
to the world not to condemn it, but to save the world. Have Mercy upon us,
look at Your Son's Holy Wounds, that are wide open now and remember the
price He has paid for us to redeem all of us. Remember His Sacred Wounds
and the two Hearts You Yourself united in Love and who suffered together,
this One of the Immaculate Conception and Your Beloved Son. O Father,
remember His Promise now and send us the Advocate in full force, the Holy
Spirit of Truth, to remind the world of the Truth and of Your Son's docility,
humbleness, obedience and great love. Father, the time has come, when the
reign of division cries out for Peace and Unity. The time has come that Your
Son's wounded Body cries out for Righteousness, that of which the world has
not known yet, but through the Immaculate Heart of Mary and the Sacred
Heart of Jesus give us Precious Father this Peace in our hearts and fulfil the
Scriptures by fulfilling Your Beloved Son's Prayer to You that we may all
be one, one in the Divine Holy Trinity so that we worship and praise You,
all around one single Tabernacle. Amen."[9]

Notes:

1.   J. Galot, S.J., *Pour une Théologie du Père*, in *Esprit et Vie*, 38 (1984) 497-503; 49, 661-
      669; F.X. Durrwell, *Le Père: Dieu et son Mystère*, Paris, 1987; Dictionnaire de Spiritualite
      XII, *Paternité de Dieu*, W. Marchel, J. Ansaldi, 413-437; *Concilium* 163 March 1981
      (several articles); *Lumiere et Vie* 104 (1971) (several articles); ample bibliography including
      recent biblical studies in M. O'Carroll, *God the Father, Our Father*, in Festschrift Heinrich
      Beck, Bamberg 1993; cf. also articles *Abba* and *Father*, in M. O'Carroll, *Trinitas*,
      Wilmington 1987 1f, 107f; id., *Verbum Caro*, Collegeville, 1992, article *Abba* 1f;

2.   7 September, 1986, Volume I, page 2;

3.   7 March, 1987, Volume I, page 53;

4.   1 May, 1987, Volume I, page 88;

5.   15 May, 1987, Volume I, page 100;

6. 19 May, 1987, Volume I, page 108;

7. The reader is reminded of the prayer for unity through the Two Hearts quoted in chapter 7. There is also a prayer spoken directly to the Father by Jesus for the unified Easter "Am I, Father to drink one more season of the cup of division or will they unify the Feast of Easter alleviating part of my pain and sorrow?..." 25 October, 1991, Volume II, page 387;

8. 25 May, 1987, Volume I, page 115;

9. 25 March, 1991, Volume II, page 298f; Much has been made by critics of Vassula about what she hears from Jesus on His relationship with the Father, and likewise with the Holy Spirit. Take this instance, "Pray that my fold be one, as I and the Father are one and the same." (29 March, 1989); or again, "Unite and be one as I and the Father are one and the same." (26 July, 1989); or, in regard to the Holy Spirit, "anyone who rejects the works of My Holy Spirit is rejecting Me for the Holy Spirit and I are one and the same." (11 October, 1988). Let the reader recall first the words of Jesus Himself "I and the Father are one" (Jn 10:30), "If you knew Me you would know My Father also" (Jn 8:19), "He who has seen Me has seen the Father." (Jn 14:9).

The French theologian René Laurentin, rightly interprets these statements of Vassula's as acceptable in the light of authentic Christian doctrine, that the three divine Persons are one in substance, distinct in Person. He does question the French and Italian translations, which unfortunately may lead to confusion.

Some further reflections are in order. First, Jesus was instructing a person wholly ignorant of theology. He wished to teach her His divinity clearly and fully. He knew full well that He was later to enlighten her, as readers of the message will make clear, on the separate interventions of each Person in her life. Is there any contemporary writer who so repeatedly, clearly and cogently, records the interventions of the three Persons as their sanctifying work continues. Nor let the reader forget the advice of Benedict XIV that any book must be judged as a whole, not by extracts taken out of context, isolated from the whole thought-content of the work. The thought content of Vassula's writings is splendidly Trinitarian.

Objection has been made likewise to the fact that Jesus has spoken of Himself as Father of Vassula. This is to forget the important truth of circumincession or perichoresis, which shows how the three divine Persons communicate with each other, may, up to a point, share mutually their attributes. Thus the Church speaks of the Holy Spirit in a great hymn *Veni Pater Pauperum*. Our divine Lord in the prophecy of Isaiah (9:5) is designated "Wonder-Counsellor, Mighty-God, Eternal Father, Prince of Peace." The risen Jesus appearing to the Apostles spoke to them thus, "Children have you any fish?" (Jn 21:5)

Another phrase picked up and held against Vassula is "Many of you tend to forget that I am Spirit and that you too are spirit." First it would be to manifest total ignorance of the writings of Vassula if one were to think that they deny that Christ is the eternal Son of God in the flesh. Her very core doctrine of the Sacred Heart cries out against such misinterpretation; so do the many passages where there is question of the physical suffering of Jesus, in His historical existence and in His Mystical Body. When Jesus said that unless we eat His flesh and drink His blood we shall not have life in us (Jn 6:53), he was not denying that He also had a human soul.

Vassula has felt the Eucharist in the sense of the flesh of Christ. This should be an object of thanksgiving for all with the faith. That it should be held against her is an intrusion into the sacred domain of personal communication with the Lord. Miracles of the Eucharist, well known as that at Lanciano, recently in the Orthodox Church in Amaan, Jordan reveal the same act of divine condescension.;

APPENDIX I

THROUGH THE HEART OF THE MOTHER
WE DISCOVER THE LOVE OF THE SAVIOUR

His Holiness Pope John Paul II

(On September 22, 1986, the Holy Father received in a special audience the participants of the Fatima Symposium. To the group which was led by Jaime Cardinal Sin, the Holy Father spoke this message:)

Dear Friends in Christ,

1. I am pleased to welcome all of you who have taken part in the International Symposium on the Alliance of the Hearts of Jesus and Mary that was held this past week in Fatima. I wish to greet in a special way Cardinal Sin, the President of your Symposium, and together with him all who were responsible for formulating and carrying out the specific plans of your week of theological study.

The title of your Symposium was taken from my Angelus Address of September 15, 1985, when I made reference to that "admirable alliance of hearts" of the Son of God and of His Mother. We can indeed say that devotion to the Sacred Heart of Jesus and to the Immaculate Heart of Mary has been an important part of the "sensus fidei" of the People of God during recent centuries. These devotions seek to direct our attention to Christ and to the role of His Mother in the mystery of Redemption, and, though distinct, they are interrelated by reason of the enduring relation of love that exists between the Son and His Mother.

2. Much research has been done on devotion to the Sacred Heart of Jesus. Hence you have made it your specific aim to reflect upon devotion to the Immaculate Heart of Mary in the perspective of Sacred Scripture and Tradition, while at the same time concentrating on the intimate link that unites the hearts of Jesus and His Mother. Devotion to the Heart of Mary cannot be traced to the early centuries of Christian history, though the Heart

of Mary is indeed mentioned in the Gospel of Luke. There are some references to the Heart of the Mother of God in the commentaries upon the Scriptures by the Fathers of the Church, but for the most part it was not until the seventeenth century that under the influence of Saint John Eudes this devotion became widespread. In our own century we see that the message of Our Lady of Fatima, the consecration of the world in 1942 to the Immaculate Heart of Mary by my predecessor Pope Pius XII, and theological initiatives such as your own, have helped us to appreciate the importance of this devotion.

It is worthy of note that the Decree by which Pope Pius XII instituted for the universal Church the celebration in honour of the Immaculate Heart of Mary states: "With this devotion the Church renders the honour due to the Immaculate Heart of the Blessed Virgin Mary, since under the symbol of this heart she venerates with reverence the eminent and singular holiness of the Mother of God and especially her most ardent love of God and Jesus her Son and moreover her maternal compassion for all those redeemed by the divine Blood" (S.R.C., 4 May 1944; AAS 37, 1945, p.50). Thus it can be said that our devotion to Mary's Immaculate Heart expresses our reverence for her maternal compassion both for Jesus and for all of us her spiritual children, as she stood at the foot of the Cross.

I presented this same thought in my first Encyclical *Redemptor Hominis*, in which I pointed out that from the first moment of the Redemptive Incarnation "under the special influence of the Holy Spirit, Mary's Heart, the Heart of both a virgin and a mother, has always followed the work of her Son and has gone out to all those whom Christ has embraced and continues to embrace with inexhaustible love" (No.22).

3. We see symbolized in the heart of Mary her maternal love, her singular sanctity and her central role in the redemptive mission of her Son. It is with regard to her special role in her Son's mission that devotion to Mary's Heart has prime importance, for through love of her Son and of all humanity she exercises a unique instrumentality in bringing us to Him.

The act of entrusting to the Immaculate Heart of Mary that I solemnly performed at Fatima on May 13, 1982, and once again on March 25, 1984 at the conclusion of the Extraordinary Holy Year of the Redemption, is based upon this truth about Mary's maternal love and particular intercessory role. If we turn to Mary's Immaculate Heart, she will surely "help us to conquer the menace of evil, which so easily takes root in the hearts of the people of today, and whose immeasurable effects already weigh down upon our modern world and seem to block the paths towards the future" (No.3).

Our act of consecration refers ultimately to the Heart of her Son, for as the Mother of Christ she is wholly united to His redemptive mission. As at the marriage feast of Cana, when she said "Do whatever He tells you", Mary directs all things to her Son, who answers our prayers and forgives our sins. Thus by dedicating ourselves to the Heart of Mary we discover a sure way to the Sacred Heart of Jesus, symbol of the merciful love of our Saviour.

The act of entrusting ourselves to the Heart of Our Lady establishes a relationship of love with her in which we dedicate to her all that we have and are. This consecration is practised essentially by a life of grace, of purity, of prayer, of penance that is joined to the fulfilment of all the duties of a Christian, and of reparation for our sins and the sins of the world.

My esteemed friends, I encourage you to continue your scholarly efforts to promote among the People of God a better understanding of devotion to the Hearts of the Son and of His Mother. I thank you for your presence here and I assure you of my prayers for your worthy endeavours. In the love of the Hearts of Jesus and Mary I impart to all of you my Apostolic Blessing.

APPENDIX II

Vassula Rydén

PART I

That all may be one, even as thou,
Father, in me and I in thee. (Jn 17:21)

If our Lord had not allowed me to touch His Heart and make me witness the Riches within It, if He had not bestowed on me innumerable favours, I should not have had the courage nor the strength, in these perilous times, to continue the work He has given me in tranquillity and with such peace of mind. I would not have endured either the trials, the oppositions, the false witnesses, the criticism, nor the assaults of the devil if God had not showered me with a downpour of extraordinary favours to aid me in my mission, and enable me thus to surmount them.

In the beginning the persecutions troubled me, but gradually God helped me to overcome them so that He thrusts me into the heart of the world and to be His Echo.

Before I begin writing anything about these extraordinary favours, I would like to mention immediately, that I had never sought to obtain a divine revelation, (since to begin with, I never knew they existed). I had never heard either that God could manifest Himself in such special ways to "speak" so intimately with His people after the Scriptures. Since I never sought God and was not interested in religion how then would I desire a private revelation?

I am not a professional writer and it will be difficult for me to describe this magnificent work of supernatural charity, but may it please God to guide my thoughts and my words to make it possible to clarify and bring to light some of the many things that are to be said and of which God revealed to me.

Father Marie-Eugène de l'Enfant Jésus, a Carmelite Father, in his book "I am a Daughter of the Church", tells us the following about extraordinary favours:

"Extraordinary favours are produced by a direct action of God that eliminates all co-operation on the part of the soul other than a passive receptivity.

Imaginary visions and intellectual visions, declare the two Saints, (Saint John of the Cross and Saint Teresa of Avila), are produced in the faculties without any activity on their part, being communicated to them in a supernatural way... extraordinary lights, otherwise called intellectual visions of spiritual substances and revelations, are infused by God directly into the intellect.

"...the first sign, negative it is true, but important, of the divine origin of extraordinary favours is that they present nothing that is contrary to reason or to faith. God adapts Himself, even in His extraordinary modes of acting, to the natural order that governs us. Visions and divine revelations do not shock. In them God speaks our language. Everything about them is proportion, sincerity and truth, balance and simplicity.

"On the other hand, pathological disturbances and the action of the devil declare themselves by lack of proportion, by strangeness, by ridiculous details, by pride, which shows itself in the care one takes to be seen by others or to surprise them, and by lies that very soon are caught in their own snare. When God manifests Himself, He speaks the language of the good man who is a good Christian; the devil and the mentally sick pose as supermen.

"The positive signs are more convincing if not more clear. One of them alone does not constitute a proof. Each one is an indication; the convergence of all engenders certitude. Although adapting Himself to the human, God could not conceal His transcendence. In extraordinary manifestations, this expresses itself by a certain majesty, a strength, an authority that produce in the soul reverence and humility."

Saint Teresa says that the first and the surest sign that locutions come from God, is

"...the sense of power and authority which they bear with them, both in themselves and in the actions which follow them." (VI Mansions, iii; Peers, II, 280)

I had heard now and then, especially from the clergy during the course of this revelation, that God does not speak anymore as He did with the prophets of the Old Testament, because all that He had to say was said through His Son Jesus Christ, and Revelation was closed at the death of the last apostle. Yet I know now that God, does not ask our permission to manifest Himself when He wants and feels free to reveal Himself on whom He wishes without asking anyone's consent.

Later on I discovered that private or prophetic revelations during history have been numerous. Saint Margaret Mary's revelations were meant to spread devotion to the

Sacred Heart; the apparitions to Saint Bernadette set crowds moving to Lourdes. Then there are many others, such as Saint Brigid of Sweden, Saint Catherine of Rue du Bac, Saint Catherine of Sienna, and I could go on and on.

With the help of Our Lady, these passages written here quoting Saints, were given me to clarify the mystical language and phenomena occurring in this prophetic revelation.

Let us hear what Saint John of the Cross, one of the greatest mystics, tells us on supernatural communications:

"God brings man to perfection according to the way of man's own nature, working what is lowest and most exterior up to what is most interior and highest. First, then, He perfects his bodily senses... And, when these senses are in some degree prepared, He is wont to perfect them still further, by bestowing on them certain supernatural favours and gifts, in order to confirm them the more completely in that which is good, offering them certain supernatural communications, such as visions of saints or holy things, in corporeal shape, the sweetest perfumes, locutions, and exceeding great delights of touch, wherewith sense is greatly confirmed in virtue and withdrawn from a desire for evil things. And besides this He continues at the same time to perfect the interior bodily senses...

"And, when these are prepared by this natural exercise, God is wont to enlighten and spiritualize them still more by means of certain supernatural visions, which are those that we are here calling imaginary; wherein, as we have said, the spirit, at the same time, profits greatly, for both kinds of vision help to take away its grossness and gradually to reform it.

"and after this manner God continues to lead the soul step by step till it reaches that which is the most interior of all." (Ascent, Book II, xxii, 162-3).

He clarifies that God's chosen soul need not be saintly to receive extraordinary favours. Saint Theresa says:

"...there are many saintly people who have never known what it is to receive a favour of this kind, and there are others who receive such favours, although they are not saintly." (VI Mansions, ix; Peers, II, 314 ff).

She also remarks that rejection of favours must not turn to scorn of them, because supernatural favours, they too are a means or even a way to go to God. God's gift must be respected and used. Saint John of the Cross says:

"For, since they are a means and manner whereby God guides such souls, there is no reason for thinking ill of them or for being alarmed or scandalized by them." (Ibid., xxii; 172).

Here is another opinion that Saint Maximus the Confessor expresses:

"A soul can never reach knowledge of God, if God Himself does not condescend to it and touch it, raising it to Himself. And the human mind could never soar high enough to receive Divine light, if God Himself did not lift it up, as far as the human mind can be lifted up, and did not enlighten it with Divine illumination." (Philokalia 1,31).

Since I had never studied theology nor read the Scriptures or had any proper catechetical instruction, hardly went to church or prayed, through lack of interest, from where then would all the theology found in this revelation come? From where would all the information concerning today's Great Apostasy in the Church come?

One of the objections raised during this revelation by certain critics was that I was not led by the Holy Spirit but by an evil spirit, who uses my hand as in automatic writing, a form of spiritism. In other words, the communications I am receiving, do not come from God but from another obscure source, therefore, the evil one.

In that case from November 1985, either Satan lost his mind or got converted, attracting those who read "True Life in God", (the title given by God for these revelations), to return to God, return to the Holy Sacraments, learn to pray the rosary daily, obey the Pope, fast twice a week on bread and water and go to confession!

But we know that Satan did not lose his mind or got converted, and he would use any means to stop people from converting and returning to God. He would use even good people to combat what comes from God's Infinite Mercy and is one means for our salvation.

He would make their zeal turn into fanaticism giving him thus a sturdy foothold, Satan's next step would be to work in them and feed their weak points. He will dull their senses of right and wrong to confuse them, so they would take the blessings from God for a curse, the Truth for a lie, the glory of God for a worthless imitation, the loving merciful calls for a malicious trap from the evil one. Satan would have succeeded in blinding them to the Truth flashing in front of them, and all they would see is darkness.

This is what Saint Symeon replied to his opponents that one should know the WORD here below, "not only from words, but in truth and through the working of grace."

(Eth 10, 478, 480).   "They do not believe that in our generation there can be someone who is moved and influenced by the divine spirit, who perceptibly sees and apprehends Him.   For every man judges them by his own condition, by what he is himself - in virtue or in vice." (Cap 1.85)

Knowing that Satan would influence people to judge me wrongly on this point, God said to me on the 8th November 1988:

> "...today you shall write down My Message with your own handwriting, so that those who have not yet fully understood that I have filled you with My graces, may understand that I have also given you the grace of hearing My Voice; allow me to dictate to you today, hear Me and write..."

Then He gave me His message all in my normal handwriting, and at the end of the message, He said:

> "This, Vassula, is also for those who think that your hand is pushed by Me without you hearing Me at all.   Some of them would not have believed that I, the Lord, am inspiring you.   Now we will continue the way I like it..."

Then the Lord continued His message with the writing that He chose and that pleases Him.

But I would also like to add what Saint Teresa of Avila says on physical phenomena. She shows us that not only one member of the body could be arrested by God, but the entire body.

This is what she says:

> "Do you suppose it causes but little perturbation to a person in complete possession of his senses when he experiences these transports of the soul? We have read in some authors that the body is transported as well as the soul, without knowing whither it is going, or who is bearing it away... Can any means of resisting this be found?   None whatever: on the contrary, resistance only makes matters worse.   This I know from a certain person... it must realize that it is no longer its own mistress, and so the violence with which it is transported becomes markedly greater.   This person, therefore, decided to offer no more resistance than a straw does when it is lifted up by amber (if you have ever observed this)... And, speaking of straw, it is a fact that a powerful man cannot bear away a straw more easily than this great and powerful Giant of ours can bear away this spirit." (VI Mansions, v; Peers, II, 293)

We could call it an attack of supernatural power, or a transcendent force.

Here is a striking experience of how God allows men to <u>touch</u> and <u>feel Him</u>; this passage is taken from the experiences of Saint Symeon and from the book "In the Light of Christ" by Archbishop BASIL KRIVOCHEINE: God gives Symeon His almighty hand and then removes it: "I give You thanks with my whole heart, because You did not avert Your gaze from me when I was lying in darkness, down below. Your divine hand touched me (...)."

From the beginning the devil took all sorts of ways and is still using all sorts of tactics to stop me from receiving God's favours, favours that united me and many others to God and have helped our souls to grow spiritually and in His Love.

Father Marie-Eugène clarifies even more how Satan, in his jealousy reacts when he loses a soul. This is what he says:

"Among the powers of evil, Satan stands out as a subtle and powerful strategist. His hateful jealousy cannot remain unmoved in the face of this soul that is about to escape him definitively and very soon to do him considerable harm. Such a soul has become his personal enemy. And so he uses against it all his resources. To the type of action that we have already mentioned, he will certainly join a more exterior activity. In the external domain of the senses, he finds all his best means and a certain superiority. To stop the progress of the soul and paralyse its action, the devil will enlist both persons and things. He will turn everything to his profit, the passions of men as well as their good desires, as also the laws of nature, which he will disturb in order to create agitation and trouble, contradiction and persecutions."

Some of the readers who criticised these messages with excessive severity were those who disjoined paragraphs, sentences and words, tearing them out of their context. For these, I would say, that it is important to bear in mind the teaching of Benedict XIV, in the Constitution which he prefixed to the Index:

"We give warning that it must be diligently remembered that a correct judgement of the true sense of an author cannot be arrived at unless the book be read all through, in all its parts, and the things found in different places be compared one with the other, and unless the whole scope and end of the author be attentively considered and examined. The author is not to be judged by one or other proposition torn from its context, or disjoined from other propositions to be found within the same book. For it frequently happens that what an author says carelessly or obscurely in one part of his work is explained clearly, fully, and distinctly in another part; so that the darkness which seemed to conceal something wrong is afterwards altogether dissipated, and the proposition is seen to be free of all error."

In the beginning of the revelation, my soul was confused and many times perplexed by God's choice. Why would he come to me and allow me to taste Him? Why would He reveal to me His entire Face and adorn my soul with the intimate knowledge of Himself?

When I asked Him, He simply said:

"I have not chosen you because of your merits since you have none; I chose you because you are wretched and a nothing. In your wretchedness I will reveal My Mercy, in your nothingness, My Greatness and that I AM. In your frailty I will reveal My Power and My Authority. So remain nothing and let Me do My Will."

In other words grace is not earned. As Scriptures say:

"There is a remnant chosen by grace. By grace, you notice, nothing therefore to do with good deeds, or grace would not be grace at all." (Rm 11:5,6)

God has a different pedagogy from ours. The messages in the beginning especially are very repetitive, but this is His divine technique for teaching a soul. Sometimes one or two words were given me and the lesson was over.

Some of the messages appear to be almost like a telegram. By this I mean, that the sentences given were brief, containing only the main context. My "training" and teaching from my angel and from the Lord, might put off any reader reading these first messages. They might even have the temptation to put them aside saying that they could not be from divine Wisdom because they sound like children's simple language, with a touch of naivety in them.

But although these messages would appear very simple, in reality they are not, because even if one brief word is uttered by the Lord, He would let the soul penetrate into that word to discover inside it many more profound teachings going into the depths of many truths.

With this transcendent light, my soul would perceive insights beyond my natural understanding, for example, of Scriptures. These insights that God would favour me with would appear as though He had allowed me to read His mind, but then He would give me only the things He would want me to see and understand.

Here is how Saint Teresa explains this phenomena:

> "In a genuine locution one single word may contain a world of meaning such as the understanding alone could never put rapidly into human language." (Ibid)

> "...the divine words instruct us at once, without any lapse of time, and by their means we can understand things which it would probably take us a month to make up ourselves." (Life, xxv; Peers, I, 159).

> "...frequently, not only can words be heard, but, in a way which I shall never be able to explain, much more can be understood than the words themselves convey and this without any further utterance." (VI Mansions, iii; Peers, II, 284).

Father Marie-Eugène would describe this infusion of understanding like a parchment which unrolls itself revealing its riches. This is what he says:

> "The faculties are at first dazzles by them. The soul cannot keep its gaze fixed on the vision. But the light that is imprinted in it and that it will never forget becomes for it like a luminous parchment which, unrolling progressively reveals its riches; or like a beacon, which at frequent intervals casts its shafts of light over the road the soul is travelling."

I noticed how God lowered Himself to adapt to me. He would have sometimes my expressions. He would use a vocabulary I would understand. But now and then it would please Him to use words I never use myself.

Father Marie Eugène says the following:

> "God's direct action, being thus grounded in the human of which it makes use, is marvellously adapted to the psychological life of the soul. This adaption of God should be underlined as an important characteristic of His interventions."

> "God, who consent to speak the language of human signs to give us His light, pushes condescendence to the point of adapting Himself to our temperaments and our particular needs in the choice of these signs, so as to reach us more surely. For a faith that has kept its purity and its simplicity, He will speak in a language of external brilliant signs that will make faith vibrate. For a faith that rationalism has rendered prudent and critical, He will have a more intellectual language. Visions and revelations will be more numerous for the Spanish sixteenth century. To reach and touch our modern minds that tend

to scepticism, God seems to leave aside the language of extraordinary external signs, to infuse His light directly in souls. Fewer extraordinary favours, but gifts of pure and dry contemplation distributed more widely: thus divine mercy, adapting itself, descends to the spiritual poverty of our time.

"The care God takes to adapt Himself to us is manifested with touching delicacy in the extraordinary interventions themselves. Visions and words reveal the transcendence of their origin by the weight they bear and by their effects; but they are so simple, so human, so near to us by their constitutive elements that they do not disturb nor shock us. Through them God comes down near to the soul and makes Himself known as God, but by making himself into Man. To speak to the Hebrews, he uses the picturesque richness of their symbols in order thus to fix His teachings in their soul. It is in the "patois" of Lourdes that the Blessed Virgin answers Bernadette's question and reveals that she is the Immaculate Conception. The divine and the human, the transcendent and the ordinary are so admirably united in the extraordinary manifestation, that the simple harmony which results becomes a sign of its supernatural origin."

I had noticed that some people were confused by the intimacy of our Lord or by the sweetness of the language. They confuse the divine love with the human love, the spiritual marriage with the human marriage. Others cannot accept the fact that Jesus lowers Himself even to become a beggar for our love. There are pages and pages I would have like to quote from Saint John of the Cross, Saint Teresa of Avila, Saint Symeon the new theologian, Saint Maximus the Confessor, Nicholas Cabasilas and the Fathers of the Church to show how deep their intimacy with our Lord was, and how the Lord was intimate with them. But it would take several books, so here are only a few words, first from Father Marie-Eugène, then of Saint John of the Cross.

Father Marie-Eugène writes:

"Spiritual marriage is a contract in good and due form. God gives Himself definitively and reveals Himself constantly in an intellectual vision. There is no ring, however, to seal the union, but rather a nail which attaches to the Cross. Nor is there a call to nuptial intimacy, but rather an invitation to work like a true bride for the honour of the Spouse. The tranquil possession of God in this union is not a goal nor a coming to rest; it is a means for working more efficaciously. Christ Jesus espouses souls here below only to associate them more closely to His works of His Church.

"...everything comes to the souls from its union with the Beloved. Saint John of the Cross insists so much on this truth that one might think that the soul had already arrived at spiritual marriage. 'Our flowery bed', sings the bride in the fifteenth stanza; Saint John of the Cross comments:

"This flowery bed is the bosom and the love of the Beloved, wherein the soul, that has become the bride, is now united; the which bed is flowery for her by reason of the union and bond which has now been made between the two, by means whereof are communicated to her the virtues, graces and gifts of the Beloved." (Ibid., st. xv; 87).

Father Marie-Eugène writes:

"In the centre and depth of the soul, in its pure and inmost substance, the Word and Spouse dwells secretly and in silence; He is there as in his own house, on His own bed of repose. He rules it as master, and holds the soul intimately and closely united to Himself. Thus He makes the soul His, and the soul can call Him its Spouse. Does not the love given it by the single operation of the Holy Trinity identify it with the Word Son of God? It is daughter by grace as the Word is Son by nature. By its union with the Word, it enters into the cycle of the Triune life and participates in the divine operations. It breathes the Holy Spirit by grace as the Word does by nature.

"Deep within, the soul has an experience of the Word-Spouse, the source of all its good. He rests in the shadows, asleep, it seems. Yet His breathing evinces His presence and His action. What great desires the soul has to know Him! When it begs to enter farther into its depths, it is in truth a more profound penetration and more intimate knowledge of Christ and His mysteries that it longs for.

"The Word-Spouse is the soul's, and the soul is His. This mutual possession and compenetration bring the soul effectively into the deep caverns that are the mysteries of Christ, into that inexhaustible mine with its countless veins enclosing riches ever new. The mysteries that the soul has known by faith, has studied in theology, or penetrated with the simple gaze of its prayer, become more clear in its depths. The light that illumines them, the gaze that grasps them, are no longer from the outside. The experience of love has entered farther into 'the thicket of wisdom,' where the multitude of God's marvellous works are seen under the light of an inner fire.

"This perception ordinarily takes place as a subtle awareness of the presence of the Word in the shadows. The divine Spouse seems to sleep in the bosom of the soul. But the Word, the Spouse, awakens. He appears to move on the bed where He lies.

Saint John of the Cross writes:

"This awakening is a movement of the Word in the substance of the soul, of such greatness and dominion and glory, and of such intimate sweetness, that it seems to the soul that all the balms and perfumed spices and flowers in the world are mingled and shaken and revolved together to give their sweetness; and that all the kingdoms and dominions of the world and all the powers and virtues of Heaven are moved. (Ibid.; 188)

"By this simple movement, the Word, the Spouse of the soul, reveals His intimate secrets, causes His treasures to shine forth, communicates His excellences. In Him all things are life; in Him they live and are and move. Hence, when this great Lord moves, He seems to carry with Him all creation, of which He is the centre. Such is the Spouse who dwells in the inmost substance of the soul, holding it in the sweet and close embrace of His love.

Then I would like to note too what Nicholas Cabasilas (b.c. 1322) says:

"God pours himself out in an ecstasy of love. He does not remain in the Heavens and call to Himself, the servant He loves. No, He Himself descends and searches out for such a servant and comes near, and lets His love be seen, as He seeks what is like Himself. From those who despise Him He does not depart: He shows no anger toward those who defy Him, but follows them to their very doors, and endures all things, and even dies, in order to demonstrate His love. All this is true, but we have not yet declared the highest thing of all: for not merely does God enter into close fellowship with His servants and extend to them His hand, but He has given Himself wholly to us, so that we are and become temples of the living God, and our members are the members of Christ. The head of these members is worshipped by the Cherubim, and these hands and feet are joined to that heart." (Sacrae liturgae interpretatio II, 132)

And in the Mystagogy 24:

"God made Himself a beggar because of His solicitude towards us (...) suffering from His tenderness till the end of times, in proportion of the suffering of each one (...)"

And finally from Saint Symeon the new theologian:

"He embraces me entirely. He gives Himself totally to me, the unworthy one, and I am filled with His love and beauty. I am sated with pleasure, I share in the light (...) For I was searching Him, the One I desired, for Whom I had passion, (...) I was burning, my entire being was aflame. (...)"

And about spiritual marriage:

"For He becomes the Bridegroom each day....and all the souls to which the Creator is joined becomes brides. (...) they are enamoured of the most Beautiful One (...) they inwardly possess God in His fullness, God who has taken form. (Hymns 15, 220-231. (...)"

These excerpts of Saint Symeon the New Theologian were taken from the book called, "In the Light of Christ", written by Archbishop Basil Krivocheine. In his book he says: "Saint Symeon uses the two expressions, 'agape' and 'eros', and apparently does not differentiate between them, although one sees that he speaks of a passionate longing for God." (page 362)

Since I have been accused of blasphemous language probably about Jesus' words to me showing that we are bound in love and that His Cross is our matrimonial bed, my answer to such people is, 'Read the biographies of the saints.' This is what they will find in the autobiography of St. Margaret Mary:

"Immediately a large cross was shown to me, the extremity of which I could not see, but it was all covered with flowers. "Behold the bed of my chaste spouses on which I shall make thee taste all the delights of My pure Love. Little by little these flowers will drop off and nothing will remain but the thorns, which are hidden because of thy weakness."

And then the language in which the Saint speaks of Him:

"My Divine Master gave me to understand that now was the time of our espousals by which He acquired a new right over me, and that I was now doubly bound to love Him with a love of preference. He gave me further to understand that after the manner of the most passionate of lovers, He would, during the time, allow me to taste all that was sweetest and most delightful in the tokens of His love."

I noticed how the Lord delights in simplicity and in the prayer of the heart. The simple dialogue is His delight! Love is exchanged by simple words. This dialogue becomes continual when love has sealed the bonds of union. How many times God showed His joy by these childish words I used that came with a flame of love from my heart:

"You are my joy, my smile, my breath, my life and my bounce!"

And Saint Symeon writes:

"Come my breath and my life. Come consolation of my contemptible soul.
Come, my joy, my glory and my delight forever."

The Lord said to us:

I am the vine, you are the branches. (Jn 15:5)

Since God is love, God in this revelation, that He named: 'True Life in God', calls
us to Him to unite with Him and in Him. God establishes a close relationship
between Himself, the Creator, and us, His creatures. He desires that this
relationship becomes intimate. He wants the soul to be in Him and He in it, because
through love the two beings who love live one in the other. This is why the Lord
in many of these messages reminds us of this union with two simple words: we, us.
Everything we do should be done together with Him. God wants to conquer the soul
and unite it to Him and place it in Him. He conquers it with love.

Saint John of the Cross stresses that this seduction takes place especially in the
direction of increased envelopment and penetration to the soul's centre:

"Love unites the soul with God, and, the more degrees of love the soul has,
the more profoundly does it enter into God and the more is it centred in Him;
and thus we can say that, as are the degrees of love of God, so are the
centres, each one deeper than another, which the soul has in God.... And
thus the soul which has one degree of love is already in its centre in God,
since one degree of love suffices for a soul to abide in Him through grace.
If it have two degrees of love, it will have entered into another and a more
interior centre with God; and, if it attain to three, it will have entered into the
third. If it attain to the last degree, the love of God will succeed in
wounding the soul even in its deepest centre - that is, in transforming and
enlightening it as regards all the being and power and virtue of the soul, such
as it is capable of receiving, until it be brought into such a state that it
appears to be God. In this state the soul is like the crystal that is clear and
pure; the more degrees of light it receives, the greater concentration of light
there is in it, and this enlightenment continues to such a degree that at last it
attains a point at which the light is centred in it with such copiousness that
it comes to appear to be wholly light, and cannot be distinguished from the
light, for it is enlightened to the greatest possible extent and thus appears to
be light itself." (Living Flame, st. i; Peers III, 23)

And I will end up by these words of Jesus:

> "Happy are the pure in heart: they shall see God." (Mt 5:8)
> "He who loves Me will be loved by My Father, and I will love him and manifest Myself to him... If anyone love Me, he will keep My word, and My Father will love him, and we will come to him and make Our abode with him." (Jn 14:21,23)

APPENDIX II

Vassula Rydén

PART II

The Approach of My Angel

In the beginning one of the first things my guardian angel put on paper was a drawing of a heart; from the centre of the heart he drew a rose as though it was growing out from the heart. Then gently and still to my great astonishment he introduced himself as my guardian angel, Daniel. He left me bewildered but with great joy at the same time. I was so happy that I was almost flying around the house, my feet barely touching the ground and I was repeating loudly: "I am the luckiest person on earth, and I am probably the only person on earth who could communicate in such a way with her angel!"

The following day my angel returned to me as before. I spent endless joyful hours communicating with him. Again, the next day he returned, but his time, to my great surprise, he brought with him a multitude of angels of different choirs. I felt that the gates of heaven were suddenly wide open because I could easily sense this great movement of angels from above. They all appeared excited and happy, just like when someone is expecting something wonderful to happen. From the way they rejoiced, I understood that heaven was having a feast and they were celebrating. Then, the angels all together sang in one voice these words: "A happy event is about to come!" I knew that whatever that event would be, it concerned me directly, but, although I tried hard to guess, I could not tell what it was. This chorus was sung all day long, with the same words and only a few minutes of silence in between this chorus. Every time heaven opened, the angels repeated the same chorus.

The first words my angel pronounced about God were the following: "God is near you and loves you."

I must have wounded the Lord very much this minute, because his words had no effect on me whatsoever. When my angel pronounced these words about God, I remember that I thought it was a normal thing for an angel to say, since angels lived near God. I did not reply and my angel did not add anything more.

Only a few days later, my angel suddenly changed attitude with me and I noticed how very grave he became. In a very solemn voice he asked me to read The Word. I pretended I did not know what The Word meant and asked him the meaning of it. With this, my angel became even more grave telling me that I knew very well what he meant, nevertheless, he told me that it was the Holy Bible. I already had my answer on my tongue and told him I did not have one at home. He said that he knew that I did not have one. He asked me to go and fetch one. Arguing still with him, I said that he was asking me the impossible, because in a Moslem country in which I lived then, (Bangladesh), the book stores did not sell Bibles. He said that I should go immediately to the American School, where my son went, and fetch one from their library. I was debating whether to go or simply stay at home and refuse. The other thing that was embarrassing me was how would my husband and all my friends react to all this. I simply could not see myself standing in front of them with a Bible! Already I was thinking of places in the house where I would hide it, were I to bring one home. But seeing again the grave look on my angel's face I decided to obey him. So I drove to the school and saw several Bibles on the shelves. I chose one and brought it home and opened to read it just as my angel had asked me to do. My eyes fell on the psalms: I read, but could not understand a single word. This was a sign from God, showing me how blind I was.

The Purification

My angel came back to me still very grave and reproached me for certain acts I had done in my lifetime that displeased God very much. Then he reproached me of how I had thrown at God's Face His gifts, gifts that He had given me but that I had not appreciated at all.

With this he started to remind me and show me the sins I had never confessed. He showed them to me as on a screen. He reminded me of the event and of how much it offended God. But the most severe reproaches I received were about the rejection of God's gifts. My angel told me that it was a great offence to God to deny and throw away His gifts. He made me see my sins with the eyes of God, the way God sees them and not the way we see them. They were so monstrous that I despised myself while weeping bitterly. This state I was put in was, I understood later on, a grace from God so that I would repent sincerely. I was shown my sins so crystal clear, exposing the interior of my soul so openly, that it was as if I was turned inside out. I suddenly realized how Adam and Eve must have felt after they had sinned, when God approached them in His Light, facing them. My soul was uncovered and at display; it felt naked, loathsome and ugly. I could only tell my angel between my sobs that I do not deserve a decent death, and that being like I am, so utterly wicked, I should die and be cut into small pieces and thrown away to the hyenas.

This purification must have gone on for almost a week. It felt like fire, a cleansing fire purifying the interior of my soul, and it was a very painful experience indeed.

The Our Father Taught By Our Creator

After this experience that had left me shattered, God our Eternal Father revealed Himself to me. I did not see Him with the eyes of my soul, as I used to see my angel, but I knew it was Him and heard Him. I remember that my reaction was one like, "ah, it is God and He can help us now!" This is why He asked me, "do you really believe I can help you?" And I answered Him, "yes!" then I remember going near the window saying to Him, "look! look how the world has become!" I wanted to show Him how the world had become. God did not comment but asked me to pray to Him the Our Father. I prayed to Him the Our Father while He was with me, listening, and when I finished He said that He was not pleased with the way I said it because I prayed it too fast. So I repeated it all over again to him but slower. Again he told me that He was not pleased because I was moving. He asked me to pray it again. I prayed it again and in the end God said that it was not satisfying Him still. I prayed it several times but every time He said He was not pleased. I started to wonder, I started to wonder whether He was making me pray all the Our Fathers that I had not been praying all these years in one single day! I had started in the morning and now it was night. Suddenly He was satisfied, for every sentence I pronounced, He said, "good!", with delight. I will try to give an example to explain what really happened:

If you were visited one day by a relative you had never met before because he lived in another country; in the beginning of your encounter you might tend to feel distant to him and maybe formal. But the more time would go by during that day you would seem to feel closer to him than in the very beginning, and so by the end of that day you would notice that a sympathy developed in you that was not there before.

And this is how it was with my first encounter with God. When I was praying the Our Father, to God, in the beginning I was distant, but His visit which lasted the whole day changed me because when I was saying this prayer to Him, I was enjoying His presence and the words I was telling Him took some meaning. He was so fatherly, very tender and very warm. The intonation of His Voice was making me feel so much at ease, that somehow, during that day, instead of responding, "yes Lord," I found myself saying, "yes Dad." I had later on apologized to God for saying, "Dad," but He said that He had taken that word like a jewel. He seemed so very pleased. And that is how finally I realized that God had feelings and that He wanted me to tell Him this prayer with MY HEART.

Satan's Assaults

Before I come into this paragraph I would like to write what Father Marie-Eugène says in his book, "I am a Daughter of the Church," about demoniac attacks.

"What is at stake in this encounter between the human and the divine, the purity of God and the soul's impurity, is too important for the devil not to intervene in it with all the power at his disposal. Yet a little while and the soul purified by the dark night will be secure against his attacks and will be to him a terrible thing. Hence the devil makes use of the advantages he still possesses over it because of its imperfections and its attachments to the sensible. Saint John of the Cross notes that: 'the evil one takes his stand, with great cunning, on the road which leads from sense to spirit.'" (Living Flame, st.iii; Peers, III, 83)

"The darkness of these regions, the soul's disarray, disconcerted as it is by the newness of its experiences and the intensity of its suffering, create conditions particularly favourable to the interventions of the prince of darkness and of lies.

"By certain exterior signs of calm and of deep silence in the senses, the devil easily guesses that the soul is receiving divine communications. Our mystical doctor says:

'Of those favours which come through a good angel God habitually allows the enemy to have knowledge: partly so that he may do that which he can against them according to the measure of justice, and that thus he may not be able to allege with truth that no opportunity is given him for conquering the soul, as he said concerning Job.' (Dark Night, Bk.II, xxiii; Peers, I, 449)

"Such are the facts in the problem of the dark night of the spirit, and the causes that produce it. This night is an encounter, or rather a real combat, organized by loving Wisdom. God establishes His perfect reign in the soul only after taking away its unfitness for the divine and conquering all the forces of evil that have any power over it."

This was so that the reader would understand better why God allows Satan to intervene.

Just after this delightful day I had spent with our Father in Heaven, all the fury of hell broke out! In a very savage way Satan attacked me. The first thing I heard from him sounded more like the growl of a wild animal than a voice. That growl seemed to say, "GOOOO!" I guessed that "go", meant that I should stop having communications with my angel and with God. All distressed I turned around in search of my angel, but Satan seemed to have taken all the space and with great hatred began to call me all sorts of names. He produced such anguishes and such terrors in my soul that I could have died had it not been that God had a plan for me. I never sensed such fury before. I ordered him to go away and this seemed to raise his fury even more. It was like the fury of a madman. Fuming with rage and like someone out of his mind he growled, his voice was very hoarse when he said: "EH? withdraw from here you b....., withdraw, or else, fire in hell does the rest!" I heard myself answering him: "No!" With my "no", I meant that I will NOT LEAVE the presence of God nor my angel's. Then he snapped back that I was cursed and called me all sorts of dirty names.

It is difficult to explain this anguish the devil can infuse in the soul. This phenomenon that occurs is something that although your logic tells you you're not mad, you yourself yet cannot control. This anguish used to come in waves, as if Satan himself were not enough, he sent other demons too to attack me. When they used to attack me it was something frightening growing within me, nothing to do with exterior fear. It was a feeling I was unable to push away.

My poor angel, in these terrible moments, moments that made me believe sometimes I would lose my mind, could only tell me one word, "PRAY!" I prayed and begged my angel to help me come out of this experience, for it seemed to last forever.

The Battle Between My Angel and Satan

As though it was not enough to be tormented in the daytime, Satan came too at nighttime. He would not leave me sleep. Every time I was about to fall asleep, he would try to suffocate me. I sometimes would feel him like an eagle who would put his claws inside my stomach, and squeeze all the breath out of me. I felt the battle around me, I felt how I was in the middle of this battle, between my angel and the devil. Then one day, as if nothing had happened, everything ceased. Satan abandoned his attacks and I had a few days peace. All this experience left me rather weak, but more attached than ever before to my angel.

In my eyes my guardian angel began to be everything, and he filled my life. I clung to him for dear life so to say. I realized how much our guardian angels protected us, loved us, cared for us, guarded us, cried for us, prayed for us, suffered with us and shared everything with us. Sorrows and joys were shared.

To the horror of the devil, since he guessed what God had in store for me, he came back into the scene. Cunning as he is, this time he changed strategy. He used the classical way to deceive me and appeared to me like my angel. He attached a great importance on how to portray God to me. His aim, since he guessed that God would approach me for a mission, was to make me fear God in the wrong way, so that when God's time came to communicate with me, I would run away from Him.

I admit that in the beginning he managed to deceive me and I believed what he said about God, because he used my ignorance to feed my brain with a false image of God. He portrayed God to me as a fearful judge, with little tolerance for His creatures, and that with the slightest error on our part, He would punish us in a terrible way. This went on for a few days.

I came to the stage where I could not discern who was who. I could not tell if I was with my angel or if it was the evil one aping my angel. I had nobody to turn to for consulting or take advice from either. I was quite alone. I also did not want to share this with my husband, for fear of upsetting him. Satan believing he had now the upper hand, started to tighten the knot, by showing signs of evil, wickedness, confusing me. To make things worse, every day that went by, he brought more and more demons with him, to invade me making it very difficult for my guardian angel to protect me. God allowed me to overhear the devil once, while he was giving orders to his angels to go and attack and paralyse me. These fallen angels surrounded me, mocked me, lied to me and called me all sorts of dirty names. They also nick-named me "Pia" but with mockery. God allowed all this to happen, for this too was another way that He made use of, to purify my soul.

My Purification Continues

A few days passed and suddenly my angel asked me to go to the seminary to find a priest and show him the messages. I did exactly as he told me. But I was very disappointed. I had great expectations and what I got was a blow. The priest thought I was going through a psychological crisis and believed I was on the verge of schizophrenia. He wanted to examine both my hands. He took both my hands and analyzed them. I knew what he had in mind, he was trying to find traces of any sort of abnormality in my hands as in certain mental cases. He believed that now God had given him this heavy cross, that was me, to carry. He pitied me and asked me to come any time to see him. I went every second or third day to visit him. I did not like going to him because he treated me as a mental case in the beginning. This went on for about three or four months. The only reason why I persevered in visiting him was so that I should prove to him I was not mental. Finally after some time he realized that I was sane. One day he even said that what I had might be a charisma from God.

My guardian angel in the meantime was leading me towards God and one of the first lessons that he gave me was on discernment. These teachings on discernment infuriated the devil even more because it meant that even though he would appear like the angel of light, I would know the difference.

My angel told me that Jesus will approach me and that his mission (my angel's) was coming towards its end. When I heard this news I was sad. I did not want my angel to leave me. He tried to reason with me explaining that he was only God's servant and that now I should turn towards God. He tried to explain that his mission with me was to take me to God and hand me safely over to Him. But this was all the more painful for me. I could not bear the idea that from one day to the other I would not communicate with my angel.

As my angel Daniel foretold me, one day Jesus came in his place. When he revealed Himself to me, he asked me, "which house is more important, your house or My House?", I answered Him, "Your House." I felt him happy with my reply, He blessed me and left.

Again, instead of my angel, the Lord came to me, and said, "it is I," and when He saw I was hesitating, He said clearly, "It is I, God." But instead of rejoicing I was unhappy. I was missing terribly my angel. I loved my angel deeply and the mere thought that he would not come again because his place would be taken by God was disturbing me. I would like to mention here, what the Lord told me regarding the love I had for my angel. He said that no one ever loved his angel as much as I have, and he hoped to say one day to me these words: "No man ever loved Me in your era as much as you have."

Now my angel kept in the background. God asked me, "do you love Me?" I said I did. He did not blame me for not loving Him enough, but instead He said very gently, "Love Me more."

The other time the Lord revealed Himself to me He told me, "revive My House," and again, "renew My House." I could not remember replying, but I knew that what He was asking me was impossible.

The following days were visits either by my angel or Jesus, sometimes both at the same time. My angel was preaching to me, he was asking me to make peace with God. When he asked me that, I was very surprised, and I told him that I was not at war with God, so how was I to make peace with Him?

God asked me again to love Him. He asked me to become intimate with Him as I was with my angel, meaning to speak freely to Him, but I could not. I still felt Him as a stranger and not as a friend. My angel was reminding me that he was just

God's servant and that I should love God and glorify Him. The more he was pushing me towards God, the more I was panicking for fear that he leave me. He was telling me to abandon myself to God, but I was not doing it.

Meanwhile Satan had not given up, he still hoped to get me in my weak state. I was allowed by God once or twice to hear a conversation between Jesus and Satan. Satan was asking from Him to put me to the test. He said to Jesus: "We will see about your Vassula... your dear Vassula will not keep faithful to you, she will fall and for good this time, I can prove it to you in the days of her trials." And so Satan was allowed again to place on me all sorts of temptations. Incredible temptations! Every time I realized that it was a temptation and I overcame it, he put on my way yet another bigger temptation. Temptations that had I succumbed to them, my soul would be bound for hell. Then his attacks started all over again. He splashed boiling oil on my mid-finger where I place the pencil to write. Immediately the blister appeared and I had to dress it to be able to hold the pencil when I was writing. The devil was trying once more and ever so hard to stop me from communicating with God and from writing. I wrote with great pain. Whenever my finger got healed, he repeated the same thing over and over again, and so for week I wrote, but not without suffering.

When my family and I went on a holiday to Thailand, we went with a boat to visit an island. On the way back as soon as we were pulling in, the boat shook and I lost my balance. So that I do not fall I grabbed the first thing in sight and it was the exhaust pipe of the boat, burning hot. I burned the whole palm of my right hand. My first thought was, "how am I to write?" My hand swelled, was red and very painful. We were half and hour from the hotel but by the time we arrived there all the swelling and pain had left me. I had no sign of burning. The Lord told me later on that He had not allowed Satan to go as far as this, and so He healed my hand.

The devil tried another way to stop me from writing. He appeared to my son, (he was ten years old then), in his dream. He took the shape of an old man and told him while sitting near his bed, "You'd better tell your mother to stop writing, and if she does not, I shall do to you the same thing I had done to her when she was young. I shall come while you are lying in bed, pull your head back and strangle you."

This was what I experienced when I was maybe six years old. I had seen one night right in front of me, while I was in bed, just above my throat, two terribly ugly hands of an old man. The next thing I knew was that something pulled my head backwards, exposing my throat. Then nothing. But this left me trembling.

Satan had hounded me from my early age, for almost every night at about the age of six, he appeared to me in dreams to terrify me, taking the shape of a big black dog. It was always the same dream. I would be walking in a dimmed corridor and there at the end would be this dog snarling, ready to jump on me and tear me to pieces, and I would flee terrified.

When I was about 10, I saw Jesus in my dream. He was at the end of some sort of corridor. I only saw His portrait. I saw Him only all the way to His waist. He was smiling and saying, "come, come to Me." I was suddenly seized by an unknown current that drew me closer and closer to Him. I was afraid of this unknown current and Jesus realizing my fear, smiled at me. This current drew me all the way to Jesus until my face stuck on His face.

At about twelve years of age too, I had another mystical experience. It was my spiritual marriage to Jesus. Again in a dream, I was dressed as a bride and my spouse was Jesus. Only I could not see Him but I knew He was there. The people who were present were cheering us cheerfully with palm leaves in their hands. We were supposed to walk the nuptial walk. Just after the marriage was over, I stepped in a room. There was our Blessed Mother with St. Mary Magdalene and two other holy women. Our Blessed Mother was very happy and came to embrace me. She started immediately to fix my dress again, my hair and I realized that She wanted me to be presentable for Her Son.

Satan Continues With Different Attacks

The devil knew what a horror I have for cockroaches. I hate to write this, but I feel I must, to show how the devil fought me. One day while going out of a room, I shut the door. I suddenly felt on my face a wet liquid that was sprinkled on me. I could not understand where it came from. I heard suddenly Satan laughing and he mockingly said to me: "This is the way I baptize. This is the kind of holy water you deserve!" Then I saw what had happened. I had squashed on the frame of the door a big cockroach.... I could have died there and then from my disgust! I do not like writing so much about Satan's attacks, but I would like to show how much he fought me to prevent this message from coming out and prevent me from the mission the Lord was preparing for me.

One day he decided again to change strategy. To deceive me, he took the exact image of my deceased father. Even the manner he spoke to me was the same. A perfect imitation. He spoke to me in French as my father now and then did and said: "My dear, look.... God, out of pity is sending me to you to tell you that you are wrong. How could you believe that He communicates with you in this way? These things are, as you know, impossible, and you are only offending and angering God. Think.... God speaking to you? Where did you every hear of such a thing before? Only madness can lead you to believe such a thing!" I asked, "Well what about my angel, with angels it is possible?" When he said, "Oh that one..." his voice was filled with hatred and I recognized Satan once more.

The Desert, Then the Total Surrender

That is why I am going to seduce her and lead her out into the wilderness and speak to her heart. (Ho 2:16)

Now God wanted me to surrender fully to Him. He wanted to unite me to Him and make me His. He wanted to mould me and transform me. I was not surrendering according to His desire and so I had to undergo another sort of purification for my total abandonment to God so that I make peace with Him. This is what happened: I called to God and to my surprise I had no response. I panicked and turned around to look for my angel, but he was not there either. Instead, I felt a few souls around me, they came like beggars, approaching me.[1] They begged me for prayers, blessings and for holy water. I went to the church immediately and brought with me holy water for them. They asked me to sprinkle it on them and so I did. This gesture attracted even more souls and in no time I had around me a big crowd. To my surprise it seemed to relieve them from their pains and their joy was great. One of them asked me to pray for him there and then and give him just one blessing. I did not know how, so he told me to just pray a simple prayer and bless him. I prayed as he asked me and blessed him. He thanked me with joy and he himself blessed me too. All this was new to me, but I felt that they were relieved and pleased. I took the opportunity to ask them whether they knew where my angel was, the One whom my heart already begun to love. But I did not get any answer.

Every day that went by in this loneliness seemed like a year. I was looking for peace and I could not find it. I was surrounded by many friends and people but I never felt so lonely and abandoned as that time. I felt as though I was going through hell. Many a time I cried out for my angel to return to me, but no, he had vanished! My soul failed at his flight. I sought him but I did not find him, I called to him but he did not answer. I roamed for three whole weeks in the desert, more dead than alive, until I could not bear it any longer and in this terrible Night that my soul was going through I cried out tearfully with all my heart and as never before to Yahweh: "FATHER!!.... where are You?... Father?... Why did You leave me? O God, take me! Take me and use me as You wish!... Purify me so that You are able to use me!"

With this piercing cry that came from the depths of my heart, heaven suddenly opened and like thunder the Father's voice, full of emotion, cried back to me: "I GOD LOVE YOU!" These words were like a balm pouring on those impressive wounds my soul received and they healed me instantly. I felt in those words uttered by God His Infinite Love.

Just after these words of love, it seemed to me as though I dropped out of a tornado into a beautiful peaceful garden. My angel reappeared and with great tenderness began to dress my wounds, those wounds I received while crossing by night this endless desert.

Yahweh then asked me to open the Bible and read. The first passage I read brought me to tears and converted me, for it revealed to me in an amazing way the Heart of God. I read in Exodus 22:25,26, these words:

> "If you take another's cloak as a pledge, you must give it back to him before sunset. It is all the covering he has; it is the cloak he wraps his body in; what else would he sleep in? If he cries to me, I will listen, for I am full of pity."

God did not explain to me immediately what happened in these three weeks for His own reasons but much later on in December 22, 1990, He gave me this explanation, here are His own words:

> "...My Heart, an Abyss of Love, cried out for you. You had accumulated sorrow upon sorrow in My Heart, treason upon treason. You were wrestling with Me, puny little creature... but I knew that your heart is not a divided heart and that once I conquer your heart, it would become entirely Mine. An object of your era, you were wrestling with Me, but I have thrown you down in the battle and dragged you in the dust and into the desert where I left you there all alone. I had provided you with a guardian angel, since the beginning of your existence, to guard you, console you and guide you. But My Wisdom ordered your guardian angel to leave you and to let you face the desert on your own. I said: "you are to live in spite of your nakedness!"[2] because no man is able to survive alone[3], Satan would have taken over completely and would have killed you. My order was given to him too. I forbade him to touch you. Then in your terror you remembered Me and looked up in Heaven searching desperately for Me. Your laments and your supplications suddenly broke the deathly stillness surrounding you and your terrified cries pierced through the heavens reaching the Holy Trinity's ears... "My child!" the Father's voice full of joy resounded through all heaven. "Ah.... I shall now make her penetrate My Wounds[4] and let her eat My Body and drink My Blood. I shall espouse her to Me and she will be Mine for eternity. I shall show her the Love I have for her and her lips from thereon shall thirst for Me and her heart shall be My headrest. She shall eagerly submit daily to My Righteousness, and I shall make her an altar of My Love and of My Passion. I, and I only shall be her only love and

passion, and I shall send her with My message to the ends of the world to conquer an irreligious people and to a people who are not even her own. And voluntarily she will carry My Cross of Peace and Love taking the road to Calvary." "And I, the Holy Spirit shall descent upon her to reveal to her the Truth and the depths of Us.[5] I shall remind the world through her that the greatest of all the gifts is: LOVE." "Let Us* then celebrate! let all heaven celebrate!"

God gave me a vision to understand better the situation. He made me understand why Satan was so aggressive with me. So long as I was not fully converted, the devil did not disturb me and felt content. He did not show any aggression. But the moment he felt I was turning towards God, and he would lose me, he attacked my soul.

This was the vision: I saw myself standing in a room and I saw a snake (Satan) crawling. Apparently that snake was my pet. But as I had lost interest in it, I stopped feeding it. Hungry and astonished it came out of its hole to look for food. I watched it going towards its dish and there it found a couple of grapes. The snake swallowed them but it did not seem satisfied. So it crawled towards the kitchen in search of food. In the meantime, it started to sense that I had changed my feeling towards it and that now I had become its enemy instead of its friend. Because of that, I knew it would try to kill me. I feared, but just then, my guardian angel appeared asking me if I had any problem. I told him about the snake. He told me that he will take care of it. I hesitated whether I should join in the battle or not, and I decided that I should join my angel and do the work together. My angel took a broom and opened a door which led outside, then went to the snake and frightened it away. He then slammed the door shut and we watched from the window how the snake reacted. It panicked. We saw it heading back again towards the door. But the door was safely shut. It went speeding down the staircase and out in to the street. The minute it slithered out, it transformed into a huge ugly toad and again into an evil spirit. The alarm was given and the people out there caught it and tied it up.

The Priest Condemns the Messages

I had been going regularly to the seminary to meet with the priest. One day he asked me to see this phenomenon when I was communicating with heaven, and when my communication started, he came over me and touched my hand to see if he could stop me. He immediately felt a sort of tingling current penetrating into his arm. He did not tell me anything, but later on, since this electric feeling still was with him all afternoon, he went to tell another priest in the seminary what he experienced. The other priest knew about me. When he told him of the incident, he classified it as diabolical rather than Divine and asked him to bring me to him.

He sprinkled his room with holy water, the chair I was to sit on, the desk, the paper and the pencil he would let me use. I went there and he asked me to call "whatever" I was communicating with and ask "it" to write "Glory be to the Father, to the Son and to the Holy Spirit." I prayed and asked God to write this for me. And He did, but with such power than the pencil broke and I had to complete it with a pen. The priest was furious and also very frightened. He started to tell me all about Satanism, evil, magic, and dumb spirits and that the spirit I was communicating with was not Divine, but a dumb spirit. He filled my head with terror. When I got up to leave he said that I should not come anymore to the seminary and the church unless I stopped writing, at least for some time; and that I should also leave alone the other priest. He gave me three prayers to recite daily, (Saint Michael's, the Memorare of Saint Bernard, and a novena to the Sacred Heart of Jesus. He also gave me a rosary in my hand.)

Shattered I went to the first priest who, at least was more gentle and told him what happened. I said that he did not like me visiting him, and that these visits should stop. He looked down, bent his head on one side and did not answer. With this I knew he agreed. I clearly saw and understood that by not visiting him, he would be relieved instantly from a huge cross. I knew I was a persona non grata, so I got up and cried out to him: "You will never see me again in your premises, not until I feel welcomed!" And so I left, thinking I was leaving the Catholic premises for good.

I went back home and wept my eyes out. My angel came to console me, caressing my brow. I lamented to God, "I am confused and my soul is grieving beyond anyone's imagination, I do not know anymore, You say it is You and my heart feels and knows it is You, but he says it is the devil. If it is You, then I want that this priest would say and admit one day that my communications are Divine, and I will believe!" God simply said, "I will bend him..."

The angel was very tender with me. He dressed my spiritual wounds very gently. I prayed every day these prayers and did exactly what the priest asked me to do. I stopped using the charisma God had given me and I avoided writing.

Since I was living in a Moslem country, I bought a Koran to study it and compare it with our Holy Bible. One day when I was taking notes, to my surprise our Heavenly Father approached me. His mere presence filled me with an inexplicable joy and He said to me: "I God love you, daughter, remember always this. Yahweh is My Name." And while I was holding the pencil, He used my had to write it on my note paper. A little later on, He descended near me and again He came and said, while using my hand: "I God love you. Vassula, remember always this. I it is who am guiding you. Yahweh is My Name." This was so touching that I broke into tears. There I was like a prisoner, forbidden to talk to my Father, forbidden to have any sort of communications with heaven, forbidden to use the charisma that God Himself had given me and forbidden to use the way I could approach My Father in heaven, and in all these prohibitions, who comes to visit me in "prison"? The One who loves me most! The most Tender Father, the One who holds the whole universe in the palm of His Hand, to show me His affection and His love.

Persecutions From The Priest

The priest though did not give up. He wrote letters to me to tell me that all what I had was a mass of rubbish and that I should just look at myself and understand that such a grace will never be given to me. Such graces were for people, who worked for God, and with a gesture of his hand, showed me his books on the shelves, or for people, he said, like Mother Teresa or the like. Then he tried to frighten me saying it was diabolical, so that I abandon the writings and he partly managed, for every time after that, when God approached me, I chased Him away. I could barely accept my angel. If I heard from God these words "I Yahweh love you," I would pretend I heard nothing and would not allow this to be written. If Jesus approached me and told me, "peace My child" I would turn away from Him and chase Him away, taking Him for the evil one. The priest managed to put in my head that God cannot communicate with a person like me because God goes only to saintly people. I would sometimes become quite aggressive when Jesus would come and speak to me, thinking it was the devil, I would fiercely chase Him away, over and over again.

In the end Wisdom found a way. My angel came telling me that he had a message from Jesus and would tell it to me. He became the go-between. This was a way I could accept, but not always, for I still was under the influence of the priests' words. How and why would the Holy One's Eyes turn and look at a contemptible soul such as mine, let alone speak to me! How could I have believed that God, the Almighty, would speak and communicate in such a simple way with me! In my life I had never heard this. Yes, only in the Holy Bible, with people like Moses, Abraham and the prophets, but this was another story and other times. A fairy-tale, that's what it was, an illusion, my mind reeled because I knew it was happening and I was not mad! Slowly and with time only, these wounds I received from the priests started to heal.

My angel gave me so much peace, preaching to me every single day for hours. Now and then he would leave space for Jesus to quote His Divine words. The first time this happened, I was about to erase the words, since I had allowed myself to write them down. The angel intervened asking me to understand and leave these words since then were truly from Jesus. The words were, "I, Jesus, love you." These were the first written words from Jesus after the crisis. They were written on the 23rd June 1986. Slowly, slowly, step by step and ever so gently, Jesus again made His approach to me.

On the 9th of July 1986, God said, "I God love you." My angel immediately, noticing my hesitation, asked me to keep these words saying that every word was given by God, and that God was near me. The next direct message from God was in July 1986. The message was: "I have fed you, (spiritually), I came to give the food to you. Please help the others by giving them this food too. Flourish them, leading them to Me. I fed you, flourished you, fragranced you. Feed the others too. Help them and lead them to Me. I have given you Love, so follow Me. I have favoured you by giving you this food. Give it to the others too, to delight on it."

Then again, the 31st of July 1986, this time Jesus came as the Sacred Heart and said to me: "In the middle of My Heart, have a place, My beloved. There you will live." On the 7th of August 1986, the Father once more spoke to me giving me this message: "I God bind you with Me." Fearing, I asked Him very sharply because I was suspicious, that He name Himself. He answered, "Yahweh". I was filled with joy and love and already I had a burning in my soul from the yearning I had for Him. I said: "I love you Eternal Father." He replied, "Love me, praise Me, your God, I am your Eternal Father." I asked Him then: "Do you feel my happiness, my anguishes, my fears, my love, my confusions?" He replied, "Yes." Then I said: "In that case you know how I feel right now. You understand me fully," and He said with great tenderness: "Yes, I do, My beloved."

This again was my first communication for a long time after the rejection I had (out of fear). God went on saying, since He knew that I was wondering why He speaks to me. He said, "I love you all. This is just a reminder to remind you how your foundations began. Deliver My message."

The very first messages I was receiving were very short, as I explained in the beginning, they sounded more like telegrams than messages.

In the meantime, in spite of everything, I had not lost contact with the priests. But I had stopped talking about the messages to the one who had condemned them and had given me so much sufferings. However, after some time, I decided to tell him that I was still receiving messages and writing them. So I showed him the notebooks instead of loose papers as before. I used any plain paper where I could write on, but when the time came to start my mission, the Holy Spirit inspired me to open notebooks and number them.

I remember inviting the priest to my house so that I could tell him that I was still communicating with God. I thought I should inform him. I told him and he did not like it very much, but he asked me to show him the notebooks. I gave them to him to keep for a day. The next day I received a very harsh letter from him, telling me to burn all my notebooks and to go and tell all my friends who were reading them, to forget everything. Somehow, I recognized Satan's harshness. I told my friends what he said, and they were very cross with him. I went over to tell him of their reaction and take my notebooks away from him. He said that God is probably very angry with me now and that He abandoned me to my fate. He said that God was patient once and twice, but now, since I was not listening, He left me with the devil.

Already, the lessons of discernment from my angel were taking their effect and they became very useful to me in this particular moment. This time I could not be deceived. I answered his letter and told him that his God is not my God. For his God, is a cruel God, quick to anger, impatient, intolerant and lacking love. His God forgives once or twice and then turns His back and throws the souls to hell, if they do not listen, whereas the God I know of, the One who communicates with me daily, my God, is all love, infinitely patient, tolerant and tender. My God who speaks to me, and bends all the way from heaven, is meek, slow to anger, all merciful and envelops my soul with only love. My God who visits me every day in my room, the One whom he treats as the devil, surrounds my soul with peace and hope. My God nourishes me spiritually, augmenting my faith in Him. He teaches me spiritual things and reveals to me the Riches of His Heart.

After this he asked me to try once more for just a few days to stop writing to see what happens.

I allowed a few more days to pass without writing, as I had been asked by the priest. I prayed and asked again in my prayer, who was really guiding me in this special way? I had asked, that if the messages were really from Him, then I would like Him to tell me and hear Him say these words: "I Yahweh am guiding you." Nothing more. And this is what happened and God answered according to my prayer.

My communications continued and one day on December 15, 1986, God gave me this message: "Daughter, all Wisdom comes from Me. Do you want Wisdom?" Without me realizing what God was offering me, I simply said, "Yes," to Him. He then said that He will give me Wisdom but that I had to acquire Wisdom if I wanted Her. When He saw how I was questioning myself on how to do this, He said that He is the Almighty and that He will teach me. I mediated on what God had offered me and the more I mediated the more I was realizing the tremendous Gift He was offering me. I realized too that I had not even thanked Him. So the following day I thanked Him and again He said that I would have to earn Wisdom, but He will help me and I should not get discouraged.

Do You Want To Serve Me?

The next thing I noticed was that Jesus was taking more and more the place of my angel. He came as the Sacred Heart. One day He surprised me by His question. He asked me if I wanted to serve Him, (for this mission). Fear overtook me and I hesitated. I did not allow this to be written like the rest of the other things. I was afraid that He might tell me to pack and leave my house to join a convent and become a nun. I was not ready and did not wish to do so either. My distrust disappointed Him, and His sadness did not escape me, since it was so obvious in the tone of His voice when He said these words, "I can abide in you in spite of your awesome weakness". I was very unhappy, because I had disappointed Him; on the other hand I was afraid of the unknown. These are the exact words:

> ..."were you to serve Me, I would reveal in you nothing but passion." I repeated, "passion", without understanding, and He said, "yes, passion. Will...." I lifted my hand not to write it, but I heard it all.

The whole night I spent my time thinking of this; then I decided to plunge into the unknown and surrender to His Will. So I came back to Him with His question. I asked Him, "do you want me to serve You?"

I immediately felt His joy and He said,

> "I do. I want very much, Vassula. Come, I will show you how and where you can serve Me.... work and serve Me as now, be as you are. I need servants who are able to serve Me where love is needed most. Work hard though, for where you are, you are among evil, unbelievers. You are in the vile depths of sin. You are going to serve your God where darkness prevails; you will have no rest. You will serve Me where every good is deformed into evil. Yes, serve Me among wretchedness, among wickedness and the iniquities of the world. Serve Me among Godless people, among those that mock Me, among those that pierce My Heart. Serve Me among My scourgers, among My condemners. Serve Me among those that recrucify Me and spit on Me. O Vassula, how I suffer! Come and console Me!.... strive and suffer with Me, share My Cross..." (24th May 1987).

The teachings with God continued, and His communications were daily and to this day that I am writing, they are going on, for He said that His charism will stay with me up to my last day on earth.

Notes:

1. When I was a teenager, I used to see with the eyes of my soul many souls surrounding me. When I used to see these souls then, I used to say to myself, "ah, here are again the dead people." They used to fill the room I was in. They seemed to sit all close to each other on the floor. I felt they enjoyed my presence. All of them seemed alike. They appeared thin with no hair and grayish in their looks. Their whole self was grayish like ash. They did not make any sound and in fact they seemed like they did not want to disrupt me. This was a very common scene that occurred for several years. Later on, Jesus explained to me all this. He said that these souls were waiting for my prayers when I would be converted.

2. I became "naked" as soon as my guardian angel and all Heaven had turned their back to me.

3. Abandoned by Heaven

4. the Son then spoke

5. the Holy Trinity

APPENDIX III

=====

Handwriting analysis of the writing of Vassula by J.A.
Munier, graphological consultant, SGF. GGOF.,
Expert in handwriting for the Court of Appeals of Paris.

I (Fr. Rene Laurentin) submitted the messages of Vassula to J.A. Munier, a licensed graphologist of the highest reputation. I did not tell him anything about the matter except for the age (47) and the first name of this lady whom he did not know.

He prefaced the analysis which follows with the title: Graphological interpretation, with no previous information (and without taking into consideration the text itself due to lack of knowledge of the English language).

Interpretation of the large letters dictated by Jesus.

- Extraordinary telluric force.
- A controlled enthusiasm with a touch of delight, i.e. seems to be the source of some kind of well-being.
- She is filled with a force that goes beyond her normal self.
- She is filled with invisible forces to which she reacts with a kind of primitive simplicity, whereas there is also in other areas a refined element.
- She is convinced of this invisible power which she perceives with intensity.
- She is an intermediary, like a center of transmission and amplification.
- She has the faith of a mystic.
- She experiences a kind of tranquil enthusiasm, a kind of fullness.
- She is very redoubled, nourished by an invisible force that seems indestructible.
- The writing in any case appears a bit strange from an ordinary point of view.
- She is very hard-working, she is a docile pupil.
- She is in a kind of second state, indifferent to the exterior world.
- She can perceive invisible worlds quite well, like a medium.
- She has a very great concentrated force; she is profound in meditation.
- She does not belong to herself. There is a certain firmness. She has great self control, probably in her demeanor as well. She is dignified.

An additional interpretation of the fragments of
handwriting in smaller letters between the lines:

- She is a person who lives in her own world.
- She is not mentally ill.
- She is of at least above average intelligence.
- She follows her own logic.
- She is capable of some integration.
- She conducts herself with tenderness, kindness, docility.
- She has a goal and she is dedicated to it.
- She experiences an inspiration from a high level.
- Her life is inspired by an ideal.
- Nothing else really matters for her.

A new analysis by Mr. J.A. Munier of a note by Vassula
(in long hand) with her signature: March 3, 1990.

- Direct simplicity. She has a kind of simple seriousness without exaggeration. She
has a great sincerity; without pretentiousness.
- Her temperament is very well balanced. Her personality seems to dominate very
well her physical state. Her emotional balance seems excellent.
- She has a good intellectual level; she is lucid, serious, and has a sense of essential
values. She has measured judgement, and is capable of intellectual precision. She
notices detail and is free from confusion. She is capable of serious critical
discussion: she is careful to be objective and not to delude herself. She is careful to
be clear-thinking and free from illusions, with a positive intellectual curiosity that is
even above average.
- Her social personality is not showy, she is simple and candid. She is a person to
take seriously, though she appears to be "just like everybody else". She is serious
without being tense, with a sort of calm severity. She is not easily affected by
events, but has a high level of sensitivity. Perhaps at times there is a possible touch
of playfulness or pleasant imaginativeness for recreation.
- Her moral level is excellent. She has a firm conviction in her beliefs. Her will is
calm and steady enough to dominate her weaknesses. She has dignity and also a very
notable goodwill.
- Some other notable qualities are: a certain reserve in relation to the phenomena that
are affecting her and her states of awareness as well. She has something much more
than just a "rich subconscious". She has an ability to be simultaneously both present
and beyond. Because of her equilibrium, her emotions, her intelligence, she herself,
as well as others are all in their proper place.

APPENDIX IV

European Cities and Overseas Countries visited by Vassula

1989 Biarritz, Nice (2)

1990 Paris, Milan, Auch, Nice, Toulouse, Mazemet, Marseilles, nr. Albi Lens (4) Broc (4) Martigny, Villeneuve.

1991 nr. Breistroff la Grande, Gera Lario, London, Beckenham, York, Manchester, Strangeways Prison, Auchinleck, Motherwell, Belfast, Dublin, Athenry, Cork, Besancon, Milan, Brussels, Pistoia, Toulouse, Quebec, U.S.A., (Pittsburgh), Clay Detention Centre (Prisoners), Philippines.

1992 Geneva (World Council of Churches), Nice, Paris, Ars, Milan, Gera Lario, Rome, Basel, Florence, Genoa, Brussels, Villeneuve, Porrentruy, Verona, Oporto, Fatima, U.S.A. (5), Canada (2), Russia, Japan, Philippines, Australia, Germany, Greece, Ireland (2), England (2).

1993 Arles, Geneva (World Council of Churches), Mexico (3), Martinique, U.S.A. (2), Canada, Lisbon, Oporto, St. Gallen.

1994 Romania, Greece (2), Rhodes, Italy, France, USA (6), Canada (2), Russia, Portugal, Spain, Ireland, England, New York, Mexico, Peru, Brazil, Chile

Planned Visits: Hungary, Indonesia, Bangladesh, Japan, Austria, Belgium, Paris, California, Puerto Rico, Panama, Israel.

N.B. This a bare, incomplete list of cities and countries. A more detailed list with exact chronology is being prepared. But already the reader will have the evidence to show that the word of Jesus to Vassula is being fulfilled: the work would begin like a small stream, that would grow into a river, and then become an ocean.

APPENDIX V

Rev. Michael O'Carroll, C.S.Sp. Brief Curriculum Vitae and Outline Bibliography.

C.V.

Education: Blackrock College, Dublin; University College Dublin (B.A. Philosophy; H.Dip. Education) Fribourg University (D.D. Dissertation: Spiritual Direction according to Ven. Francis Libermann, 1939).

Career:

Education: Professor Blackrock College (Religious Knowledge, History, French Language and Literature);

Journalism: *Catholic Standard* (14 years sole editorial writer, Features especially on Vatican II in session, book reviews); *The Leader* (10 years identical service); much occasional work elsewhere;

Pastoral Ministry: *Lay Apostolate*, chaplain to College Scout Troop; Spiritual Director three praesidia Legion of Mary; Adult Education courses in Social Science and Practical Psychology, Dun Laoghaire Technical College; chaplain annually to Irish Handicapped, Banneux Shrine; care of adopted children;

Spiritual Training: Retreats and lectures; chaplain Blackrock Carmelite Convent;

Ecclesial Collaboration: Deep cultural and intellectual attachment to the Church in France with diocesan service (Beauvais) annually for twenty years;

Ecumenism: Member of the Mercier Society (1941-1944) for dialogue with Protestants, and of the wartime Pillar of Fire Society for dialogue with Jews; first chairman of Irish branch of the Ecumenical Society of the Blessed Virgin May;

Recognition: Elected to General chapters C.S.Sp., 1968 (continued to 1969), 1974; Member of the Pontifical Marian Academy; *Associé des Bollandistes*; Member of the French Society of Marian Studies.

BIBLIOGRAPHY

1. Articles in religious periodicals e.g. The Irish Rosary, Missionary Annals of the Holy Ghost Fathers, Blackrock College Annual, *Maria Legionis* (organ of the Legion of Mary), Hibernia, Madonna, Knock Shrine Annual;

2. Articles in theological reviews, Clergy Review, Homiletic and Pastoral Review, Irish Ecclesiastical Record, Irish Theological Quarterly, The Furrow, Doctrine and Life, *Marianum, Ephemerides Mariologicae*; prefaces to a number of books;

3. Contributions: International Mariological Congresses, Rome, Saragossa, Malta, Kevalaer, Huelva; dictionaries, *Dictionnaire de Spiritualité* (25 articles); Marienlexikon (Regensburg) (24 articles written or requested) Modern Dictionary of Theology (1 article) Encyclopedia of Catholic Practice (12 articles); commemorative volumes: Dom Columba Marmion, Fr. René Laurentin, Fr. G.M. Besutti, O.S.M.; Fr. Theodore Koechler, S.M.; Professor Heinrich Beck (Bamberg);

4. Five pamphlets, Ven. Francis Libermann (2), The secret of Knock, African Glory (Mgr. Alexander Le Roy), Disciples of St. Thérèse of Lisieux, Lourdes Centenary Year.

Books: twenty on Marian theology, hagiography and the Papacy, among which: *Joseph, Son of David*; *Mediatress of All Graces*; *Medjugorje, Facts, Documents, Theology*; *Le Sanctuaire de Knock* (awaiting publication in Paris); *Pius XII, Greatness Dishonoured - A documented Study*; five theological encyclopedias, *Theotokos* (Our Lady), *Trinitas* (the Holy Trinity), *Corpus Christi* (the Eucharist), *Veni Creator Spiritus* (the Holy Spirit), *Verbum Caro* (Jesus the Christ); *John Paul II, A Dictionary of His Life and Teachings*; *Vassula of the Sacred Heart's Passion*; *Bearer of the Light - Vassula, Mediatrix of Divided Christians*.

NATIONAL DISTRIBUTORS (ENGLISH EDITION)

United Kingdom

Chris Lynch
J.M.J. Publications
PO Box 385
Belfast BT9 6RQ
United Kingdom
Tel: (1232) 381596
Fax: (1232) 381596

Australia

Center for Peace
c/o Leon LeGrand
91 Auburn Road
AUBURN Victoria
Australia 3123
Fax: (03) 882-9675
Tel: (03) 882-9822

New York (USA)

John Lynch
PO Box 533
Bethpage
N.Y. USA 11714-0533
Fax: (516) 293-9635
Tel: (516) 293-9635

Philippines

MARY AND DAVID
PO BOX 146
Lapulapu City 6015
Cebu,
The Philippines.
Fax: (6332) 310305

South Africa

Winnie Williams
Friends of Medjugorje
PO Box 32817
Braamfontein 2017
Johannesburg
South Africa
Tel: (011) 614-3084
Fax: (011) 614-3417

Republic of Ireland

D.M.Publications
"Maryville"
Loughshinney
Skerries
Co Dublin
EIRE
Tel: (1) 8491458
Fax: (1) 8492466

Malawi

Rui Francisco
PO Box 124
Lilongwe
Malawi
Africa

Fax: (265) 721504

Denmark: Niels Huidt, Mysundegade 8V, DK 1668, Copenhagen V, Denmark (Fax: 45 331 33115)

Switzerland: Parvis, CH-1648, Hautville, Switzerland (Tel: 41 29 51905)

Holland: Stichting Het Ware Leven in God, Timorstraat 16, 6524 KC Nijmegen, Holland

'True Life in God' books are available in the following languages:

Switzerland: Tom Austin True Life in God, PO Box 902, CH-1800 Vevey, Switzerland

Phillipines: Center for Peace Asia, Shaw Blvd Cor. Old, Wackwack Road, Manduluyong Metro, Manila, Philippines. Tel: 795-622. Fax: 922-8358; and Mary and David Thomas, PO Box 146, Lapu-Lapu City 6015, Cebu, Phillipines

French: 1. Edition du Parvis, CH-1648 Hauteville, Switzerland
2. 'La Vraie vie en Dieu', Editions FX de Guibert (OEIL), 27 Rue de l'Abbé-Grégoire, F-75006 PARIS

German: Das Wahre Lebe in Gott, Mariamverlag, D-7893 Jestetten, Germany

Italian: 'La Vera Vita in Dio', Edizioni Dehoniane, Via Casale San Pio V, 20, 1-00165 ROMA, Italy

Spanish/: Centro de Difusion 'Grupo Reina', Belisario Dominguez 1302,
Mexican "Laboratorios Jema", Mazatlan, Sin, Mexico CP 82000 Tel: (91-69) 82-11-59

Portuguese: Ediçoes Boa Nova, 4760 Vila Nova de Famalicao, Famalicao,
and Spanish Portugal. Tel: 75-165. Fax: 311-594

Polish: Vox Domini, Skr Poczt 72, 43-190 Mikolów, Poland

Greek: Candy Jeannoutsikos, Essex SA, Fokionos 8 Ermou, 10563 Athens, Greece

Russian: Cyril Kozina, Foyer Oriental Chrétien, 206 Ave de la Couronne, B-1050 Bruxelles, Belgium

Korean: Father R Spies, Father Damien Center, PO Box 36, Anyang-Shi, Kyeong-Gi Do 430-600, South Korea

Flemish: Mevr Lieve Van den Berre, Epsomlaan 34, 8400 Oostende, Belguim. Tel: (059) 503-752

Danish:	Niels Christian Huidt, Louis Petersenveg, 2960 Rungsted-Kyst, Denmark
Bangladeshi:	Father James Fannan, National Major Seminary, Plot 9, Road No.27, Banani, Dhaka 1213, Bangladesh
Indonesian:	Indriati Makki, Jalan Larong no.1a, Kompleks PLN, Kelurahan Duren Tiga, Jakarta 12760, Indonesia
Norwegian:	Ingfrid Lillerud, Lerdalsvn 22, 1263 Oslo, Norway
Ukranian:	Cyril Kozina, Foyer Oriental Chrétien, 206 Ave de la Couronne, B-1050 Bruxelles, Belgium
Dutch:	Stichting Getuigenis van Gods Liefde, PO Box 6290, 5600 HG Eindhoven, Holland
Bulgarian:	Miladora Anastassova, Bd D Grover 20, 1606 Sofia, Bulgaria
Hungarian:	c/o Ilma Jordan, Szolyva v 1/b, 1126 Budapest, Hungary
Croatian:	Franjo Ereiz, Za Belaka, Za M D Vukić, Palmotićeja 33, 41001 Zagreb PP699, Croatia
Japanese/ Chinese:	Serge Bernard Kuhn, Foyer de Charite, Ai to Hakari no Ie, Sendaiji 136, Oaza, 568 Ibaragi-Shi, Osaka-Fu, Japan
Canada:	Caravan Agencies 6 Dumbarton BLVD. Winnipeg MBR3 P2C4 Tel (204) 895-7544. Fax (204) 895-8878

Queries relating to any version, please contact:

Patrick Beneston
Association la Vrai Vie en Dieu
5 Rue de Turbigo
75001 PARIS
France

(Fax: France [1] 34-93-08-13)

NEW TITLES AVAILABLE

John Paul II - A Dictionary of His Life and Teachings by M O'Carroll CSSp
A quick and fascinating guide to the life and teachings of this outstanding leader of
the Church, which will be of great help to Catholics in these confused times. What
has he said about the third secret of Fatima? What does the Pope think of Opus Dei?
the Orthodox Churches? the Jews? What was his relationship with Monsignor
Lefebvre? All these questions have been answered by this comprehensive dictionary,
compiled by one of the outstanding theologians of our day, Father Michael O'Carroll
CSSp.

Bearer of the Light by M O'Carroll CSSp
This is the second book by Father Michael O'Carroll on Vassula and the messages
'True Life in God.' In this book Vassula's most recent visit to Russia is recorded.
Other themes include: pre-history of her conversion; extraordinary signs; the Passion;
Chastisement and Purification. The book includes some extraordinary personal
testimonies from people all around the world who experienced supernatural events
in her presence. A must for any reader of the 'True Life in God' messages.

Volume IV (Notebooks 65-71)
This most recent volume of the messages of 'True Life in God' contains, among
other things: prophecies on Russia explained - resurrection of the Church - repairing
what was undone - unity by intermarriage. Daniel explained - the Rebel - the
"enemy enthroning himself in 'my sanctuary'" - abolition of the Perpetual Sacrifice.
Message to Cardinals, bishops and priests (17 March 1993).

Fire of Love
In this book prepared by Vassula Rydén from the complete works of 'True Life in
God' to date are those passages she considers, the most important references to and
by the Holy Spirit. 'Note to the Reader' is written by Emil Castro and the Preface
os written by Fr Ion Bria, Professor of Orthodox Theology, World Council of
Churches, Geneva.

When God Gives a Sign by René Laurentin
Father Laurentin has long been recognised for his scientific and theological approach
to claimed apparitions and his search for the truth. In this book he skillfully and
with discernment answers questions arising in relation to Vassula Rydén's charism
and the 'True Life in God' messages.
**(This book is available in the UK from Sue Ellis, Spring House, Spring Bottom
Lane, Bletchingly, Surrey, England Tel: 0883 346365 and in the USA from
Trinitas, PO Box 475, Independence, MO, USA 64051)**

OTHER TITLES AVAILABLE

<u>**Volume II**</u> (Notebooks 32-58)

Jesus teaches that God is alive and very near, desiring a return to love, Adoration, sharing His Passion, consoling Him; return of Jesus. He teaches about the state of the Church, His shepherds; the renewal of His vineyards; Devotion to the Two Sacred Hearts of Jesus and Mary; expands on the ten commandments and Beatitudes; Apocalypse 12. The rebellion in the Church and the Great Apostasy; the suffering of His Peter; the minature judgement; unrolling of the 'scrolls.' Many prayers, of consecration, of adoration, of consolation, praise etc... to Father, Son and Holy Spirit.

<u>**Volume III**</u> (Notebooks 59-64)

Among the contents in this volume: Jesus marks foreheads with the consecration to him, Judgement Day, the time of sorting, the lamb's seal, the three days of darkness, and a strong message when the earth will shake and the sky will vanish.

<u>**Prayers of Jesus and Vassula**</u>

A beautiful assortment of prayers, some given by Jesus, others by Vassula, inspired by the Holy Spirit. A section on the Devotion to the Two Hearts; Daily Prayers and quotations of Jesus' teaching how to pray.

<u>**Vassula of the Sacred Heart's Passion**</u> by Michael O'Carroll C.S.Sp.

A 220 page book giving an outline of Vassula's life, her charism and analysis of Jesus' messages in the light of the teaching of the Church. Also a message to cardinals, bishops and priests of 'The Rebel' with a warning not to listen or follow the teaching of anyone except the Holy Father, John Paul II. (17 March 1993)

<u>**'True Life in God Magazine'**</u>

Available quarterly - annual subscription £5 (incl p&p). USA $15. This glossy magazine will keep the True Life in God reader in closer touch with Vassula, her travels, important new messages, videos, new books and new testimonies. Articles by Fr M O'Carroll, Vassula and Fr James Fannan. News of 'True Life in God' prayer groups worldwide.

True Life in God
Original Handwritten Version

'When God Gives a Sign' (Vassula Rydén) by Réné Laurentin

'My Angel Daniel' - early dawn of 'True Life in God'

Videos and Audios

Available from: Pat Callagan
                 Trinitas
                 Independence
                 PO Box 475
                 Missouri
                 USA 64051-0475

                 Tel: (816) 254-4489
                 Fax: (816) 254-1469